RIDGEFIELD LIBRARY ASSOCIATION

3 4010 11265 631

S0-AAJ-634

14 Day

DATE DUE

• Moscow

• Maikop

Grozny •

Baku •

RIDGEFIELD
47 MAIN STREET
RIDGEFIELD, CONN. 06877

WITHDRAWN

SEP 1 9 2008

A Sixth Sense

Cas des terrains très réd.

Fig 2

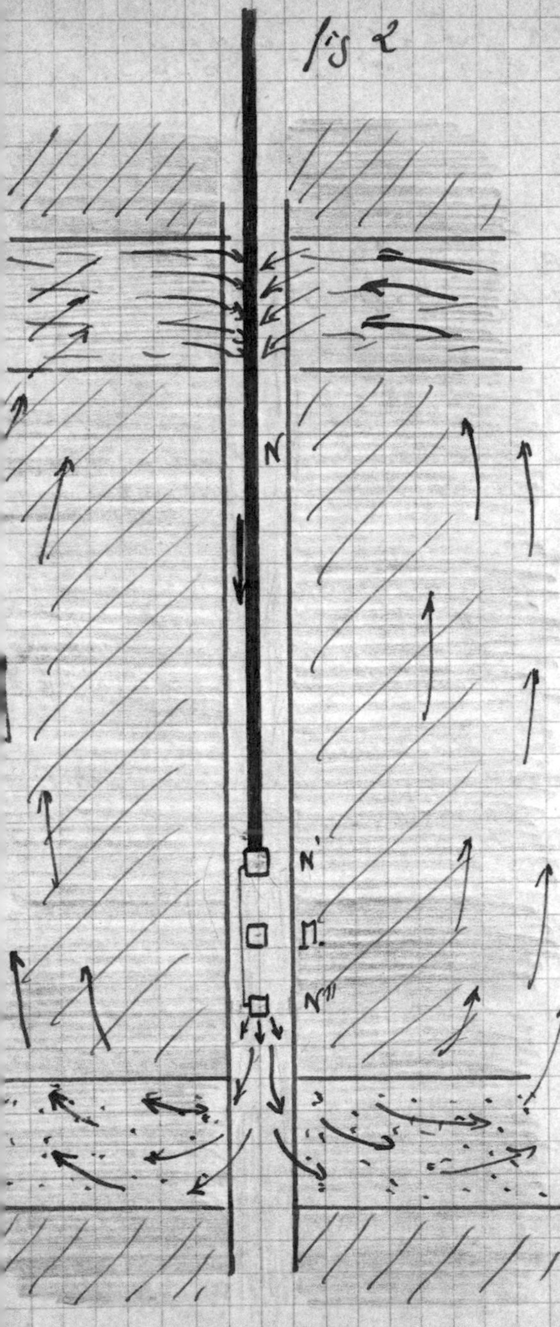

Dans le cas représenté ici où le terrain bleu est supposé (par exemple 100 fois plus r. les boues ou les couches condu. en rouge) le courant dû à l'é. ou à l'électroosmose dans la poreuse conductrice suit le t. sur la figure.

Le courant se répand dans poreuse à grande distance . pour pouvoir traverser le co. résistante sous une très grand. Il revient vers le sondage par l. conductrice non poreuse, est p. entièrement capté par l'él. dans la paille il circule, arriv. (anneau de garde) N', pass. à l'électrode (anneau de gard. en empruntant le connexion. qui relie ces deux électrodes N. se répand dans les boues en t. la résistance de contact l. avec ces boues, circule le long dans les boues pour rejoindre poreuse, pénètre dans le ca. en traversant le cake dan. le potentiel est élevé par la c. etc. — — .

Si la résistance de contact aux vaguement défini) de l'. avec les boues est trop grande du courant peut s'échapp. N' pour rejoindre à travers les région N" et se joindre au itou de N" pour rejoindre la

Evaluation très grossière de la résistance de contact d'un. de garde.

On peut considérer que la résistance à partir de l'anneau de garde N" se décompose très grossièrement en deux :

1° La résistance entre l'anneau de garde et une sph. S de contact N" et ayant le diamètre du sondage.

2° La résistance entre cette sphère et l'entrée de la

A Sixth Sense

The Life and Science of Henri-Georges Doll

Oilfield Pioneer and Inventor

Michael Oristaglio & Alexander Dorozynski
Preface by Jean-Pierre Causse

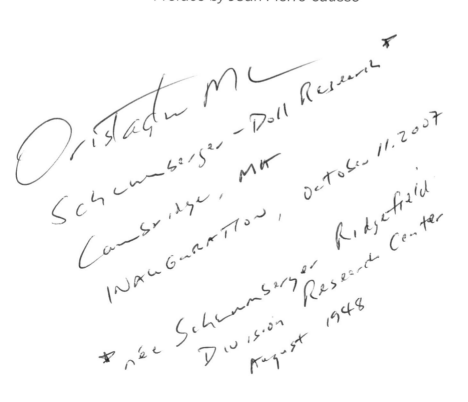

Copyright © Michael Oristaglio and Alexander Dorozynski, 2007

All rights reserved. No part of this publication may be reproduced,
stored in a retrieval system, or transmitted by any means, electronic,
mechanical, photocopying, recording, scanning, or otherwise, without
the permission in writing of the authors.

Creative Direction by Milton Glaser
Design by WORKSHOP NYC, LLC

Printed in the United States by The Hammer Company

This book is dedicated

to Henriette de Vitry (1934–2007),

daughter of Henri-Georges Doll and Anne Schlumberger.

Her visit to Ridgefield in June 2004

inspired this project.

CONTENTS

Preface

THIS BOOK NEEDED TO BE WRITTEN and it comes at the right time. Soon there will be no one left to testify personally about the person of Henri Doll. The closing of the Schlumberger research center in Ridgefield, Connecticut, and its transfer near the campus of MIT mark the end of an era and offer the opportunity for a fruitful glance into the past.

The saga of Schlumberger has been told in various publications and is fairly well known, even to the public at large. Carefully nurtured by the company and the family, the saga also perpetuates a myth, not unfounded, of an absolute symmetry between the family's two branches – that of Conrad and that of Marcel – as their father had wanted it when he launched his sons into their enterprise with astonishing foresight and audacity. But this somewhat rigid edifice tends to relegate to a secondary role and to blur the image of Henri-Georges Doll. Aside from specialists in applied geophysics and petroleum prospecting, only a few are familiar with the name and career of a man who can be considered as one of the greatest French scientists, and surely as one of the must prolific inventors, of the 20th century.

After completing his studies at École Polytechnique and École des Mines in Paris, Doll became Conrad's son-in-law and collaborator and, after Conrad's premature death, his successor. Few families have produced as many brilliant minds as did the Schlumberger family – protestant descendants of the statesman and historian François Guizot – who, though sometimes divided by rivalries, always united when needed and who with hard work, personal sacrifice, tenacity, and daring built in a few years an immense industrial empire. It does not diminish anyone to say that among these two or three generations of men and women (and, in the Schlumberger family, the women were in no way inferior to the men) that Henri Doll stood out with his stature as an inventor and scientist. It is impossible of course to ignore the essential contributions of the managers, administrators, and financiers, or those of the thousands of other engineers and scientists without whom such success would not have been achieved. But at a time when innovation comes mostly from teamwork, is it not worthwhile to note the occasion, very rare today, when invention can be traced to a single person, without whom – and there is no doubt about this – there would not have been any lasting enterprise at all?

This book takes the opportunity to relate again, for a wide public and in a lively manner, the path taken from the initial inventions of Conrad and Marcel Schlumberger – the Schlumberger "adventure" – through the life and work of Henri-Georges Doll. One could also say, to relate the life and work of Doll against the background of the development of a new technique, of which he was in practice the chief inventor and which revolutionized the search for petroleum, the "black gold" that was the motor of the 20th century.

Starting from initial idea of Conrad Schlumberger to characterize rocks by their electrical resistivity – a method that eventually failed to compete seriously with the seismic method in surface prospecting for oil – Doll succeeded in applying it in the borehole, thus inventing logging and making it indispensable to this day. He also discovered the spontaneous potential effect in oil wells and provided its correct scientific explanation. He devised a constant stream of new remote-sensing instruments based on these principles and worked ceaselessly at improving their interpretation. He was the chief proponent of the method despite the difficulties it had getting started in the 1930s.

At one time or another, and often at the same time, Doll was scientist, soldier, and oilfield pioneer – in fields stretching from wild Chechnya, already rebellious against central power, to the vast deserts of the American West. He was also businessman and chairman of a large multinational corporation. As he was nearing his fifties, he understandably sought a quiet setting for his remaining work. In creating the Schlumberger research laboratory at Ridgefield, Connecticut, he gave himself a magnificent tool for this work and infused it with grand ambitions. He devoted himself passionately to it for ten years, at severe cost in his personal life. The laboratory, which was rightly renamed in his honor upon his retirement, has continued to this day, under the direction of his successors, to sustain the indisputable technical leadership of Schlumberger in its business.

The book brings out the character of this likeable man of enormous intelligence, who also had his weaknesses. Also vividly present is Annette, his first wife and the oldest daughter of Conrad, who was herself a remarkable person and who as if freed by their separation in the 1950s undertook her own exceptional endeavors. Her life deserves its own book.

As in a Greek tragedy, it was Annette who watched over Henri-Georges in his final days and who, by burying him at Val-Richer and joining him there herself two years later, inscribed their names together again forever.

Jean-Pierre Causse

Member, The National Academy of Technologies of France
Paris, November 2006

Henri-Georges Doll in uniform at École Polytechnique in 1923.

Chapter 1

Introduction –
An Average
polytechnicien

On Monday, March 18, 1940, a
French army lieutenant came to the
United States embassy in Paris to
give a deposition before American
Vice-Consul John R. Wood.
Europe was at war. In September
1939, the German army had invaded
Poland. England, France, Australia,
and New Zealand had declared
war on Germany, while the United
States, Ireland, Belgium, and Italy
remained neutral.

Most of the world expected Hitler to launch his next offensive toward the west, across the German border with France. But for six months, nothing happened. The French were calling this period *la drôle de guerre* ("the phony war"); the Germans called it *Sitzkrieg* ("the sitting war").

The French lieutenant was Henri-Georges Doll. He was an engineer, a graduate of École Polytechnique and École des Mines, two of France's prestigious *grandes écoles* (literally, "great schools") of science, engineering, and civil service. Doll was also a reserve commander in the French artillery at the start of the war, and had been mobilized to the French-German border with a battalion of 150 men. But early in 1940, the French Ministry of Armaments had summoned him to Paris to work on a new system for detecting land mines, which as French intelligence had learned, the Germans were deploying on a vast scale.

Doll's new detector was not like the fragile, handheld devices that soldiers had to wave carefully over the ground while advancing across a mine field one foot at a time. His new device could be mounted in front of a tank or other moving vehicle. To protect its magnetic coils and electronic circuits, and to avoid false alarms, the device was mounted on rubber wheels, which absorbed shocks and glided smoothly over the surface when the vehicle bounced and turned on rough terrain. The mounting system had been devised by another French officer, Marcel Lebourg, a mechanical engineer who had worked with Doll before the war in a small private company.

The American vice-consul who took Doll's deposition most likely knew nothing about the French officer's secret project at the Ministry of Armaments. In response to the question, "What is your current occupation?" Doll had given his rank and field command, adding only that he had returned to Paris to work on "an electrical apparatus of which I was called upon to submit a prototype last Saturday and on which I shall have to continue working for some weeks."

The deposition had nothing to do with the war. Lieutenant Doll had come to the American embassy that morning to testify in a case pending before the United States District Court in Houston, Texas. The case was a patent lawsuit, *Schlumberger Well Surveying Corporation v. Halliburton Oil Well Cementing Company.* It marked one of the first great industrial battles for control of the science and technology of oil and gas exploration.

At the start of the war, Henri-Georges Doll, 37 years old, was the director of research for *Société de prospection électrique (Procédés Schlumberger)*, a French company. Translated literally the name means "Company for Electrical Prospecting (Schlumberger Methods)." Its employees affectionately called it *la Pros* (pronounced like the first syllable in "prospecting"). The headquarters of *la Pros* was in Paris, at 30 rue Fabert, near the northeast corner of the Esplanade des Invalides, the large open park in central Paris that connects the national military hospital, Les Invalides, to the left bank of the River Seine. Doll was also a director of the company's American affiliate, Schlumberger Well Surveying Corporation, whose offices were in Houston, Texas.

The "Schlumberger method" used electrical current to explore beneath the earth's surface. In its earliest form, the method involved creating an electrical circuit in the ground by passing current through two metal stakes, which functioned as electrodes, and measuring the differences in electrical potential (the voltage) between two other electrodes placed in the ground at different distances from the first two. The technique eventually became known as "the resistivity method," because the relationship between the electrical current injected into the ground and voltage measured on the surface could be used to determine the resistance that different types of rock or soil showed to the passage of an electrical current.

Since the 19th century, geologists and physicists had experimented with electricity as a way of "seeing" into the earth. The reasoning was simple: Because different features of rocks and soils – their chemical composition, moisture content, and degree of compaction, for example – determine their electrical resistivities, it should be possible to characterize and identify rocks and soils by electrical measurements.

This reasoning, however, was deceptive. Precisely because different features of rocks and soils determine their electrical resistivities, it is possible that many different combinations of features – corresponding to different rocks and soils – can give rise to exactly the same resistivity. Plato's ancient allegory of the cave comes to mind: If one is confined to a cave and can see only the shadows cast on its walls by objects passing near the entrance, it is not easy to discover the true nature of the three-dimensional world outside. Nor is it easy to discover the nature of the earth using measurements made only on its surface.

Doll took up this field of research at the age of 24, after finishing his graduate studies at École des Mines, France's top school of geology and mining engineering. Pursuing its many paths led him to the discovery of new methods of prospecting for oil, of locating buried land mines, of measuring blood flow, and even of helping astronauts navigate in space.

Doll worked for *la Pros* and its successor, Schlumberger, for 42 years; in 1987, he was appointed an officer of the *Legion d'Honneur*, one of France's highest decorations. To all who knew him in his public and private life, he was unmistakably French. Yet by the time of his death, on July 25, 1991, in Monfort-l'Amaury, a small town outside Paris, he had been an American citizen for nearly 30 years and had become one of the great, but little known, American inventors of the 20th century.

Today, more than a century after his birth, whenever instruments are lowered into a well to send back measurements of the location and quantity of water, oil, gas, or mineral deposits deep underground, one can be certain that the technology bears the mark of Doll's inventive genius.

"Man has a dual interest in the study of the interior of the earth on which he lives," Doll wrote in 1960 in a special issue of the trade journal *Electronics*. "He naturally has the desire to unearth the buried resources – petroleum, minerals, water – which he can use to improve his living conditions. And being a creature of curiosity, he has the urge to inquire, speculate, and increase his knowledge of the planet on which he will spend most, if not all, of his life." (*Electronics*, 19 July 1960).

Doll's life (1902-1991) paralleled – and his work enabled – one of the most dramatic and sweeping eras of technological innovation and material advancement. The changes were fueled to a large extent by exploitation of a new portable source of energy. In 1900, just prior to his birth, worldwide oil production was only 400,000 barrels a day; by 2000, it had reached 75 million barrels a day, an increase by nearly a factor of two hundred. The demographic explosion during this same time only quadrupled the world's population, from about one-and-a-half billion in 1900 to about six billion in 2000. In the 20th century, the average per capita consumption of oil increased by nearly a factor of 50. It is still growing.

> A barrel of oil is equivalent to about 160 liters in the metric system or about 42 U.S. gallons. Most statistics on oil production and consumption still use this traditional measure, although the standard unit of the International System (S.I.) is now the metric ton. The density of different grades of oil varies, but on average is about 80% that of water. A liter of oil therefore weighs about 0.8 kilograms. A barrel of oil weighs about 0.14 metric tons.

Henri-Georges Doll was born on August 13, 1902, at the home of his parents, Henri Doll and Thérèse (née Braun), on boulevard Saint-Germain, a fashionable street near the center of Paris which begins and ends on the left bank of the Seine. The oldest of four brothers, Henri-Georges attended primary school in the capital before the family moved to Caluire, a suburb of Lyon, where his father managed a multinational textile conglomerate. Lyon was (and still is) the second largest city in France and one of the country's major industrial centers. At the start of the 20th century, it was also a center of the textile business in Europe.

Family life was comfortable for the Dolls. Their home in Caluire included a park and tennis courts. Henri-Georges continued his studies at the public school (*lycée*) in Lyon, which he remembered as being "strict." In July 1918, he was admitted to the first stage of the French *baccalauréat* (which is roughly equivalent to an American high school diploma) in Latin and the sciences. A year later, on July 4, 1919, he was "judged by the faculty of sciences at the University of Lyon to be worthy of the bachelor's degree of secondary education in Latin, science and mathematics, with a passing grade."

Like the rest of France, Lyon was predominantly Catholic. The Dolls were Protestant, but the family was welcomed socially in the city. Henri-Georges recalled a certain resistance in some matters – for example, when he wanted to attend dance classes with the Catholic children – but things were usually worked out.

The Doll family was part of what has been called France's "Protestant high society" (in French, *haute société protestante*, often abbreviated "HSP"). The group traces its origins to the Huguenots in the 16th century, and includes such prominent names as the Havilland family in the porcelain business of Limoges, the Hine family in the wine business of Cognac; and François Guizot in national politics and literature. This influential minority thrived to the point of imposing what Clarisse Schlumberger, author of a long history of her family, called "a kind of Protestant Imperialism" throughout the country.

Clarisse Schlumberger, *Schlumberger, racines et paysages* (Éditions Oberlin, 1997).

The Dolls were close to the Schlumberger family, whose pre-eminence in the textile, finance, and wine industries, as well as in arts and letters, dates to the 17th century. Henri Doll's brother, Albert Doll, had married Pauline Schlumberger, the only daughter of Paul Schlumberger and Marguerite de Witt. Marguerite was the granddaughter of François Guizot, the son of a Protestant family of Nîmes and one of the leading public figures in France during a career that spanned most of the 19th century. Guizot began as a lawyer in Paris in 1805, became a professor of history at the Sorbonne, and then entered politics as a deputy from the city of Lisieux in Normandy, eventually becoming minister of public education (1832–1837), and finally premier (1847) during the restoration monarchy of Louis-Philippe. Guizot's two major historical treatises, *History of the English Revolution* and *General History of Civilization in Europe,* are considered seminal works of modern European history.

Henri and Thérèse (née Braun) Doll.

The young Henri-Georges was allowed to attend surprise parties and receptions with the Catholic children of Lyonnais society, and to participate in activities like tennis, golf, and bridge, normally reserved for the elite. He was an excellent tennis player and often played with another young student from Lyon, Jean Borotra – the "Bounding Basque" who would win five Grand Slam singles titles, including two Wimbledon championships, and who with the other "Four Musketeers" would help France win five consecutive Davis Cups starting in 1927.

As a student, Henri-Georges was also attracted to music and dance, a fascination that stayed with him for life. During the intense period of study for the entrance examination of École Polytechnique, he slipped away on two separate evenings to see Diaghilev's Russian Ballet, featuring Léonide Massine, on tour in Lyon.

He passed the examination for École Polytechnique near the top of the entrance class of 1921, ranking 27th out of 250 candidates accepted (there is no record of the number who took the examination, which is open to all students in France). His admission is recorded in the registration book on September 14, 1921, in the sweeping stokes of the steel-nibbed *Sergent major* pen favored by French bureaucrats:

Hair: Black
Eyes: Brown
Forehead: Normal Slope
Nose: Average (There was no further comment on the size and
   shape of this rather imposing feature of the young student.)
Face: Oval
Height: 1.76 m (5 feet 9 inches).

École Polytechnique was the first of France's *grandes écoles* of science, engineering, and civil service. The school was created in 1794 by the National Convention that ruled France from 1792 to 1795, the middle years of the long French Revolution (1789-1799). Its purpose was to help the country stem a crisis of technical competence caused by the loss of a generation of scientists and engineers in the chaos of the early Revolution. Gaspard Monge, creator of the field of descriptive geometry and an early promoter of the metric system, was one of its founders. In 1804, Napoléon gave École Polytechnique a new role as a national military academy, along with its motto: *Pour la patrie, les sciences et la gloire* ("For the fatherland, the sciences, and glory"). He also moved the campus to a site on the ancient College of Navarre along rue de la Montagne Sainte-Geneviève in Paris (in 1976, the campus moved again to its current location in the city of Palaiseau, about six kilometers, or nearly four miles, southwest of Paris).

École Polytechnique's military character grew during the Third Republic (1870-1940), when it became the main source of the army's artillery officers and engineers. But it never lost its standing as France's leading institute of technology and science; many of the country's most famous scientists and mathematicians, including Poisson, Cauchy, and Fresnel, were trained as *polytechniciens*. The school's insignia symbolizes its dual mission with two cannon crossed in the shape of an "X" – the symbol traditionally used to represent the unknown quantity in a mathematical equation.

> One of the pieces by John Lienhard for the series *The Engines of Our Ingenuity*, produced by KUHF-FM Houston for National Pubic Radio (NPR), is about "The Polytechnic Legacy" and its influence on the history of engineering. See www.uh.edu/engines/asmedall.htm.

Henri-Georges matriculated at École Polytechnique on October 7, 1921, and received a placement in artillery training, his first choice. He did not shine academically and admitted later that he devoted little time to his studies. In the first semester, he was elected class treasurer (*caissier*), a position whose long list of responsibilities included representing the class before the school administration, arranging aid for less fortunate students, overseeing the hazing of new students, and organizing class events such as parades, balls, banquets, comedy shows, practical jokes, and most important, the thunderous entertainment for the feast of Saint Barbara, the patron saint of gunners and artillerymen. "All that took a lot of time," he wrote later, "too much time to allow anyone to be at the head of his class."

He was far from the head, ranking 138 in a class of 251 at the end of his first year, and 142 at the end of 1923. His best subjects were mathematics and chemistry. Along with the rest of his classmates, Henri-Georges also received the traditional military training of the school. In June 1922, he trained at Camp Mailly in the Aube region, southeast of Paris; the next June he was at Camp Coëtquidan, in Morbihan, Brittany, near the northeast coast of France. (Camp Coëtquidan is France's most famous military training facility and has also served as a training ground for American troops. Harry Truman was stationed there in 1918 during his service with 129th Artillery Regiment in World War I.)

On October 1, 1923, Henri-Georges was promoted to second lieutenant in the artillery reserve, attached to the 32nd Artillery Regiment, and was assigned to the artillery training school at Fontainebleau, south of Paris. In 1924, after a second artillery training school, an evaluation by the training officer read simply:

Judgment: Unsure
Character: A little soft
Conduct and character: Very good
Demeanor: Very good.

The overall assessment was mixed: "Needs practice. Lacks precision and is not well grounded in artillery techniques. Has self-confidence and can do better. Probably best adapted to the role of deputy officer for his good demeanor and education." He ranked 24th out of the 68 cadets at Fontainebleau, with a grade of 13.5 out of 20 in general aptitude.

The evaluation was much better a few months later, in October 1924, after a training course with the 54th Artillery Regiment of the 14th Army Corps: "...excellent second officer, very intelligent, energetic and a hard worker. Did first-class work on the firing range."

In the traditional graduation photo, a formal military portrait, Henri-Georges looks handsome in a black-caped uniform with red striped pants; the bicorn hat of the French army rests on his left arm, folded across a belted waist; white gloves are held tightly in his right hand, pressed against the hip. His hair, mustache, and eyebrows are jet black, and a large, but well-proportioned nose dominates a long oval face, marked by a light dimple at the exact center of his chin.

Henri-Georges liked to joke and probably enjoyed the playful words used to describe him during his time at École Polytechique: *lambda, coëtard, pantoufler.* It meant: An average student (*lambda*), who had trained at Camp Coëtquidan (*coëtard*), and was destined for the private sector (the *pantoufle*, or slipper, being the opposite of the *botte*, or military boot).

After graduation, the life of the new second-lieutenant took a decisive turn. Conrad Schlumberger, also a *polytechnicien* and a professor of physics at École des Mines, had taken notice of the young man. At École Polytechnique, Henri-Georges had been attracted mainly to chemistry, but Conrad Schlumberger encouraged him to continue his studies at École des Mines and specialize in geology, because, he said, "...if there is a place for you in my company, you will be better prepared after studying geology."

Conrad also encouraged a courtship with his oldest daughter, Anne Marguerite Louis Marie, called "Annette." Annette danced with Henri-Georges at the traditional graduation ball of École Polytechnique, held at the Hotel Continental in Paris. A year later they were married at the town hall of Saint-Ouen-le-Pin, a small town near Pont-l'Evêque in the Calvados region of France.

The reception was held at Val-Richer, the magnificent Schlumberger family estate at the site of an ancient Cistercian abbey, which had belonged to François Guizot and had been purchased by Conrad's father, Paul Schlumberger. (Today the estate is shared among the 350 descendants of Paul and Marguerite Schlumberger.) Pierre Schlumberger, the son of Conrad's younger brother Marcel, was the young groomsman, who held his cousin's bridal train in the photo-graph of the bridal party taken on the front porch of the estate. The paths of Henri-Georges Doll and Pierre Schlumberger would cross again twenty years later in Texas, under less happy circumstances.

Marriage of Henri-Georges Doll and Annette Schlumberger, September 24, 1924, at Val-Richer, the Schlumberger family estate in Normandy.

An arranged marriage? Perhaps. It was common at the time, and not just among the Protestant high society of France. Conrad had three daughters, but no sons, and he was heir to an industrial fortune. In her memoir published in 1977, *La boite magique, ou les sources du pétrole* (Éditions Fayard), Annette wrote, "In the person of my husband, Henri Doll, I had given my father the son he had always hoped for: Brilliant and gifted with a imagination so practical that ideas and problems seemed to clarify and lose their rough edges whenever he touched them. Did he know that the pursuit of research, where his life would find its meaning, held little for the young girl that he was marrying?"

Izaline, the oldest daughter of Henri-Georges and Annette, said of her mother's marriage, "She didn't have a choice."

Even more surely than a son, Doll became the intellectual successor of his father-in-law. With his ingenuity, his relentless work ethic, and his knack for picking the right collaborators at the right time, he would help transform a small family enterprise – a "start-up" in today's terms – into the world's largest and most successful oilfield services company.

The literal translation of the title of Annette's memoir is "The magic box, or the sources of oil." It was published in English as *The Schlumberger Adventure* (Arco Publishing, New York, 1982).

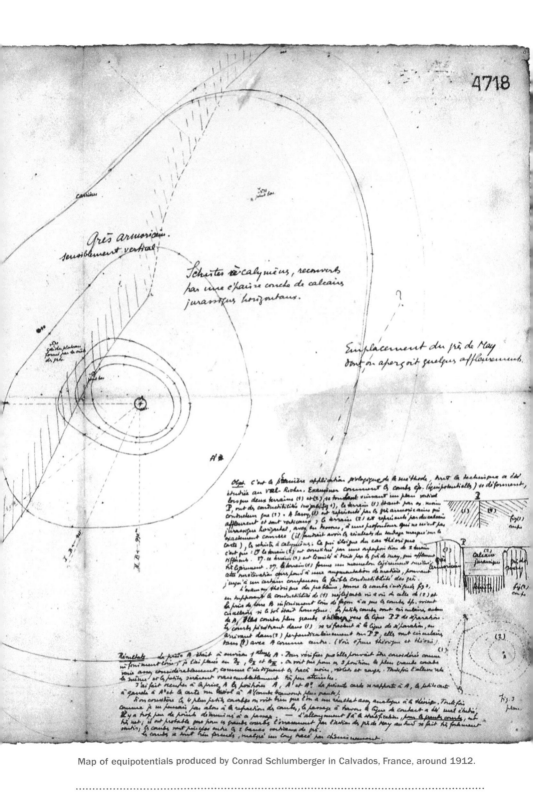

Map of equipotentials produced by Conrad Schlumberger in Calvados, France, around 1912.

Chapter 2

Why Measure the Earth's Resistivity?

Conrad Schlumberger, born in 1878, was the descendant of a long line of industrialists from Alsace who first made their fortune in cotton mills and looms. His father, Paul, wanted to study science, but eventually had to take over the family's textile business, first at Guebwiller in Alsace, then later in England. Paul Schlumberger married Marguerite de Witt, the granddaughter of François Guizot.

She was an early champion of women's rights and later directed the International League for Women's Suffrage.

Paul and Marguerite Schlumberger had five sons and a daughter. Two of the sons studied science: Conrad, at École Polytechnique, and Marcel, at École Centrale des Arts et Manufactures in Paris. École Centrale is also one of France's top engineering schools; its graduates (*centraliens*) can be found at the highest positions in French industry and civil service. (Gustave Eiffel, creator of the Eiffel Tower, was a *centralien*.) Maurice, the youngest of the five sons, became a banker; Jean, the oldest, followed a career in literature. With André Gide, Gaston Gallimard, and Martin du Gard, Jean was one of the founders of the *Nouvelle revue française* (*New French Review*), which became France's most prestigious literary magazine. The family's third child, Daniel, died in his mid-thirties. The daughter, Pauline, married Albert Doll, the uncle of Henri-Georges.

In 1910, Conrad Schlumberger, then professor of physics at École des Mines and France's chief mining engineer (*ingénieur en chef des mines*), had the idea of using electrical currents as a way of "seeing" underground. A few other scientists around the world, notably Frank Wenner at the National Bureau of Standards in Washington, D.C., and Richard Ambronn in Germany, also had the same idea.

Although mining is an ancient human activity, the methods used for mineral prospecting at the start of the 20th century were still crude. They were limited mainly to the search for surface geological features, such as hills, valleys, or rock outcrops, that were known to correlate with subsurface structures of interest – the faults, folds, and fractures often found near mineralized zones, or the buried domes and sequences of permeable and impermeable layers that contained groundwater or oil and gas. Drilling a shallow hole into the subsurface was the main way of confirming the conclusions drawn from studies of surface geology.

Prospectors had also known for some time – at least since the publication of William Gilbert's *de Magnete* in 1600 – that magnetic minerals could be located by the disturbances they created in the earth's natural magnetic field. At the turn of the 20th century, a sensitive compass was still the main tool of geophysical exploration.

> William Gilbert (1544-1603) was an English physician and natural philosopher, and served for a time as the personal physician of Queen Elizabeth I. The full title of his major work was *De Magnete, Magneticisque Corporibus, et de Magno Magnete Tellure* (On the Magnet and Magnetic Bodies, and on the Great Magnet the Earth). It is considered the first treatise on geophysics.

In the early 19th century, the English geologist Robert Were Fox had also carried out experiments using electrical currents in the tin mines of Cornwall. Unlike the earth's magnetic field, which is always pointing north unless disturbed by local magnetic objects, there is no natural electric field at the earth's surface that can serve as a steady reference for electrical experiments. So it was necessary for Fox to use batteries to inject artificial electrical current into the ground and to try to measure carefully how the injected current spread through the subsurface. But the electrical equipment available at the time – and throughout most of the 19th century – was either primitive or too delicate for field work. As a result, no systematic methods had been developed for determining the electrical properties of rocks and soil, or for understanding the relationship between these properties and the kinds of minerals and fluids they might contain.

Conrad Schlumberger did his first electrical experiments in a bathtub filled with soil in the basement of École des Mines. In August 1912, he moved the experiments outdoors to the family estate at Val-Richer. He planted two electrodes – simple metal stakes – into the ground a large distance apart and connected them with wires to opposite poles of a battery, which drove electrical current into the earth. Using two other electrodes connected to a sensitive instrument called a potentiometer, he then measured at different locations along the earth's surface the electrical voltage created by the current flowing through the ground. The map he sketched from these measurements at first glance looked like a relief map; its contour lines, however, did not connect points of equal altitude, but rather points of equal electrical voltage ("equipotential" lines) caused by the flowing current. It was the beginning of a new method of exploring the earth's subsurface using electricity.

Conrad's idea was simple. Electrical current can flow through any material. When injected into the earth, it spreads out in all directions from the point of injection. If the ground is homogeneous, the current also spreads uniformly and occupies an ever-expanding hemisphere in the ground, as individual filaments of current flow straight from the point of injection along all directions pointing into the ground and along its surface.

But if the ground is not homogeneous – if it is composed of layers with different types of rock with different compositions or different amounts of water at different locations, or if layers themselves have been distorted over geologic time into folds, faults, or other geologic structures – then the current spreading from the point of injection will not follow straight-line paths, but will seek out the "path of least resistance."

The property that determines the current paths in the ground, or in any material, is called the "electrical resistivity," or simply the "resistivity." Resistivity, like density, is an intrinsic property of materials and can vary from one point to another in the subsurface (or in any object) according to the type of material present and according to its state, for example, its temperature and pressure.

Density is simply the quantity of mass per unit volume. The standard unit for measuring density is the kilogram per cubic meter. A more practical unit is the gram per cubic centimeter; at room temperature and atmospheric pressure, water has a density of about one gram per cubic centimeter.

Resistivity is the ability of a material to resist the flow of electrical current. The standard unit for resistivity is the ohm-meter (written "ohm-m"); its definition is more complicated than that for density.

Consider a one-meter cube, composed of uniform material. The value of its electrical resistivity in ohm-m is the difference in voltage that must be placed on two opposing faces of the cube to force an electrical current of one ampere (A) to flow between the two faces. One volt (V) is needed to create a current of 1 A through a cube of material with a resistivity of 1 ohm-m; 100 V are needed for a more resistive material of 100 ohm-m. A cubic meter is a huge volume of material. A way of measuring resistivity on a smaller scale is to take a one-centimeter cube. The material has a resistivity of 1 ohm-m if it passes a current of 1 A when connected to a 100 V battery.

Another way of defining the resistivity of a material is as follows: The resistance (in ohm) of a piece of material through which electrical current flows is proportional to the resistivity of the material and to its length, and it is inversely proportional to the cross-sectional area of the flow.

Most scientific units in electricity and magnetism are named after famous figures in the subjects' history. The volt is named after the Italian physicist Alessandro Volta (1745-1827), who constructed the first battery in 1900; the ampere, after the French physicist André-Marie Ampère (1775-1836), who elaborated the connection between steady electrical currents and magnetic fields; and the ohm, after the German physicist Georg Ohm (1789-1854), who first studied the relationship between voltage and current in electrical circuits.

Electrical resistivity can range from zero to infinity. A perfect vacuum has infinite resistivity, while a superconductor has a resistivity of zero. The resistivities of ordinary materials also span a very large range. Metals have resistivities on the order of one-millionth of an ohm-m, whereas most plastic materials are excellent electrical insulators, with resistivities of the order of a million ohm-m. Sea water (and human blood) has a resistivity of about 0.25 ohm-m; ordinary tap water, about 4 ohm-m.

Rocks and dry soils, including dry sand, generally have very high resistivity, about 1000 ohm-m or more. But below a certain depth in the earth, nearly all rocks are saturated with water, meaning that water fills all void spaces – the "pores" that exist between the solid grains of rock. If the pores of the rocks are connected, electrical current can be carried by ions in the water occupying the pores, which lowers the electrical resistivity of most water-saturated rocks to a range from about 0.1 to 10 ohm-m. Some rocks containing clay minerals, which trap water in their crystal structures, also have low resistivities in the range of near one ohm-m, even if they appear dry at their surface. Another way of lowering the natural resistivity of a rock is to add small amounts of metallic minerals, such as copper, silver, or gold.

But the only way – or nearly the only way – to raise the resistivity of a rock is to fill its pores with oil or gas (electrical insulators), instead of water (an electrical conductor).

When Conrad Schlumberger began his research in 1910, information about the electrical resistivity of rocks and soils was still fragmentary. He understood nevertheless its potential importance for mineral exploration. In a monograph describing his early research, he wrote: "Among all the methods of prospecting imaginable, those based

Conrad Schlumberger performing electrical experiments on the grounds of Val-Richer in 1911. Conrad's brother Marcel, the young *polytechnicien* Eugène Léonardon, and Roger Jost, the nephew of the steward who managed the estate, all participated in these first experiments.

on the electrical conductivity are especially attractive. They require precise measurements, but they allow one to address a large variety of geological problems, and even to target directly metallic minerals that are good conductors of electricity."

Étude sur la Prospection Électrique du Sous-sol, Conrad Schlumberger (Gauthiers-Villars et Cie., 1920, préface, p. v-vi).

To make "precise measurements" possible, Conrad had refined a new potentiometer, which he had had built by the firm Hartmann-Braun of Frankfurt, Germany, the leading manufacturer of precision electrical instruments at the time. The instrument, mounted on a tripod, was rugged, simple to operate and portable. It could not only create and measure a calibrated series of voltages down to a fraction of a millivolt (one thousandth of a volt), but was also integrated with a

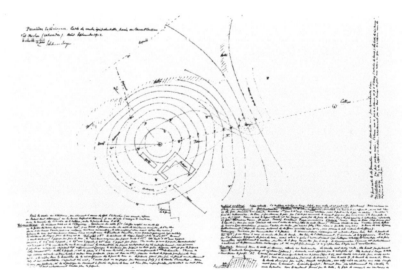

Map produced by Conrad Schlumberger from electrical experiments at Val-Richer. The lines are curves of "equipotential" (equal electrical voltage) centered on an electrode – electrode *A* in Conrad's terminology – which injected current into the ground from a battery. A second electrode (*B*), which collected current from the ground to complete the electrical circuit, was placed a large distance away. The experiment was done on a wide flat lawn, above sandy soil at the back of the house, whose outline appears at the bottom center of the figure. On a perfectly flat surface above homogeneous ground, the equipotential curves would be perfect circles centered on electrode *A*. Deviations indicate inhomogeneities in the subsurface.

galvanometer capable of measuring very weak electrical currents, on the order of a few microamperes (a millionth of an ampere).

Conrad continued to improve his "black box" over more than a decade of laboratory and field research. Its amazing sensitivity allowed him to make electrical measurements over long distances, and he often carried a megaphone into the field to communicate with his assistants the instructions to open or close the circuit on the batteries or on the generator that injected electrical current into the earth.

Conrad was close to his brother Marcel, who shared his enthusiasm for science and engineering. Six year younger than Conrad, Marcel was fascinated by mechanical engineering, automobiles, and aviation. After trying unsuccessfully to perfect an automatic transmission for cars, he turned his interests to the design of instruments for the mining industry. Paul Schlumberger, seeing that two of his sons had arrived at the same field of endeavor by different routes, encouraged them to team up. He believed strongly in the future of the science and technology that Conrad was developing.

In 1914, however, World War I engulfed Europe. Conrad was mobilized as an artillery captain. While serving at the front lines, he invented a system for locating enemy artillery by measuring the sound waves propagated through the air and along the ground after a shot was fired. (Similar systems developed by German and American scientists would lead after the War to the development of methods that use sound waves to probe inside the earth. The "seismic method" would eventually compete directly with Conrad's method of electrical currents.)

Conrad was profoundly shaken by the horrors of the Great War and began to question his future and his role in the world. In her memoirs, Annette recounts a conversation that her father had had with a friend in the trenches at Verdun: "I am ashamed," Conrad said, "to belong to a family of industrialists whose workers get up at dawn, walk kilometers to work in the cotton mills, and slave away twelve or fourteen hours a day. Not one of them has had a decent life."

Conrad Schlumberger around 1920.

Marcel Schlumberger during World War I.

Decommissioned after the end of the War in 1919, Conrad considered devoting his life to social and pacifist activities. He began to write a book on world peace and supported the socialist newspaper *L'Humanité*, which had been founded in 1904 by Jean Jaurès, the leader of the French socialist party. (This was before the French Communists took control of *L'Humanité* in 1920 and made it their official party newspaper.) Even Conrad's closest friends and colleagues were surprised by his turning away from science.

His father intervened. Paul Schlumberger offered to support his two sons, Conrad and Marcel, in a new enterprise that would develop Conrad's technology of electrical prospecting. The support came with one important condition: that the two brothers devote themselves fully to the new endeavor and refrain from efforts in other areas. "The field of endeavor," he wrote, "is wide enough to satisfy their scientific curiosity. The scientific interest in research must take precedence over financial interests. Marcel will bring to Conrad his remarkable qualities as an engineer and his common sense. Conrad will be the wise physicist. I will support them." He offered 500,000 francs of his own money for the endeavor.

> It is difficult to compare directly the old *franc-or* ("gold franc") of the early 20th century, supported by the gold standard, with today's French currency, the euro. But to give an idea, 500,000 *francs-or* represented about 160 kilograms of gold at the time, which at 2007 prices, is worth about 2,500,000 euros – or at current exchange rates, about $3.5 million.

Conrad and Marcel accepted their father's offer. On November 12, 1919, in Paris, they signed a formal covenant (*convention*) embodying the agreement before a notary public.

Conrad abandoned the writing of his pacifist book and resumed his teaching at École des Mines. The period that his older brother Jean described as "undoubtedly the most painful personal crisis that [Conrad] had ever undergone" was over. He set up an electrical laboratory again in the basement of École des Mines and continued the experiments he had started before the war, filling bathtubs and tanks with soils and materials of different composition, arranging them to simulate geological structures on a small scale, and carrying out miniature prospecting experiments. In one test, he used sand saturated with water and sheets of ebonite (an insulating material) to simulate sequences of conducting and resistive layers in the subsurface. He also called on Alfred-Marie Liénard, the deputy director of École des Mines and one of France's most talented mathematical physicists, to help develop the mathematical tools needed to understand how electrical current spreads through complex geological structures. Soon after resuming his electrical research, Conrad's attention turned naturally to a subject whose importance had been emphasized by the Great War.

The subject was oil exploration.

Chapter 3

The Age of Oil

The modern exploitation of oil began
in the second half of the nineteenth
century. Crude oil, or its byproduct
kerosene, was first used mainly
for lighting, in oil or kerosene lamps.
Supplies, however, were limited
until Edwin Drake drilled the first
successful oil well in Titusville,
Pennsylvania, in 1859. The wells of
western Pennsylvania, and then
Ohio, provided an abundant supply
of crude oil, which gradually began
to replace vegetable oils as a
lubricant and whale oil for lighting.

The rapid development of the automobile after the turn of the century dragged the oil industry along in its wake. The "rush for liquid gold" had begun.

The military and political importance of the new resource also soon became apparent. In 1912, the British Royal Navy under the direction of First Lord of the Admiralty Winston Churchill converted its fleet from coal to oil. The Germans and Americans quickly did the same. Motorized transportation of troops began in sensational fashion on September 7, 1914, when General Joseph Gallieni of the French army requisitioned the taxicabs of Paris to transport some 10,000 soldiers as reinforcements for a counter-offensive against the Germans, who had advanced within 50 kilometers of Paris. General Gallieni's "taxis of the Marne" became legend.

World War I also saw the first use of the modern tank at the Battle of the Somme in September 1916, one of the bloodiest battles of the war. The first vehicles were actually modified farm tractors. The British clad them in metal armor and called them "tanks" (as in "containers") to conceal their purpose as assault vehicles. As the infantry motorized, air forces also developed rapidly; thousands of airplanes were manufactured for use in World War I.

Georges Clemenceau, the French Prime Minister during the war, declared oil to be "the blood of the earth" and made an urgent appeal to President Woodrow Wilson to provide oil supplies to the Allies, without which, he wrote, "our armies are paralyzed." The United States was the leading producer of oil, a position it had held since the start of the oil age. By the time of World War I, the U.S. oil industry had already seen several booms and busts, as vast new fields were discovered in Texas, Oklahoma, and California. John D. Rockefeller's Standard Oil Company, established in 1870, had become the world's largest corporation by the turn of the century, and was broken up by the United States Supreme Court in 1911.

Soon after signing the agreement with their father, Conrad and Marcel Schlumberger envisioned setting up their own company for electrical prospecting. The first field experiments had shown that electrical methods could be used to find metallic mineral deposits, but Conrad had also recognized the method's potential for identifying underground oil reservoirs, which are perhaps the most difficult resources to discover with remote measurements.

Oil forms from organic material buried deep underground at high temperature and pressure. Its density, once formed, is only about 80% that of water; so buried oil will migrate inexorably to the surface unless it is trapped underground by impermeable layers – that is, by layers of rock whose pores are clogged or too narrow to permit the flow of any fluid. The structures most favorable for the accumulation of oil are porous layers, usually sandstones and limestones, which have been bowed up by geological forces into underground "domes" or into arch-like ridges called "anticlines" and which have been capped by impermeable layers – usually shales, which are rocks formed by compaction of very fine-grained silt and clay.

Sandstone is formed from larger grains of sand, cemented or packed together. Limestone is composed mainly of calcium carbonate from the shells of marine organisms. The "porosity" of sandstones and limestones – that is, the fraction of the total volume of rock that is void space between the solid grains – is often as high as 30%. The porosity of shales is close to zero.

To prospect for oil from the surface, it was necessary not only to identify these structures deep underground, but also to determine whether their pores were filled with water or with oil.

Conrad's method of electrical prospecting had advanced significantly since the end of World War I. Eugène Léonardon, a graduate of École Polytechnique who had worked with Conrad and Marcel before World War I, came back to work with them as their first full-time engineer. Others followed as Conrad obtained exploration contracts from the government or local mining companies. Some recruits were attracted by a small advertisement in the French *Journal des Mines* (Mining Journal), asking for "athletic engineers to carry out field surveys after carrying miles of cable across fields, thickets, vineyards and other obstacles."

The brothers had a preference for engineers from the French *grandes écoles*, such as Polytechnique, Mines, and Centrale, but they also recruited from Institut Agronomique (Agricultural Institute) and École des Maîtres Mineurs (School of Mining Administration). Sherwin Kelly, an American graduate of École des Mines, joined their enterprise in 1922 and was sent to the United States with Léonardon, where the two carried out successful electrical surveys for copper mines in Tennessee and Michigan and for coal deposits in Pennsylvania.

Conrad and Marcel continued to improve their equipment, including the now famous "black box," and to refine field procedures so that ever larger areas could be covered quickly. They also developed procedures to measure and account for natural electrical currents, which exist in various forms underground and can be a source of "noise" for electrical prospecting. Some natural currents, which the French field engineers called *vagabonds* ("wandering"), are purely random, caused by motion of ions in water-filled pores of underground rocks. Others, called "telluric," are driven by electrical fields generated in the atmosphere by thunderstorms and by interactions between the earth's magnetic field and the solar wind. Some natural underground currents are relatively steady, driven either by the flow of salt water in underground aquifers or by electrochemical reactions between mineral ores and surrounding fluids – both of which can create a kind of natural underground battery. Whatever their origin, these natural currents needed to be taken into account when using Conrad's method of injecting current into the ground to measure the earth's resistivity.

During the summer of 1923, a crew employed by the Schlumberger brothers undertook a large survey in the district of Plahova, west of the city of Ploesti, in Rumania. The survey outlined a zone of high resistivity a hundred meters (330 feet) or so below the surface, which subsequent drilling revealed to be a large underground deposit of salt, which is almost a perfect insulator. Oil deposits were later discovered near the flanks of the Ploesti "salt dome." It was the first oil reservoir to be discovered by surface geophysical mapping. The discovery was actually inferred, since the resistivity map did not reveal directly the oil reservoir, but rather the zone of high resistivity associated with the salt itself.

Despite this and other successes, demand for use of the new technology of electrical prospecting was slow to develop. The resistivity maps gave only indirect indications of the shape, size, or depth of underground structures that *might* hold or trap oil. The technology of electricity was still new, and to the practical men of the oil business, Conrad's method inspired skepticism or was confused with fanciful schemes based on the even newer science of radio waves.

These schemes, and others like them, are described in a delightful article entitled "Black Magic," which appeared in January 1936 in the inaugural issue of the scientific journal *Geophysics*, published by the newly formed Society of Exploration Geophysicists. The author was Ludwig Blau, a geophysicist with Humble Oil & Refining Company, which had maintained over the years a file on the dubious methods it (and other oil companies) had received from prospectors in search of a contract. There was a "radio condenser," which could indicate directly by the turn of a knob the size and depth of an oil field, and the "hertzian wave and cathode ray detector," which located oil reservoirs, groundwater levels, or mineral veins with a range of several kilometers. Other devices included an instrument for detecting the "corpuscules of radiation" given off by underground oil; a vial of "oil bait" hung on a walking stick, which oscillated back and forth over a reservoir; and a special "masculine liquid" with an affinity for oil, which the inventor had determined to be feminine in character.

Credulity for schemes capable of finding oil in bold new ways was of course not limited to the early days of oil exploration. A catalog of modern examples would include *les avions renifleurs* ("sniffer planes") which flew at high altitude and detected newly discovered atomic particles emanating from oil fields. The French Interior Ministry allegedly spent millions of dollars on the device before discovering that it was simply printing out existing geologic maps stored in its software. A version of the radio condenser for discovering oil by turning the knob on a new type of radio receiver also made a comeback in the 1990s, mounted in a vintage model Cadillac.

At the end of 1923, Conrad Schlumberger resigned his professorship at École des Mines to work full time with Marcel on the enterprise their father had funded. The next year, Conrad encouraged his new son-in-law, Henri-Georges Doll, to enroll at École des Mines, mainly to study geology, but also to improve his skills in physics and mathematics. Doll also worked as a research assistant in the offices that Conrad and Marcel set up in a small house at 30 rue Fabert, along the northern end of the Esplanade des Invalides, about a hundred meters from the left bank of the Seine. Three of the five rooms were converted into offices; the remaining two became a machine shop and a laboratory. Conrad and Marcel shared the same work desk, along with all other aspects of the business, from designing and building new equipment, to drafting contracts with clients, ordering supplies for the crews, and keeping the books. Rue Fabert would remain the headquarters of Conrad's and Marcel's endeavor for the next twenty years.

Doll and Annette lived on rue Casimir-Périer, a small street just west of the Esplanade des Invalides, a short walk from rue Fabert. Annette came to the office often to have lunch with her husband and her father. She remembered often finding her father pacing up and down the office, looking at the floor and talking about his views on technical questions or on relationships with clients. Conrad was his own secretary: he typed his own letters, organized his own files, and sharpened his own pencils. He and Marcel smoked constantly. "Marcel," Annette wrote, "always seemed to have a cigarette in his lips."

Marcel also carried with him a copybook – the kind used by French schoolchildren – which he filled with sketches of new equipment, as he reviewed its design on the drafting tables and followed its construction in the machine shop on the first floor, which had been converted from an old café bar.

On December 1, 1925, Annette gave birth to her first child, a daughter, which she and Henri-Georges named Izaline, after Izaline Plan, the wife of Ernest Guizot, the first cousin of her great-great grandfather, François Guizot.

Doll became a full-time employee of the Schlumberger brothers in 1926. "Conrad and Marcel were alone at the offices in Paris," he later recalled. "I was their employee, but had no special title. I did field work, mostly in France, often in Normandy, to prospect for deposits of iron ore. We were also using the same methods to study dam sites, to look for the former river beds, filled with alluvial soil that needed to be cemented in before the dam was built, to prevent underground leaks."

Photographs show him wearing the field outfit of time – knicker-bockers flared at the thighs and stuffed into long field boots laced up to just below the knee – which he combined with his own preference for conservative dress. He is usually seen wearing a tie, even in the field. The natural, almost casual, elegance that shines through these early pictures would never desert him.

Doll was also developing an uncanny intuition for visualizing the complicated paths that electrical current follows through the earth. "The deposits we were looking for," he recalled in an interview after his retirement, "were usually covered by 400 to 500 feet of recent sediments. It was necessary to 'see' through this cover, as if you were peeling the layers off one at a time from the surface." At École des Mines, moreover, he had become an excellent mathematician. With Conrad and Marcel at rue Fabert, he was also learning how to develop new geophysical equipment.

In addition to Conrad's electrical method, *la Pros* had begun to experiment with using magnetic fields for mineral prospecting and wanted to develop better methods for measuring the distortions of the earth's magnetic field caused by buried magnetic minerals, especially iron deposits. The magnetometers of the time were delicate to handle, subject to random drifts, and required a long time (several minutes or more) to make an accurate measurement.

Doll took up the project and designed and built at rue Fabert a new instrument that used electromagnetic induction to the measure the earth's magnetic field. The device consisted of two large circular frames, about a meter in diameter, carrying coils of wire that could be rotated about a horizontal axis by a crank. (The motion of the coils as they turn in the earth's magnetic field creates a voltage that is proportional both to the magnetic field and to their rate of rotation. This "induction" effect is the same principle that is used to generate electrical power, for example, in hydroelectric plants that use falling water to turn a large coil suspended in a powerful magnetic field.) The entire apparatus, except for the wire coils, was constructed from non-magnetic materials – plywood, Bakelite (the first synthetic plastic), and aluminum.

Doll tested the new device on the Esplanade des Invalides. As he was performing the experiment, a crowd gathered to inspect the large rotating instrument. A cyclist circling the equipment and the current from electric trains passing in the nearby Metro station kept disturbing the measurement. A policeman, attracted as much by the curious device as by the gathering crowd, came over and put an end to the show. Doll finished the tests at Marcel's property at Cormeilles-en-Parisis, about ten kilometers (six miles) northwest of Paris. Six years later he would use a version of the instrument in the oil fields of the Soviet Union, and it would be the subject of his first paper at an international scientific conference.

In 1926, electrical prospecting had two remarkable successes. The target was neither metallic mineral nor oil deposits, but a layer of potash sandwiched in deposits of rock salt beneath the broad flat plains that lie between the cities of Mulhouse and Colmar, near the French-German border in Alsace. Alsatian potash was one of the world's main sources of potassium chloride used in artificial fertilizers of the day. A large electrical survey consisting of about 4000 separate measurements covering 50 square kilometers (19 square miles) outlined the crest of an elongated underground arch, nearly seven kilometers (four miles) long, where the salt layer bowed up in a geological anticline. A separate survey revealed where the top of the Mayenheim salt dome, the major subsurface feature of the region, came within 100 meters of the surface. The targets identified in each of these surveys were later confirmed by drilling.

The discoveries encouraged Conrad and Marcel to incorporate a new public company in Paris, in July 1926, under the name Société de prospection électrique (Procédés Schlumberger).

An initial capital of 200,000 francs was divided into 2000 shares of common stock with a par value of 100 francs per share. The two brothers gave the new company a license to practice the technology of electrical measurements, as embodied in patents granted to Conrad Schlumberger in 18 countries, along with field equipment and the results of all of the surveys they had done so far.

In return, Conrad and Marcel each received 750 shares of the common stock and 1000 beneficial or "founders' shares," which had no nominal value but entitled them to a share of the profits. The two brothers also purchased stock in the company at 100 francs a share: Conrad bought 245 shares; Marcel, 247 shares. The eight remaining shares were sold to the family: Their two brothers, Jean and Maurice, each purchased two shares; their brother-in-law Albert Doll (the husband of their sister Pauline and the uncle of Henri-Georges) purchased two shares; Conrad's daughter Annette and Marcel's daughter Genevieve each purchased one share.

Conrad was named president of the company. Albert Doll and Maurice Schlumberger were named its auditors. The board of directors consisted of the four brothers – Conrad, Marcel, Jean, and Maurice – and Albert Doll. Henri-Georges Doll was named the company's agent with the responsibility under French law for presenting a report to the shareholders' meeting on the financial results of the first business year.

On October 15, 1926, two months after the founding of *la Pros*, Paul Schlumberger died. The agreement he had made with his two sons would soon lead to a breakthrough.

Oil derrick at Pechelbronn, around 1930.

Chapter 4

From Core to Log

A hollow tube forced into the ground at the bottom of a drill hole fills up with material and, if extracted carefully, provides a sample of earth from the region just below the bottom of the hole. Geologists call this kind of sample a "geological core," or just a "core." The origin of the term is obscure, but probably reflects the normal meaning of the English word ("central part"), as well as the shape of an apple core. The English word is related to the French for heart (*coeur*), but in French, a geological core is actually *une carotte* (literally, "a carrot").

"Coring" (*carottage*, in French) has long been a standard method for gathering samples in geology and in archaeology. More recently, long cores taken through glaciers and sediments at the ocean bottom have provided a valuable record of Earth's climate, helping scientists to precisely date glacial cycles as well as to determine the relationship between average global temperature and the amount of carbon dioxide and other greenhouse gases in the atmosphere.

Oil and mineral prospectors also learned very early the value of extracting samples of the earth from their wells, and they quickly developed ingenious methods for taking cores up to several meters long from the bottoms of deep wells and for bringing them safely back to the surface. Coring is still the most reliable way of determining exactly what the drill bit has penetrated and for providing samples that can be tested in a laboratory for the presence of oil, or evaluated for other important physical properties, such as density, porosity, and chemical composition.

But mechanical coring also has major drawbacks. First, it takes time. To obtain a core from the bottom of a well, the entire column of drill pipe in the hole has to be removed – so that the regular drill bit can be replaced with a special bit for taking cores – and then reinserted back into the hole. After the sample is taken, the drill pipe must be removed again to recover the core and re-attach the original drill bit. This process slows down drilling and increases its cost so much that it is impractical to take cores at regular intervals along the entire length of a well.

Second, coring is not reliable. Core samples often came back to the surface in poor condition, incomplete or broken (especially when the rock layers themselves are not well consolidated); the sample can also be contaminated by the mud that circulates through the well during drilling. Finally, coring is dangerous. The longer the well remains open while cores are being taken, the greater the chances that pressure deep underground will cause formation fluids, including explosive oil or gas, to erupt through the well in a "blowout."

In 1927, Conrad Schlumberger began to conceive a way of replacing mechanical coring with measurements made in the well. The idea itself was not new. Robert Fox, the English geologist credited with carrying out with the first measurements of the electrical properties of the earth, did experiments injecting electrical current deep underground in the tin mines of Cornwall in the 1820s. In *la Pros*, the idea first came up in 1921, when Conrad's brother Marcel was doing a surface electrical survey with three engineers in the coal basin of Bessèges near the city of Nîmes in the south of France. Marcel had the idea of taking measurements directly within the coal seams themselves to confirm the results of the surface survey. According to anecdotal accounts (no written report survives), Marcel cobbled together a system using flower pots to lower the electrical equipment into a nearby well that was about 800 meters (2625 feet) deep. The pots provided both ballast and protection to the electrodes during the descent. He and the crew were able to record several electrical measurements with the equipment resting at the bottom of the well.

When he returned to Paris, Marcel described these experiments to Conrad, who also had been thinking about the possibility of making electrical measurements in wells. Conrad was on the board of directors of a French-Belgian company that operated the oil fields in eastern France near the town of Pechelbronn, and he knew that the local geologists were having difficulty identifying the layers that had been penetrated by the drill bit. He believed that electrical measurements made along the well could help to solve this problem.

Conrad and Marcel discussed their ideas, but took no further action at the time. The two brothers still believed that the future of their business lay in surface electrical prospecting and wanted to respond to a challenge from a new exploration technology using sound waves that was developing rapidly in the United States.

The new method, called "seismic prospecting," had been invented almost simultaneously in Germany, the United States, and Canada near the end of World War I. In Germany, the inventor was Ludger Mintrop, a mining engineer from the University of Berlin. In the United States, many individuals were involved, but three of the most prominent were Burton McCollum, an electrical engineer from the University of Kansas; William Haseman, a professor of physics at the University of Oklahoma; and J. Clarence Karcher, one of Haseman's graduate students. The Canadian inventor, Reginald Fessenden, one of the pioneers in the development of radio, had also sketched some of the key ideas of the seismic method in a U.S. patent application filed in 1917.

Like Conrad Schlumberger in France, Mintrop, McCollum, Haseman, and Karcher worked during World War I on locating enemy cannon using sound waves. Mintrop worked with the Artillery Control Division of the German army; McCollum, Haseman, and Karcher worked together at the U.S. Bureau of Standards in Washington, D.C. After the war, they all started to apply the technology of sound-wave generation and measurement to oil exploration. The three Americans set up Geological Engineering Company in the United States in 1920; a year later, Mintrop set up the German company SEISMOS. Both companies soon had commercial crews working in the oil fields of Oklahoma, Texas, and the Gulf Coast.

> McCollum, Haseman, and Karcher worked at the Bureau of Standards with another physicist, E. A. Eckhardt, who was also prominent in the early history of geophysical exploration and helped set up the geophysical research laboratories of Gulf Oil in Pittsburgh, Pennsylvania.

The seismic method of prospecting uses sound waves generated by a source, usually an explosion, at the earth's surface. The waves propagate inside the earth, where they are refracted (bent) or reflected by geological layers, causing some of the energy to return back to the surface, where it can be recorded. By the mid-1920s, the method had proved to be effective in locating salt domes along the Gulf of Mexico, where oil and gas are often found in the jumble of permeable and impermeable layers near the margins of the domes.

Until the 1920s, most prospectors had been skeptical that measurements made at the surface could locate oil deposits deep underground, and were content to rely instead on "wildcat" wells drilled near surface geological features that correlated with earlier successful strikes. Many of the gushers that dominated the first decades of U.S. oil production were wildcat strikes, but the success rate of "wildcatting" was very low – no better than about 1 in 10.

Use of the seismic method to locate geological structures associated with oil deposits – such as salt domes or anticlines – began to change these odds during the 1920s. As a result, the rate of finding major oil fields along the Gulf Coast improved from about one per year at the start of the decade to seven per year by the late 1920s. The cost of finding oil along the Gulf Coast fell dramatically, and U.S. oil reserves, which had stagnated for several years, began to increase again steadily.

E. E. Rosaire, a geologist for the Independent Exploration Company in Houston, Texas, wrote a series of articles for the journal *Geophysics* about the early history and effectiveness of geophysical methods for oil exploration. The best article is Rosiare, E. E., and Stiles, M. E., 1936, "Exploration on the Gulf Coast, to 1936" (*Geophysics*, v. 1, pp. 142-148). Rosaire was the first vice-president of the Society of Economic Geophysicists, which eventually changed its name to the Society of Exploration Geophysicists (SEG), today the world's largest professional society of applied geophysics

While the seismic method could help locate underground structures likely to trap oil, it could not determine whether the structures were actually filled with oil and gas, or just groundwater. The hope was that electrical measurements made from the surface would be able to sense the presence of oil deposits directly.

Marcel, with his nephew Marc, carried out the first experiments for *la Pros* in Texas in 1925, including surveys at Spindletop Dome, the famous oil gusher in east Texas whose discovery in 1901 had by itself tripled U.S. oil production. The results were good enough to lead to a contract with Roxana Petroleum, a subsidiary of Royal Dutch Shell. But eight months of surveying along the Gulf Coast, in which Conrad also participated during September 1926, were not able to repeat the success seen near the Ploesti salt dome in Rumania three years earlier, or even to reproduce the encouraging results seen at Spindletop. Roxana terminated the contract in the spring of 1927.

The Pechelbronn oil refinery in a photograph taken in the late 1940s. Pechelbronn, one of the oldest oil fields in Europe, was the site of the first electrical logging experiment carried out by Doll in September 1927. (Reprinted from *The Technical Review*, Schlumberger.)

Conrad had always understood the limitations of surface electrical measurements for locating structures deep inside the earth, but the failures along the Gulf Coast were humbling. The "Schlumberger method" of electrical prospecting risked acquiring a bad reputation for oil exploration in the United States, the most important world market for geophysical services. Early in 1927, Conrad returned to the idea of making electrical measurements underground. He discussed his ideas at length with Marcel and Doll, who recalled daily meetings to go over Conrad's calculations and to discuss the design of electrical equipment that could operate in oil wells.

In a note entitled "Electrical investigations in wells," written in the spring of 1927 at the company's offices in Paris, Conrad laid out these ideas for a new method of surveying oil wells. He and Marcel would later call the technique "electrical coring" (*carottage électrique*), invoking the idea that the technique would replace mechanical coring as a way of identifying geological layers encountered during drilling. The method would eventually be known as "electrical well logging." The term "logging" derived from the trip the sensors made in the well. They were lowered to the depth of interest on a cable, and measurements were made versus depth as they were slowly drawn to the surface. Just as a ship's log is a record of its journey, so too the "well log" became a record of the journey of the sensors.

Doll was assigned the task of building the equipment for the first tests, along with another young field engineer, Paul Charrin.

Charrin gave an anecdotal account of Conrad's decision to return to downhole measurements in the article "A History of Well Logging," by Hamilton Johnson (*Geophysics*, 1962, v. 28, pp. 507-527):

"Mr. Conrad Schlumberger had a very good friend, Mr. Meganck, manager of a Franco-Belgian drilling company by the name of Foraky. One day they were talking about their professional experiences and problems. Mr. Schlumberger, who had the wonderful talent of making clear even very complicated things, was giving his friend an idea of what geophysics, then in its infancy, was trying to do, and what he especially was trying to do with electrical methods. Mr. Meganck outlined the problems of the drillers of the day, who were operating in the dark, not knowing where they were nor where they were going, except by taking some very costly and time consuming cores. From whence came the spark I do not know, since I was not present, but I do know, since it was told to me by Mr. Schlumberger, that on that day was born the idea of applying electrical methods to logging of drill holes."

The idea for "electrical coring" was simple simple and involved taking the surface electrode array Conrad had developed and standing it on its head to slide down a well. The method Conrad had perfected for surface prospecting determines the "apparent resistivity" of a geologic formation by passing an electrical current into the earth between two electrodes, A and B, and by recording the difference in electric potential (the voltage) between two other electrodes, M and N. Whenever field conditions allowed, the four electrodes, A, B, M and N, were laid out along the same line at the earth's surface, with the potential electrodes M and N between the current electrodes A and B.

One can imagine the current as passing from the battery into the earth at electrode A and returning out of the ground at electrode B (which is connected to the opposite pole of the battery to complete the

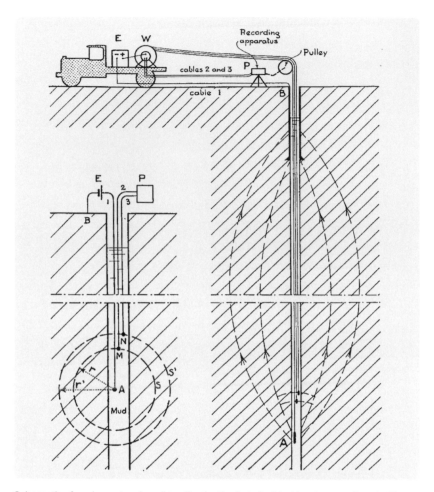

Schematic of equipment and configuration for the first electrical logging experiments. Three electrodes – a current electrode A and two potential electrodes M and N – are lowered into a well at the end of cables connecting them to surface equipment (a battery and a potentiometer). The electrical current emitted by the battery through electrode A passes from the mud filling the well into surrounding rock formations, then returns to the battery at electrode B, placed near the well at the surface. Usually the second electrode was grounded to the steel casing at the top of the well. The potentiometer at the surface measures the electrical potential (voltage) between electrodes M and N that is created by the flowing current. The ratio of the voltage to the current emitted by the battery is proportional to the average resistivity of the ground near the level of the downhole electrodes. In a typical experiment, the electrodes were first lowered to the bottom of the well, and then winched back to the surface, stopping every meter or so to record a measurement. This method of electrical logging would revolutionize the oil industry. (Reprinted with permission of the Society of Petroleum Engineers from *Transactions*, American Institute of Mining and Metallurgical Engineers, 1934.)

electrical circuit). When the earth beneath the electrodes is homogeneous, filaments of current spread out uniformly into the ground from the point of injection – including vertically straight down – until the current "senses" the presence of the second electrode B and turns back toward the surface. The depth to which the current filaments descend before turning back to the surface depends on the separation between electrodes A and B, which more or less determines the "depth of investigation" of the measurement. (This picture is only approximate: the actual path that the current takes in the earth depends on the resistivity of the ground, which of course, is not known in advance.) It had required hundreds of experiments, and many pages of complex mathematical analysis, to arrive at a set of rules giving a useful interpretation of the maps produced by the surface method.

In Conrad's 1927 note, the surface method is turned on its side. The electrodes A, M, and N were mounted a fixed distance apart on a cylindrical tube, called a "sonde," which was lowered to the bottom of the well. The current electrode A was at the bottom of the sonde, below the electrodes M and N. The electrode B, where the current returned to the battery, was placed at the surface, next to the well.

All three electrodes were connected by cables to instruments at the surface: The current electrode A was connected to the battery; the two potential electrodes M and N, to the terminals of the potentiometer. The sonde carrying the three downhole electrodes was pulled back to the surface with a winch, stopping at regular intervals to make readings.

The only large oil field in France was located near Pechelbronn, a small town in Alsace about 20 kilometers (12 miles) north of Strasbourg. (The town of Guebwiller, where Conrad and Marcel had spent their childhood, is about 50 kilometers south of Strasbourg.) Oil seepages had been exploited there since the time of Louis XIV, with the bitumen extracted from the seepages used for lighting and medicinal preparations. Since 1919, the Schlumberger family had been stockholders of the company operating the field, Pechelbronn-Société Anonyme d'Exploitations Minières (PSAEM). Conrad was a member of its board of directors.

The oil fields at Pechelbronn were old and nearly depleted. There were already more than 3000 oil wells at the site, and more were being drilled every day. Production was maintained by pumping the oil from a depth of a few hundred meters. The geology at Pechelbronn was well known to *la Pros*, who had already used the site as a testing ground for surface electrical equipment. It was a natural choice for the first tests of downhole electrical measurements. The chief drilling engineer of PSAEM, Monsieur Trouilloux, gave *la Pros* access to the information available from years of mechanical coring, so that it would be possible to compare the results with ground truth.

Early in August 1927, Doll, accompanied by two field engineers, Charles Schiebli and Roger Jost, took up residence at an inn named *L'Auberge du Cheval Blanc* (The White Horse Inn) in the town of Woerth-sur-Sauer about five kilometers west of Pechelbronn. Jost recalled in an interview after his retirement that the entire operation was carried out "discreetly, so as not to reveal anything to the occasional spectator. We knew that we were about to do something new, a great discovery perhaps that was necessary to keep secret."

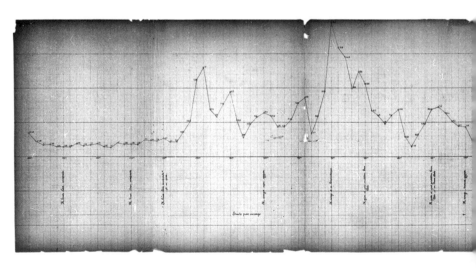

The first electrical log recorded at Pechelbronn on September 5, 1927. The log was drawn by Henri-Georges Doll several days later at the offices of Société de prospection électrique at rue Fabert in Paris. The curve shows the "apparent resistivity" of the ground (in units of ohm-m) at different depths in the well. The highest point on the graph corresponds to a resistivity of

Their equipment was more suited for a laboratory experiment. The cables were bound with insulating tape, with string wound around the outside for added strength. Doll had to teach the crew how to tie fishermen's knots to keep the assembly in place. The cable was wound around a large winch, on which a bell was arranged to sound automatically when it was time to stop cranking and make a measurement.

The first tests were carried out at night when the drill rigs were idle. Conditions were not ideal; it was raining hard and the truck got stuck in the mud while driving down to the well. The cable broke in several places during the first test. The crew spliced it back together with patches used for car tires and a special type of glue of the time called "magic paste."

The next day, the weather cleared. Doll and his crew carried out the first electrical coring experiment on September 5, 1927, in a well designated as Diefenbach 2905, tower number 7. Doll described the test in an interview more than thirty years later for the Schlumberger company magazine *Sonde Off*.

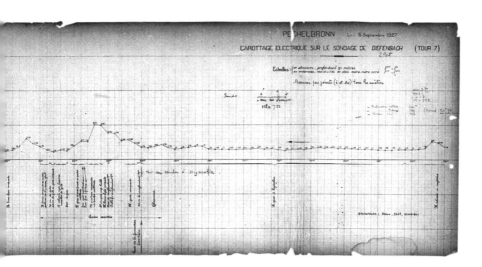

about 20 ohm-m. Text along the bottom is Doll's interpretation of the log in terms of the subsurface geology at Pechelbronn. Doll noticed a zone of high resistivity between the depths 220 and 225 meters in a porous sedimentary layer that normally had a low resistivity when filled with salt water. A nearby well confirmed the presence of oil in the layer.

"The separation between electrodes A and M was 3 meters; between M and N, about 1 meter. We made a sonde from four tubes of Bakelite fastened end to end with brass plated collars and screws. The electrodes were wires wound around the tubes. We cobbled together a ballast at the end of the sonde from a brass tube about 4 centimeters in diameter, filled with duck shot and sealed off at both ends; it weighed about 12 kilos. The entire assemblage looked like a long snake, with five segments.

"The cable, if you can call it that, consisted of three copper wires, insulated by rubber, like the wire used for spark plugs in cars. Its tensile strength was about 40 kilograms per strand. The cables were not wound together, as they were later; the three wires were just wound around the winch.

"The X-frame of the winch and its end-caps were made of wood; a large tube of Bakelite formed the core; the whole thing was held together with long strips of brass, bolted down. The winch was turned by a motorcycle chain connecting a large sprocket wheel to a smaller one. The axis of the winch was steel, with bicycle pedals mounted at both ends, so that two of us could turn it. A ratchet mechanism prevented the spool from unwinding by itself.

"For an electrical contact, we plugged the wire into a standard wall outlet mounted on one of the end caps of the winch. To turn the spool, we disconnected the wire that ran to the potentiometer.

"The frame holding the pulley wheel which fed the cable over the winch was made of wood, with an off-centered axis. There was a long counter-arm that served as a kind of force meter. We were worried that the wires would snap, and by watching the balance of the counter-arm, could judge the tension on the wire. A counting wheel on the pulley, like the kilometer-meter on a car, indicated the depth. We planned to make readings every meter. The measurements were made with a potentiometer mounted on a tripod, like the ones used in surface work.

"It was a beautiful fall day. We drove down to the well in a dilapidated old truck which had been used in surface prospecting. The well was about 500 meters deep. We only had 600 meters of cable, so we could not have gone much deeper.

"Once the experiment was underway, one of us had to disconnect the wires, another turned the winch, and the third ran down to the drilling platform to read the counting wheel…. It was back and forth continually. I wrote down the readings in a notebook, opposite the depth readings. Then, we disconnected the wire, wound the winch one meter up to the next station, reconnected, made the next reading, and so on, one meter at a time.

"At the start, we were running around in circles a little, but quickly got the hang of it, and were able to knock out about 50 stations in one hour.

"The whole thing worked well. Everything went according to plan except for one incident. While detaching the ballast from the bottom of the sonde, after it came out of the well and was hanging from the derrick, we forgot that the tube above, being hollow, had filled with mud, which sprayed out all over, covering us from head to toe. We ended the day taking baths in the local village."

Back in Paris several days later, Doll plotted the measurements on graph paper making the first "electrical log" of an oil well. Conrad's idea – that the resistivity measurement would allow the geologists to identify the different layers – seemed to work. Comparing the curve of resistivity versus depth with cores taken from the well, Doll was able to confirm that the largest changes in resistivity occurred when the sonde passed between different rock layers. The peaks of the curve (the zones of highest resistivity) corresponded to hard rocks and the troughs (the zones of low resistivity) to softer, more porous rocks.

Particularly interesting was a thick zone of low resistivity, which began at about 280 meters (900 feet) deep and was interrupted by a sharp peak of high resistivity at a depth of about 225 meters (740 feet). The zone of high resistivity corresponded to the top of a layer of porous limestone called marl (*marnes*, in French), which normally had low resistivity when filled with salt water.

A core from a nearby well confirmed that the top of the layer contained oil.

Henri-Georges Doll taking measurements in the desert near Bakersfield, California, 1928.

Chapter 5

U.S.A. – No Oil for the "Frogs"

Despite the success of the experiment at Pechelbronn, Conrad and Marcel were not convinced that "electrical coring" could become an important part of their company's business. They understood its potential value for drillers, and quickly filed patents in France and in the United States on the new method, but they still believed that surface exploration was the largest commercial market for geophysics. Decisions about *where* to drill wells seemed to dominate their clients' activities.

The field engineer Jean Mathiez remembered participating in intense discussions at rue Fabert about the significance of the results at Pechelbronn, with Henri-Georges Doll arguing strongly for the value of the new measurement and for devoting resources to answering questions his first tests had raised: Did the resistivity on the log accurately represent the resistivity of the rocks and fluids surrounding the well? How much did the presence of the well itself affect the readings? According to Mathiez, Conrad – who had spent years of his own career studying similar questions for surface measurements and knew that the answers could be elusive – felt that he needed to restrain his son-in-law's enthusiasm.

Doll also had strong support for the new measurement from Eugène Léonardon. Léonardon had been struggling since 1922 to establish surface electrical prospecting as a viable business in the United States. A few months after *la Pros* was incorporated in France, Léonardon opened an office for the company in New York City, on the 20th floor of the Cunard Building near 25th Street and Broadway. The name of the American affiliate of *la Pros* was Schlumberger Electrical Prospecting Methods (SEPM).

Léonardon first heard about the success at Pechelbronn in a type-written letter from Conrad on September 24, 1927. In the margin on the first page, Conrad had sketched the experiment, showing the electrodes in the well and the lines of electrical current leading to the battery at the surface. Léonardon immediately wrote back asking that Doll make a tour of the United States with the new equipment.

Conrad and Marcel agreed to send Doll to the United States, but decided that he would not bring along the logging equipment. In a letter to Léonardon, the brothers even suggested that he approach an American drilling company with an offer to license the new technology in return for royalties, which could help finance the growth of the surface prospecting business. Léonardon "threw a fit" at the suggestion. Having seen firsthand the success of the seismic method along the Gulf Coast, he believed that electrical methods could not compete in oil exploration and was convinced that his company would need to find a new market.

Doll embarked for the United States aboard the steamship *Rochambeau* on February 22, 1928. He arrived in New York on March 4 and spent several days with Léonardon in New York, describing for him in more detail the new equipment and the experiments at Pechelbronn. He then headed west to visit the company's field crew, who were working in the Wasco oil field in Kern County, California. (At the turn of the 20th century, California had surpassed Pennsylvania as the leading oil-producing state in the United States, but was itself quickly surpassed by Texas. Unlike Pennsylvania, however, California has remained a major oil-producing state.) The crew in California – a young Swiss engineer, Edouard Poldini, and three French engineers, André Allégret, Pierre Baron, and Jacques Gallois – were carrying out surface electrical surveys under a contract with Shell Oil.

Two months into the trip, on April 20, 1928, Doll learned that Annette had delivered their second child, another daughter. They named her after Annette's great-grandmother, Clarisse, the mother of Paul Schlumberger. At the end of April, Doll returned to New York from California and sailed to Paris. He brought a fashionable hatbox from New York as a present for Annette.

The business of *la Pros* was growing. In 1928, the company had 50 engineers in the field. Most were working on contracts in surface electrical prospecting for minerals, but also occasionally for oil, in Europe (Rumania, Serbia and France) and in Africa (Belgian Congo and South Africa). Léonardon also had a crew working on mineral prospecting in Canada.

Many of the engineers had been hired from the top universities of France, but a few were self-taught, having learned the "Schlumberger Method" while working as assistants to the field crews. Roger Jost, for example, was the nephew of the steward of the Schlumberger family estate at Val-Richer, and had been hired as Conrad's first field assistant in 1925 at the age of 17. (Jost worked for more than forty years for the company founded by "Papa Conrad," as many of the employees called him, and left a remarkable set of notebooks detailing his experiences all over the world.)

As business steadied, life at rue Fabert settled into a normal routine. Conrad still liked to pace up and down the office, expounding his ideas on both science and politics, especially on developments in the Soviet Union. Marcel generally sat at the drawing table, sketching his ideas for new mechanical devices. He was fascinated at the time by the possibility of taking rock samples, not from the bottom of the well, but from the walls of borehole itself. He had bent the barrel of a shotgun into a device for shooting hollow shells laterally into the borehole wall; the shells had chains attached at one end, which allowed them to be extracted from the wall and brought to the surface filled with rock samples.

According to Louis Chatelier, an engineer working at rue Fabert, when Doll saw Marcel's prototype, he asked to be given notice of the first test, so that he could leave the office for the day. (The prototype was in fact never used, but a decade later it did puzzle the experts sent to rue Fabert by the German army, which had occupied Paris.)

Doll's father Henri still lived in Caluire, but he also had an office in Paris and came often to visit his son. Annette occasionally came along to fetch the entire family, including her father and uncle, to lunch at the Doll family's apartment on rue Casimir-Périer.

Talking about her father in a recent interview, Izaline, the oldest daughter of Annette and Henri-Georges, said that his practical bent and love of craftsmanship came from his own father's side of the family. Conversations in her grandfather's household, she said, often turned to practical subjects such as electricity, plumbing, and woodworking. The family home in Caluire, where Doll often went during vacations, had a fully-outfitted workroom for milling and cabinetmaking. Her grandfather, Izaline recalled, "knew how to make anything with his hands."

Doll seemed to have the same natural gift. Annette described him as having the "gnarled hands of a craftsman in the best sense of the phrase. With him, and all around him, especially at work, things just seemed to work. One could not imagine that the needle of a potentiometer would make a false move, or even that the lead in his pencil would break."

Through the end of 1928 and into 1929, Léonardon continued to plead with Conrad and Marcel to send Doll back to the United States to test electrical coring in U.S. oil fields. But Conrad and Marcel did not want to drain resources from the company's growing business in mineral prospecting. Doll, however, believed strongly in electrical logging and had spent much of his own time the past two years comparing the log he had made at Pechelbronn with nearby surface electrical measurements and with cores and other data provided by the drillers.

"I learned [from studying the first logs at Pechelbronn]," he wrote in one of his notebooks, "that with any measurement there are always misleading signals, like 'enemies' opposing a true measurement." He also improved the equipment. The three cables were wound tightly with a steel member to provide more coherence and strength, and then were wrapped in tarred cotton fabric for insulation. New winches were designed and integrated with a revolving drum of paper and a pen, whose movement was linked to the needle of the potentiometer, allowing continuous recording of the measurements as the electrodes were winched up the well. "It was through Doll's tenacity," Mathiez recalled, "that the technology of electrical coring progressed rapidly during 1927 and 1928."

In July 1929, Doll got the green light to return to America. Accompanied this time by Annette, he sailed for New York in August 1929 to replace Léonardon, who was taking a long-overdue vacation. The couple rented a tiny apartment on the eighth floor of a building on East 42nd Street called Tudor City, which overlooked a park along the East River where the United Nations building now stands. For several months, Doll worked at the New York office interpreting surveys made by field crews in California, Texas, and Canada. His English was still rudimentary, but he nevertheless visited the offices of several oil companies in New York City with the American engineer Sherwin Kelly, who helped him explain and promote the potential of the new downhole electrical measurements.

In August 1929, the first electrical coring experiment in the United States was carried out near Santa Barbara, California, in an oil field operated by Shell. The test was not very successful. The crew – Jacques Gallois, Gilbert Deschâtre, and Robert Roche – collected measurements along 2950 feet of the well, but the operation took several days. The equipment failed many times and finally got stuck in the well. After extracting it and repairing the cable, the crew loaded their truck and drove to Oklahoma, where a second series of tests had been arranged for Gypsy Oil, a subsidiary of Gulf Oil. Based in Pittsburgh, where it was part of the Mellon banking and business empire, Gulf was the largest American oil company not descended from the breakup of Standard Oil in 1911.

At the end of November, Doll and Annette took a train from New York to Oklahoma. Deschâtre was waiting for them at the station in Tulsa, along with several crates of new equipment, including a new winch, which had been shipped from Paris. He and Doll modified the winch to fit onto the chassis of an American truck. The three then drove 90 miles southwest from Tulsa along rough back roads leading to the oil fields around Seminole, Oklahoma.

Seminole is located in the territory of the Seminole Nation, where the Seminole native Indian tribe from Florida was relocated by the Treaty of 1842, which ended the Indian Wars in the Southeast. The capital of the Seminole Nation is Wewoka, about 12 miles southeast of Seminole. The city of Seminole itself was a small trading post for farmers in the area. It had fewer than 1000 inhabitants until 1926, when oil was discovered by wildcat drilling in the surrounding plains.

Within two years, five giant oil fields were discovered near Seminole in what geologists would later call the Mid-Continent Oil District. Production from the gushers at Seminole glutted the U.S. oil market in the late 1920s and made Oklahoma the top oil-producing state for nearly a decade. At its peak in July 1927, oil production from Greater

Seminole oil field reached 527,400 barrels of oil per day, about 25% of U.S. production at the time. More than 20,000 workers descended on Seminole, creating the last oil boomtown before the Great Depression.

The trip was Annette's first encounter with the rough world of the oil patch, and it made a strong impression. "We arrived in Seminole after nightfall," she wrote, "and walked into a saloon that had about it something of a gambling den, something of a fancy house. Our entrance caused a great stir. The ladies (to use Henri's euphemism) who usually ventured into such places were not exactly the type who accompanied their spouses to take measurements in boreholes. An atmosphere thick with tobacco and alcohol and loud with thunderous voices and the tinkling of a piano player enveloped me. Then before I could get my bearings, I felt myself being hoisted from the floor and deposited on a table like a Chinese doll. Tearing themselves away from their fanciful schemes (which would make millionaires of them in the time it took to dig the right hole in the right place), several strapping fellows devoured my skirt with their eyes, as children would a birthday cake. I was the *chanteuse* or the dancer they were waiting for, of whom they expected great entertainment.

"Not I, alas! I was only the wife of an engineer on a field mission. Nothing funny about that, nothing funny at all for lonesome oil drillers. My husband was laughing at their frustration and found my embarrassment amusing. As for Deschâtre, the poor man, I remember a quick surge of annoyance at seeing him there, falling asleep on his feet as if nothing at all was happening. However, when I was leaving New York I read his latest report. For the period from September 15 to October 17 alone, he had to his credit 1760 kilometers by truck; 21 kilometers of cored wells; 13,600 measurements; 2600 meters of cable lost in the boreholes."

The crew made arrangements for the Dolls to stay at the local hotel, but they also insisted that Annette accompany them to the field rather than remain at the hotel. They worked mainly at night, when the drilling rigs were quiet, maneuvering their truck and equipment between the tall wooden derricks, which filled the fields outside the city and flared gas into the clear night sky. Temperatures on the Oklahoma plain in late November were glacial. One day, when the truck ran out of gas, they pushed it to a local gas station. Finding the station closed, they managed to get a pump working and filled the truck's tank, leaving some money and a note of apology attached to the pump.

"Another day," Doll recounted many years later (when he returned to Tulsa to receive an award from the Society of Professional Well Log Analysts), "one of the field engineers, myself and my wife, whom we couldn't leave at the hotel without a bodyguard, arrived in the truck at another well to be logged. A man with a shotgun quickly appeared, running toward the well and shouting at us, asking what we were doing there. I told him, 'We are going to make an electrical log of this well.' 'And who gave you permission to do that?' the man asked. We told him, the vice-president, Mr. So-and-So. (I don't remember his name anymore.) He replied, 'Yeah. Well, I'm the president and I'm giving you exactly ten minutes to clear out, or I will put you down.'"

The Mid-Continent Oil District includes the oil fields of Oklahoma, Kansas, and northern Texas, which dominated world oil production for more than a decade starting in the early 1920s. The oil reservoirs in the region are found mainly in rocks of the Paleozoic era, which form the stable core of the North American continent. The Paleozoic era is the oldest and longest of the three eras that geologists use to divide the fossil record. It extends from the explosion of life (as seen in the fossil record) in the Cambrian period about 550 million years ago, to the dawn of the age of dinosaurs, about 250 million years ago, at the start of the second era of the fossil record, the Mesozoic era. The final era, the Cenozoic, extends from the end of the age of dinosaurs, about 65 million years ago, to the present day. The names of the eras are taken from the Greek words for "ancient life," "middle life," and "new life."

Unlike in Pennsylvania, Ohio, and coastal Texas, the surface geology of the central plains provides few clues to prospectors looking for oil. Development of the Mid-Continent Oil District in the early 1920s was a triumph of geological detective work and inspired wildcat drilling based on subtle surface features, a few geological outcrops, and thousands of drillers' logs – the records that drillers make by studying the ground-up bits of rock called "cuttings" that emerge from wells during drilling.

> The early geologic work to piece together maps of the Mid-Continent Oil District was done by a small oil company called Marland Oil, led by E. W. Marland, one of the pioneers in using modern geology for oil exploration. The book to read is Edgar Wesley Owen's monumental work, *Trek of the Oil Finders: A History of Exploration for Petroleum*, published by the American Association of Petroleum Geologists (Memoir 6, Tulsa, Oklahoma, 1975), on the occasion of its 50th anniversary.

By the time of the Seminole oil strikes, geological cross sections had been developed for most of the region, cataloging the sequence of beds down from the surface. Certain geological layers called "marker horizons" were known to lie a fixed distance above the oil-bearing layers. After the drill bit reached one of the marker horizons – which could usually be determined by examining the drill cuttings – the drilling process was interrupted every few meters to take cores or to test the underlying layers for the presence of oil by allowing the well to flow. In many oil fields of the region, however, the marker horizons were thin and difficult to identify, even when cores were taken.

The consulting geologist for Gypsy Oil, Roger Knappen, wanted to see if the new electrical measurements could identify the marker horizons and accelerate the process of completing new wells. At the end of November 1929, after more than a month of continuous tests in wells operated by Gypsy, Doll and Deschâtre met with Knappen in Tulsa. Knappen was pleased with the tests, which he believed had shown that the new electrical logs could identify marker horizons in the Mid-Continent Oil District, especially in the oil fields of Kansas. He was particularly interested in using the electrical measurements to directly detect the presence of thin oil layers

"Oil! Oil!" Deschâtre wrote in a letter to Paris in mid-November. "It's the only thing that interests these companies. If only we had a direct method to detect it…. They are always asking, 'Do you know how to distinguish an oil sandstone from a water sandstone?' The answer is delicate: Obviously we can tell the difference, provided that we can determine first whether or not the layer is actually a sandstone!"

At the end of the meeting in Tulsa, Knappen told Doll and Deschâtre that Gypsy would continue the tests, but only if Schlumberger reduced its price from $2000 a month for a full-time crew to $400. He had calculated what he thought was a fair price, based on the cost of a drilling crew and the amount of time that could be saved by using electrical logging, instead of mechanical coring, to identify the major geological layers during drilling.

Léonardon refused the offer.

Doll continued his trip through the western United States, doing further experiments with the crew in Wyoming, then traveling to Denver where he met with faculty and students at the famous Colorado School of Mines, the top American university for mining engineering and petroleum geology. Annette, tired from the trip to Oklahoma, returned to New York. Doll joined her there in mid-December, and they returned to Paris in time for Christmas.

The efforts to commercialize electrical logging in the United States continued after Doll's return to Paris. Deschâtre negotiated a new contract with three oil companies – Humble, Gulf, and Shell, which operated a joint venture called "Hugush" – to log a series of wells along the Gulf Coast.

The Gulf Coast Oil District extends from the prolific oil fields of east Texas (which include Spindletop) eastward along the Gulf of Mexico into Louisiana. Most of the oil reservoirs in this region are found at the margins of towering underground geological structures called salt domes.

About 150 million years ago, thick layers of rock salt (essentially the same composition as ordinary table salt, sodium chloride) were deposited along the southern margin of the ancient North American continent, at the bottom of a shallow sea which dried up and refilled several times during a period of alternating climate in the Mesozoic era.

When wet conditions returned, at the end of the Mesozoic, the salt layers were buried under thousands of meters of sediment deposited by the ancient Mississippi River. The heat and pressure deep underground make the salt ductile enough to flow; when disturbed by tectonic movements in the region (such as earthquakes), the salt layer erupted through the denser overlying layers, forming mushroom-shaped underground structures composed almost entirely of salt. Geologists estimate that thousands of salt domes have formed along the Gulf Coast; more than five hundred have been identified during a century of oil prospecting in the region. Oil is usually trapped in permeable layers lying below the "crown" of the impermeable salt, or in the jumble of layers thrown up at the margins of the domes by the erupting salt.

The search for salt domes was one of the first great triumphs of geophysical exploration. The first successes were based on precise measurements of gravity at the earth's surface. Since the density of salt is less than that of the surrounding rocks, the force of gravity is (very) slightly less than normal above a salt dome. The first instrument capable of measuring these tiny differences in gravity was the torsion balance, invented in 1902 by the Hungarian physicist Lorand von Eötvös. The technology, originally invented to help determine the shape of the earth, had been gradually improved during the first two decades of the twentieth century, to the point where it could measure variations of gravity of about one part in ten million of the earth's normal gravitational field.

In 1920, Everette Lee DeGolyer, a geologist and general manger of the oil company Amerada, ordered two torsion balances to be manufactured in Budapest and sent a young American geologist, Donald Barton, to bring them back to the United States. In December 1922, Barton made the first survey with these instruments over the Spindletop oil field, showing large variations of gravity over the buried salt dome. Other surveys followed quickly, and in November 1924, a new salt dome was found west of Spindletop in the Nash region of the Gulf Coast of Texas.

Two years later, drilling confirmed the presence of oil at the margins of the "Nash Dome," which is usually credited as the first oil field discovered in the United States by geophysical methods.

Although the torsion balance could reveal the roughly circular zones of low gravity above salt domes, it could not precisely locate the margins of a dome because the weakness in the earth's gravity

Schematic cross section through a typical salt dome in the Gulf Coast. Thick layers of rock salt become ductile when buried beneath sediments under the Gulf and, when disturbed by tectonic movements such as earthquakes, erupt through the heavier overlying layers. The erupting salt tends to spread horizontally near the surface creating towering mushroom-shaped domes. Oil is often trapped under the impermeable crown of the dome, or in the layers thrown up at the margins of the structure. Some of the largest gushers in the history of oil exploration, including the famous Spindletop field in Texas, were discovered near salt domes along the Gulf Coast.

caused by the lighter salt layers extended many kilometers beyond the limits of a dome.

> The survey at Spindletop actually showed a larger than normal gravitational field above the salt dome, which was caused by a hard layer of cap rock squeezed between the top of the dome and the surface. It was not until surveys had been carried out over other domes in the Gulf that geologists and geophysicists realized that the situation at Spindletop was unusual and that a low gravity field represented the normal signature of a salt dome. See *Geophysics in the Affairs of Mankind*, L.C. Lawyer, C. C. Bates, and R. B. Rice (Society of Exploration Geophysicists, Tulsa, 2001).

The seismometer became the device of choice to more precisely locate the outline of an underground dome. Two seismic methods developed more or less in parallel during the search for Gulf Coast salt domes in the 1920s. The first method, called seismic refraction, was developed by Ludger Mintrop's German company Seismos. An explosive charge is set off near the surface of the earth, and a recording system measures the time of arrival of sound waves that travel through the earth roughly horizontally and then back to the surface to a series of instruments called geophones, which are placed at different distances from the explosive charge.

Because sound waves travel much faster in the highly elastic salt of the dome than in the surrounding sediments, it was possible to map accurately the outline of the top of the dome using a technique called "fan shooting," in which geophones are placed along a large semicircular arc centered on the explosive charge. The time of arrival of the sound waves is shortened along lines that pass over the buried salt.

A second technique, called seismic reflection, was developed mainly by the Geophysical Research Corporation, a company organized in 1924 by DeGolyer as a subsidiary of Amerada Oil. The seismic reflection method involves sending sound waves more or less straight down into the earth – also by setting off an explosive charge at the surface – and recording the echoes or "reflections" that are generated when waves cross boundaries between different types of rock. (Echoes of sound waves are generated at the interface between two different rock types if either the speed of sound or the density is different in the two layers.) By recording the travel time of the echo, it is possible to determine the distance to the object that generated it. This method of "echo-location" is essentially the same as that used to track objects with radar or underwater sonar. It is also how bats and dolphins map their surroundings.

The seismic refraction method dominated early oil exploration in the Gulf Coast. But in the late 1920s, when new electronic equipment allowed the recording of weak echoes from deeply buried structures, the seismic reflection method became uncannily effective at locating salt domes. In a letter to Paris in 1928 describing these developments, Léonardon wrote that "finding salt domes, even at depths of 1500 to 2000 meters, will soon become child's play."

But even after a salt dome had been located and its size and shape outlined, it was still not obvious where exactly to drill to find oil trapped along its margins. As Conrad pointed out in a reply to Léonardon, "Many oil companies now have a surplus of salt domes, but also a lot of dry holes."

DeGolyer is one of the legendary figures of the oil industry and is often called "the father of American geophysics." He set up Geophysical Research Corporation after learning about Reginald Fessenden's 1917 patent and visiting him several times at his home in Framingham, Massachusetts. DeGolyer hired J. Clarence Karcher to run GRC. Karcher, who had helped to set up the first American seismic company, Geophysical Engineering, worked at Western Electric on ocean-bottom telegraphy after Geophysical Engineering folded. DeGolyer offered Karcher a 15% interest in GRC and a $300,000 research budget to develop Fessenden's patent. He intended that GRC, though owned by Amerada, would provide seismic surveys for other oil companies, but when the owners of Amerada disagreed with this, DeGolyer secretly financed another company called Geophysical Service Inc. (GSI), which quickly became the world's leading seismic company. Karcher resigned from GRC to become president of GSI. See *Mr. De, A Biography of Everette Lee DeGolyer*, Lon Tinkle (Little, Brown and Company, Boston, 1970).

Deschâtre had convinced Humble, Gulf, and Shell that the new electri-cal logging technology would allow their geologists to discern the sequence of geological layers at the margins of the domes and identify the oil-producing layers. Léonardon signed the agreement with Hugush in New York on January 27, 1930, and put Roger Henquet in Houston to coordinate the work. Henquet was a young French engi-neer, a *centralien*, who had joined the company in May 1929 and had worked with Doll and Deschâtre in Oklahoma. Deschâtre, Gallois, Henquet, and Jean Mathieu – another young engineer who had recently arrived from France – would alternate in the two-man logging crew.

On January 24, the company's only truck, loaded with the experi-mental electrical equipment, a new automatic recording apparatus, and a winch with several thousand feet of cable, set out from Houston. Just reaching the well sites over the next few months would prove to be physically demanding and dangerous. Paved roads extended only 20 miles or so beyond the scattered towns along the Coast, most of which was still recovering slowly from the Great Mississippi Flood of 1927. In less than six months, the crew would drive more than

Logging truck stuck in the mud along the Gulf Coast, 1930.

8000 miles on back roads through bayous, swamps, and deep mud surrounding the oil fields.

Getting their equipment to the wells was just the start of the crew's problems. On January 28, 1930, one day into the first test, they sent a telegram to Paris:

STARTED LOGGING GULF COAST 27 [JANUARY] UNABLE TO PENETRATE BELOW THE TUBING DESPITE THIRTY HOURS OF EFFORTS VERY HEAVY MUD URGENTLY NEED A TWO-TON CABLE ALLOWING USE OF HEAVIER BALLAST WHEN CAN YOU SEND?

The job had to be abandoned. It took Doll and the engineers in Paris nearly a month to construct a stronger cable, supporting heavier ballast, which would allow the equipment to sink to the bottom of the well through the dense drilling mud in Gulf Coast wells. The new assembly included a mechanism for releasing the heavy ballast at the bottom of the well, so that the crew would not have to winch it back to the surface. The equipment had been in the field for nearly a year and was wearing out. The winch broke several times, cables leaked constantly, and the new recording apparatus rarely worked as designed.

Nevertheless, by July the crew had managed to log 45 wells in 22 oil fields from Laredo, Texas, just north of the Mexican border to White Castle, a small town on the Mississippi River about 30 miles north of New Orleans. All but a few of the wells yielded good electrical logs, but a problem that Léonardon had anticipated would prove insurmountable. In December 1929, while the project was still under negotiation, he sent a long letter to Deschâtre in Houston. "I rather believe," he wrote, "that work in the Gulf Coast will be composed of scattered results, which will be difficult to correlate, and that we will have a hard time to get something out of it quickly."

Léonardon had foreseen the problem. The wells of the Hugush project were not close enough to allow comparison of the logs from different wells. As a result, it was impossible to draw a consistent picture of the subsurface geology. At one point, when the logs from two wells relatively close together showed recognizable correlations, Léonardon asked the oil companies for more wells to log in the same area. He was told, in effect, "to log the wells requested, not to request wells to log."

Humble, Gulf, and Shell wanted a blind test of the technology and gave the crew almost no information about the wells they were surveying. Without this information, it was difficult to identify the geological layers in the logs. The oil companies themselves were also distracted by operational problems. The discovery of huge new fields in California and East Texas in the late 1920s had glutted the world oil market, causing enormous swings in price. The price of oil fell from $1.10 to $0.10 per barrel in a couple of months. Demand for oil collapsed as the U.S. economy, shaken by the stock market crash in October 1929, fell into a deep recession.

At the end of July 1930, the three oil companies decided to stop the tests. The crew remained in the Gulf Coast area, looking for spot work, but for the first time since Léonardon had arrived in the United States, there was little hope of new activity. Deschâtre visited his friends at the oil companies in Houston and another 120 clients in New York and Boston: "Most of the people know us," he wrote to Paris, "and are almost always very friendly. At least half of them are interested in learning more about our methods. They all express regret not to have any problems to work on at the moment, or if they do have some, no money to study them."

Earlier in the year, Léonardon had written to Paris about the difficulties other companies were having as economic recession spread through the United States. "Lundberg [a Swedish geophysicist]," he wrote, "offered to work for fifty dollars a day in British Columbia, and, of course, this is quite a disadvantage for [our field engineer] in his efforts to get work in this territory. Mason, Slichter and Gauld [American geophysicists] go a little farther than this in the reduction of fees. Since Mr. Gauld is now in Vancouver doing nothing, he has offered to go into the Cariboo district to do prospecting without charge....

"To a certain extent, the above is good news, provided we shall be able to stand the so-called Nogi 'last quarter of an hour.' In Europe, you certainly cannot imagine the depression into which American industry has been plunged."

Léonardon wrote again in August asking about placements for his engineers elsewhere in the company. In early September, Doll provided the reply from headquarters. "Business is fortunately going a little better in Europe than in the United States," he wrote. "It will be possible here to employ most of the personnel coming back from the US. But as you know very well, when it's necessary, in covering a period when there is not much work, to accept short, varied projects, we need engineers who know all of our methods and a little bit of geology, and who can present themselves suitably before the clients.... For your guidance, we have to let you know that despite all of our good will, it may be necessary to bid goodbye to two or three of our prospectors. In any case, it's not necessary to return the equipment to France."

Although he planned for the worst, Léonardon bridled at the idea of losing both his equipment and his staff and pleaded with Doll in personal letters to convince Conrad and Marcel Schlumberger to keep the American operations going. He proposed that SEPM could survive in the United States as a commercial representative for French business interests. Conrad and Marcel thought the idea was crazy and suggested that Léonardon take a vacation.

Léonardon wrote privately to Doll in the first week of September. "I can see it from here," he confided. "They're afraid we might look like fast-food merchants. I can be trusted to do the dirty work." A few days later, when it was clear that Conrad and Marcel would close his operations, he wrote again, "I think that you are still close enough to your stay in the United States to tell *ces messieurs* firmly that their plan sounds like a joke." But before a response could arrive, Léonardon sent a telegram to headquarters on September 8, 1930:

WE EXPECT BARRING UNFORESEEN EVENTS TO STOP
ABLE TO SEND THE PERSONNEL TO VENEZUELA IF
USEFUL WE HAVE NINE THOUSAND IN THE BANK AT
ISELIN DON'T TOUCH

In the end, only Mathieu was sent to Venezuela; the others remained in the United States for several months before returning to Paris. Léonardon stayed in New York. He vented his frustration in a letter to Paris on October 17, 1930. "The Swedes," he wrote, "have like us worked only a little this year: a contract in Saskatchewan or Alberta for oil…that's all. All the same, [their president] Mr. Rogers sees the future with confidence…. Do I need to confess that, personally, I admire his steadfast vision? Do you feel capable enough to emulate it? Do you have the money? Are your financial plans to stay on the chessboard worldwide as well considered? Your telegrams at the start of October lead me to think rather that America is, in your mind, something like a cottage for a summer stay in the country: When the weather turns bad, you put the key under the door."

Asked, many years later, what he had been thinking during this period, Léonardon replied: "I thought, Above all, hold on. Just six more months and we will see."

In January 1931, he returned to Paris.

Eugénia Delarova, ballerina and wife of choreographer Léonide Massine. Delarova danced with Massine in numerous productions of the Russian Ballet during the 1930s. Thirty years later, she married Henri-Georges Doll in New York City. (Published with the kind authorization of *Société des Bains de Mer Hôtel & Casinos Resort, Monte-Carlo, Place du Casino – Monte-Carlo MC 98000, Principauté de Monaco*.)

Chapter 6

Between Two Wars

When Société de prospection électrique (*la Pros*) closed its offices in the United States at the end of 1930, twenty years had elapsed since Conrad Schlumberger's first electrical experiments in the basement at École des Mines and on his family's estate at Val-Richer. During these years, the economic and political roles of oil had become more and more important.

World production more than doubled in the decade after World War I, rising from about 688 million barrels in 1920 (about 188,000 barrels per day) to more than 1.4 billion barrels in 1930 (about 400,000 barrels per day).

The growth was stimulated by new means of transportation – the automobile and the airplane – and by the public's fascination with speed. In 1910, there were about 458,000 automobiles registered in the United States; by 1920, the number had grown to more than eight million; by the end of the decade, it was nearly 25 million.

Source: www.railsandtrails.com. See also *Pivotal Decades: The United States, 1900-1920*, John M. Cooper, Jr. (W. W. Norton & Co., New York, 1990).

In 1922, Felice Nazzaro won the French Grand Prix at Strasbourg in a Fiat, completing the course at the amazing speed of 126 kilometers per hour (78 miles per hour); in 1930, Tazio Nuvolari won the Italian Grand Prix (the *Mille Miglia* from Vicenza to Brescia) in an Alfa Romeo, with an average speed above the magical number of 160.9344 kilometers per hour (100 miles per hour).

Charles Lindbergh made his solo flight across the Atlantic in 1927, while Jean Mermoz, working for the French airmail company Aéropostale, flew around the world in 1927 and 1928, and then crossed the southern Atlantic in 1930, becoming the darling of the French-speaking world.

Another boost to oil consumption came from the petrochemical industry, which started in the United States in the 1920s with the invention of thermal cracking for refining oil into various byproducts such as plastics, soap, detergents, lubricants, synthetic fibers, pesticides, and medicines. In 1927, a French engineer, Eugène Houdry, invented "catalytic cracking," a more efficient method for refining oil by using chemical catalysts in the cracking process. Houdry's new method was adopted by Sun Oil Company in the United States in 1937, and became the main industrial process of the petrochemical industry.

The oil fields of the United States still dominated, providing about 65% of world production during the 1920s. Supply, however, was becoming more diversified. Outside the United States, the known reserves of oil were concentrated in the Middle East and in Persia (in countries still under the mandate of Great Britain), in the Caucasus region of Soviet Russia, in the Dutch East Indies (primarily in Sumatra), and in Venezuela and Mexico.

Mexico's share of world production had fallen dramatically during the decade – from more than 20% in 1920 to about 3% by 1930. Venezuela's share had risen more dramatically, from less than 1% (1.2 million barrels a year) in 1920 to nearly 10% (137 million barrels a year) in 1929. By the end of the decade, Venezuela ranked second in production behind the United States. Russia was a close third at 9%. The Middle East and the Far East were each producing less than 5% of world oil.

The United States was by far the largest consumer of oil, but unlike today it was also supplying more than a third of the world's total exports. Great Britain and the Netherlands, however, controlled supplies to Western Europe, primarily through the two giant oil companies, Anglo-Persian Oil Company (which later became British Petroleum or BP) and Royal Dutch Shell. In the 1920s, Venezuela had actually become the main source of oil for both Shell and Anglo-Persian. Great Britain had also granted Russia access to part of the English market.

France imported nearly all of its oil, and more than 90% of its imports were controlled by Great Britain. France's military leaders had calculated that fighting a modern war would require 12 to 30 million (metric) tons of oil per year (about 84 to 210 million barrels of oil), compared to the country's peacetime annual consumption of about six million tons (42 million barrels). Without the cooperation of its main supplier, Great Britain, going to war was simply not an option for France. This "oil servitude" also explained in part France's economic and political concessions in the years leading up to World War II, such as its abandonment of war reparations from Germany, its withdrawal of troops from the Ruhr district, and its non-intervention when Hitler began re-militarization of the Rhineland.

The years between the wars marked the high point of the colonial empires of Western Europe. This was the last period during which "the sun never set" on the British Empire. France had colonies in north and equatorial Africa and in Madagascar, Indochina, and Guyana, along with trading posts in India and mandates in Syria and Libya. In 1931, The Colonial Exposition at the Bois de Vincennes in Paris attracted eight million visitors. Paul Reynaud, the government's colonial minister, sponsored the exposition "to make the French aware of their empire." Colonialism was accepted in Europe as part of the status quo, with an insensitivity toward local inhabitants that is difficult to imagine today. For example, in 1930, at the Grand Eucharistic Congress in Tunisia, hundreds of Muslim infants dressed as crusaders were part of the event.

In France, the Roaring Twenties were *les années folles* ("the crazy years"). Artists, especially American writers of the Lost Generation – Henry Miller, John Dos Passos, F. Scott Fitzgerald, and Ernest Hemingway – gathered in the cafes of Paris near Montparnasse. In 1924, André Breton launched surrealism with his *Surrealist Manifesto*.

Sidney Bechet and Flossie Mills starred in *La revue nègre* (The Negro Review) on the Champs-Élysées, where Josephine Baker walked her pet cheetah on stage at the end of a diamond-studded leash. Mistinguett sang her signature song *Mon homme* at the Moulin Rouge, the Folies Bergères, and the Casino de Paris. (Fanny Brice later popularized the song for American audiences as My Man.)

Max Linder introduced burlesque to Paris, and the first talking films debuted. In 1927, the Russian ballet dancer and choreographer Léonide Massine triumphed in Paris with *Pas d'acier* (The Steel Step), with music by Sergei Prokofiev. In 1928, it was George Balanchine and Igor Stravinsky with *Apollon musagète* (Apollo Musagetes). One of the dancers in *Pas d'acier* was Eugénia Delarova, who became Massine's wife. Born in Saint Petersburg, she played the role of the young flower girl in *Gaietés parisiennes* with Massine's Russian Ballet of Monte Carlo in 1938; one year later, she shared the stage with Yul Brynner at the Strand Theatre in London, singing the gypsy tune *Les yeux noirs* (The

Black Eyes). Twenty-five years later she would marry Henri-Georges Doll in New York City.

The world of science had also changed dramatically, moving away from the classical physics that Conrad Schlumberger and his generation of scientists had learned and taught. A list of some of the Nobel Prizes awarded in physics between the wars (usually honoring work done a decade or so earlier) gives an idea of the magnitude of these changes.

In 1918, the Nobel Prize in physics was awarded to the German physicist Max Planck for his discovery of the quantum of energy, which marked the beginning of modern physics. In 1921, the Prize was awarded to Albert Einstein, not for special and general relativity, his revolutionary theories of space and time, but for his use of the new quantum theory to explain the photoelectric effect, which showed that light waves sometimes behaved like particles. In 1922, the award went to the Danish physicist Niels Bohr for outlining the first consistent quantum theory of atoms and light.

In 1923, the Nobel Prize in physics was awarded to the American physicist Robert Millikan for determining the charge of the electron; in 1926, it was given to the French physicist Jean Perrin for experiments that finally demonstrated convincingly the existence of atoms. In 1929, the Prize went to another Frenchman, Louis de Broglie, for showing that electrons – then the smallest and lightest known particles of matter – sometimes behaved like light waves.

In 1933, the Nobel Prize in physics was awarded to the German physicist Werner Heisenberg for the first complete statement of the principles of the new quantum theory. Part of the new theory was the proposition that it is impossible, even in principle, to measure precisely both the position and the speed of an object at the same time. Heisenberg's "uncertainty principle" would overturn forever the Newtonian model of the world.

In 1935, the Prize was awarded to the British physicist James Chadwick for his discovery of the neutron. This new "elementary" particle completed for a time the physicists' model of the atom, with protons and neutrons bound together by an as yet unknown force in a dense positively-charged nucleus, surrounded by a cloud of electrons attracted to the nucleus by electromagnetic forces.

In 1938, the Nobel Prize went to the Italian physicist Enrico Fermi for his discovery of nuclear reactions and new radioactive elements caused by the absorption of neutrons.

> The discovery of the neutron at the Cavendish Laboratory of Cambridge University, under the direction of the "father of nuclear physics" Ernest Rutherford, is one of the great detective stories of 20th century physics. The book to read is *The Fly in the Cathedral, How a Group of Cambridge Scientists Won the International Race to Split the Atom*, Brian Cathcart (Viking, New York, 2004).

Despite its failure to penetrate the American market, *la Pros* had survived its start-up years. In 1929, the company had 56 engineers in the field, while a dozen or so employees worked at its headquarters in Paris, supporting field crews, interpreting data, fixing equipment and doing research on new equipment and measurements. The company's finances were healthy. In 1929, it made a profit of more than 1.4 million francs, mostly from surface prospecting for minerals in Europe and Africa.

The franc, however, was devaluating compared to the United States dollar and the British pound. In 1926, Raymond Poincaré led a national unity government that created the *le franc Poincaré*, convertible into gold, to stabilize the currency. The franc had lost nearly 80% of its value since 1914. To compensate for this, and to protect their father's original investment, Conrad and Marcel became expert at juggling exchange rates in the different countries where they operated.

La Pros was still a family business. Its bylaws specified that the original shareholders could not sell any shares without first making an offer to the other shareholders, who were all family members. Conrad and Marcel worked without a salary and were compensated by additional shares.

Doll was not yet a shareholder (Annette owned the family shares). "I had no particular title. I had the salary of a regular engineer," he recalled later. Nevertheless, he had become indispensable to Conrad and Marcel in running the business. Aside from his two trips to the United States in 1928 and 1929, he had spent much of his time doing administrative work at headquarters – dealing with suppliers and clients, handling personnel matters for the field engineers, and compiling the company's books. He was spending so much time on this work that he decided to take night courses in business and accounting.

Research, however, was his real passion. "I could not imagine," Annette wrote in her memoir, "an intellect as detached as his, I would even say oblivious, to any other area of interest.... I understood that I would have to live with 'electrical coring' night and day, its lines and curves writing themselves into my life. Filled with optimism, Henri-Georges wanted equipment, engineers. He believed that the men of the oil industry were hanging on his work.... He never had the least doubt about his calling. When he took aim at a target, he knew how to prepare his shot well in advance and in depth, calculating all the angles down to the tiniest details. And when he let the arrow fly, it was to hit the target."

Resistivity and spontaneous potential (SP) logs at Pechelbronn, 1931.

Chapter 7

A Battery at Seminole

In 1807, the Russian chemist F. F. Reuss discovered that he could make water flow uphill using a battery. Reuss was studying what happens when electrical current flows through water, repeating experiments done by scientists in England who had shown that a strong current could break water down into its components, hydrogen and oxygen, which were released as gases (in the process now called electrolysis).

Reuss placed a plug of powdered quartz at the bottom of a U-shaped tube, filled the arms of the tube with water, and connected them with wires to opposite poles of a battery. To his surprise, the water in the arm connected to the negative pole of the battery rose more than 20 centimeters (eight inches). In the other arm, it fell. The effect disappeared when the powdered quartz was removed, but was enhanced when the quartz was mixed with clay. In a paper presented to the Imperial Society of Moscow in 1809, Reuss noted that the battery had apparently turned the porous quartz into a pressure pump, driving water from one arm of the tube to the other. It was an unusual pump – there were no obvious moving parts.

Fifty years later, Georg Hermann Quincke, a German physics student at the University of Berlin, discovered the opposite effect. He observed that when water was forced under pressure through a porous quartz plug, it created a difference in electrical potential at opposite ends of the plug. In other words, water flowing under pressure turned porous quartz into a kind of natural battery.

In the spring of 1930, Doll realized that the effect observed by Quincke had probably been operating unnoticed in nearly every oil well that had been drilled during the last ten years. His idea would change the direction of the Schlumberger brothers' company and the future of the oil industry.

Doll had been thinking about one of the logs that he and Deschâtre had recorded in November 1929 for Gypsy Oil in the Seminole oil field of Oklahoma. The log was actually in the bottom drawer of his desk. Doll, who had been standing near the well while Deschâtre prepared the equipment, had noticed the needle of the potentiometer vibrating back and forth as the electrodes were being lowered into the well. The battery, however, was disconnected from the cable, which meant that no electrical current was flowing into the earth. With zero current flowing, the voltage between the downhole electrodes should have been zero.

A small vibration of the needle was actually not unusual. A typical logging run started with the tool being lowered to the bottom of the hole with the battery disconnected to conserve power. After it reached bottom, the battery was reconnected, and measurements were made as the tool was winched back up the well. The engineers of *la Pros* had grown accustomed to watching the needle vibrate during the tool's descent. It was generally believed that these vibrations were registering small variations of electrical potential in the drilling mud, caused by differences in its chemical composition at different depths. The mud reacted chemically with the tool's metal electrodes, changing their electrical properties.

The field engineers used the needle as a way of monitoring the sonde's motion: If the potentiometer needle was vibrating, then the sonde was moving; if the needle was stopped, then the sonde was probably stopped, too – either because it had reached the bottom of the well or had gotten stuck. In either case, it was important to stop unwinding cable into the well, where it could become tangled.

Doll knew about the effect of the mud, but the vibrations he observed at Seminole seemed too large and systematic to be caused by such small changes. As an analogy, you would not be surprised to see the speedometer needle of a car twitch as you settled in the driver's seat, but you would be very surprised if the needle rose to five miles per hour, and vibrated there for several seconds, while the engine was off.

The effect was not random. When the tool was lowered into the well a second time, the strong vibrations began again at the same depths. After the log was recorded, Doll wrote a note in the margin of the log at the corresponding depth: "Vibration of the needle. Probably SP." The abbreviation "SP" stood for "spontaneous potential," a term used for a difference in electrical potential that occurs naturally in a material when there is no apparent source of electrical current.

Doll was intrigued by the effect he had observed at Seminole, but he knew that the objective of the work was to sell electrical logs (recorded with the battery on!) to Gypsy and not to do experiments with spontaneous potentials. After the last disappointing meeting with Gypsy Oil, Doll packed the log in his suitcase, and it ended up in the bottom desk drawer of his new office at 42 rue Saint-Dominique, around the corner from the company's headquarters on rue Fabert.

"No one had been able to explain why a geologic layer with oil could have created the spontaneous potential [observed at Seminole]," Doll recalled later. "Up till then, when the spontaneous potential changed…during a logging run, one never considered that it was anything but the simple fact that the mud was not very homogeneous and…would therefore change the voltage on the electrodes.

"In fact, the situation…was just the reverse. Since the mud circulates constantly, it is relatively very homogeneous, and…where there is no other source of spontaneous potential, the 'SP line' is completely flat. One day, this puzzle, which came back to me a little every time I opened the drawer and could see the rolled-up log sitting there, gave me an idea."

Doll's idea was to put aside, at least initially, the properties of the mud and to focus instead on the fact that the effect he had observed at Seminole had occurred opposite a geological layer that *produced* oil.

As oil prospectors often discover to their disappointment, there are many more layers underground containing oil than there are layers that will produce it. What makes the difference is the rate at which oil can flow through a rock, which is determined by a property called the rock's permeability. Permeable rock allows fluid to flow easily through its pores; impermeable rock prevents flow. Both types of rock are necessary to make an underground reservoir: Porous, permeable rock must be present to contain the oil and allow it to be drained from underground. Impermeable rock – usually called cap rock by geologists – is needed to seal off the top of the reservoir. If there is no cap rock over a reservoir, then its oil will inevitably rise to the surface over geologic time (since it is lighter than water), forming an oil seep, and eventually evaporating into the atmosphere.

A well drilled into a reservoir provides a release point for fluids trapped by the cap rock. The fluids flow horizontally into the well and from there rise to the surface, driven by the large pressure difference between fluids deep underground and the lower pressure in an open borehole.

Looking again at the Seminole log in Paris early in the spring of 1930, Doll realized that the reverse process could also occur: Fluid in the well could flow *into* a permeable rock layer if the fluid pressure in the well exceeded the pressure in the pores of the rocks. He also realized immediately that this reverse flow would actually be the normal condition in wells drilled by the process of rotary drilling, which had become the standard method of drilling oil wells during the 1920s.

In rotary drilling, rock is ground up by the teeth of a drill bit placed at the end of a hollow steel drill pipe. The pipe is rotated by a motor on the drilling platform at the surface. The pipes come in different sizes, but a typical section is about 30 feet (nine meters) long. After the first section of pipe has penetrated into the ground, another section is screwed on at the top. Drilling then continues with further sections of pipe being added until the hole reaches the desired depth. As the drill string rotates in the well, drilling mud is pumped through the center of the hollow pipes down to the bit, where it emerges from a small opening in the face of the bit, flushes away the cuttings at the bottom of the hole, and returns to the surface in the narrow annulus between the drill pipe and the borehole wall.

The drilling mud is weighted with additives (usually clay particles) so that its pressure is higher than that of the fluids in the surrounding rock layers. This excess pressure (overpressure) in the mud is what prevents a blowout – an explosive rush of pressurized fluids into the well and up to surface.

Doll's idea was that overpressure in the drilling mud opposite permeable layers was actually generating the spontaneous electrical potentials observed in oil wells. It was the same phenomenon that Quincke had observed in his experiments with porous quartz plugs in the 1850s: A conducting fluid flowing under pressure through a porous medium generates an electrical potential – a natural battery. The phenomenon was originally called "electro-osmosis" or "electro-filtration." Today it is usually called a "streaming potential."

> Scientists in the 19th century following Quincke had studied the phenomenon in different fluids and materials, using it to elucidate principles governing the conversion of electrical energy into mechanical power. In 1879, the German physicist Hermann von Helmholtz developed a molecular model that is still used today to explain the effect. In Helmholtz's model, excess charge in the fluid develops when ions become trapped in a thin layer lining the walls of the channels through which the fluid flows in the porous material. This effect is similar to the static electricity that develops when certain materials are rubbed together. A small quantity of this excess electric charge is dragged along by the flow, creating an electrical current that changes the potential along the direction of flow.

Doll described his idea to Conrad, who immediately understood its importance. Conrad had been one of the first scientists to measure streaming potentials at the earth's surface, which are usually caused by water flowing through underground aquifers, and had devoted a chapter of his book to the subject.

The importance of Doll's idea was this: The streaming potential in oil wells could occur only opposite permeable layers – that is, opposite layers that were capable of producing oil. Whether oil or water was present in the layer was not important; what mattered was that the layer was permeable. Every oil company in the world wanted to know the permeability of its underground reservoirs. There was no safe and easy way to measure it directly.

Using a well-known formula, Doll and Conrad calculated that the streaming potential in a typical oil well could be large enough to explain the vibrations of the needle at Seminole. The two scientists planned a series of experiments to be done at Pechelbronn. Later that evening, Conrad confided to his daughter Annette that her husband "had made a discovery that could be very important for the company."

Experiments to test Doll's idea were done in the fall of 1930 at Pechelbronn. Two years earlier, *la Pros* had signed a contract with the operators of the Pechelbronn field, giving the company full access to the site, in exchange for logging new wells as they were drilled. (The contract also paid *la Pros* a small monthly fee.) Although it was the most convenient place to test new logging equipment and ideas, the oil-bearing layers at Pechelbronn were not ideal for measuring a streaming potential. The layers were thin and relatively impermeable, unlike the prolific sandstones at Seminole. The oil-bearing zones were also shallow, which meant that the overpressure would be small.

In planning the experiments, Doll also had to compromise with the equipment. The ideal way to measure the streaming potential in an oil well is by moving one electrode along the well, while a second electrode is placed at the earth's surface to provide a stable reference potential. In this arrangement, the streaming potential appears as a deflection, a "bump" on the curve as the electrode passes by a permeable layer.

The only equipment available at Pechelbronn was the standard logging device, which measured the potential difference between two downhole electrodes about 50 centimeters apart. To reconstruct the curve of absolute electrical potential from these measurements, it was necessary to add the readings at consecutive depths from the bottom to the top of the well.

> The calculation is like reconstructing the price history of a stock from its daily changes. Starting at 100, say, the stock moves up 2 points one day (102), down 3 points the next (99), then up 6 points (105), etc. The calculations, though easy, are tedious and prone to errors. Since each logging run at Pechelbronn would consist of about 1000 measurements, the calculation was like reconstructing a stock's price history over five years from its daily changes.

The tests started in November 1930. Paul Chabas, a young French engineer in charge of the operation at Pechelbronn, made the measurements with the local crew and mailed the results to Paris, where Doll made the tedious calculations by hand. Dozens of tests were made to verify that the results were repeatable and did not depend on the location, size, or shape of the electrodes on the sonde – or, for that matter, on Doll's calculations.

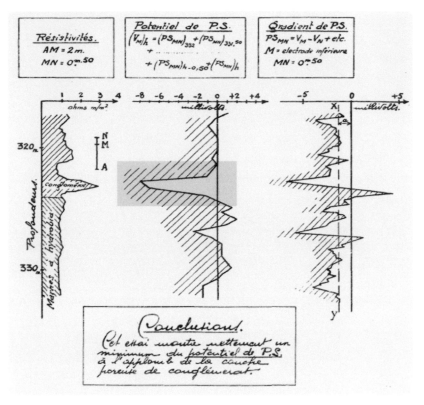

First spontaneous potential (SP) log recorded at Pechelbronn in February 1931 and published in May 1931 in *Proselec*, the internal technical journal of *la Pros*. The graph was drawn in Paris by Doll from measurements recorded by Paul Chabas. The curve on the left shows a standard resistivity log with text indicating the different geological layers. The curve on the right shows the raw measurements, which Doll used to construct the SP log (center). The log shows a "minimum of the spontaneous potential opposite a porous conglomerate."

It took nearly two months to obtain a satisfactory result. A log recorded on February 5, 1931, showed a small bump on the curve of electrical potential at two successive depths opposite a porous layer. The change in potential was small, about eight millivolts (mV), but subsequent tests showed that it was consistent from well to well. Doll wrote in the margin of the log that he showed to Conrad, "this test shows nicely a minimum of the spontaneous potential opposite a porous conglomerate."

Conrad felt that the result was convincing enough to devote an entire issue of the company's monthly technical bulletin to explaining the physics of streaming potentials and to summarizing the results of the tests at Pechelbronn. (The technical bulletin, called *Proselec*, was edited by Conrad's daughter Dominique.) A long article in the May 1931 issue ended with a directive that "every crew should whenever possible record a profile of SP in their normal logging operations."

The logs that would confirm the importance of the new measurement would not be recorded in France or the United States, but in the great oil fields of the Caucasus in the Soviet Union.

Henri-Georges and Annette in Moscow, 1932.

Chapter 8

In the Soviet Union

The oil province of the Caucasus runs for more than 1000 kilometers (620 miles) along the northern foothills of the Caucasus Mountains – from the southwestern shore of the Caspian Sea near Baku in Azerbaijan, through Grozny in Chechnya, the geographic center of the region, to the northeastern shore of the Black Sea near Maikop (in what is now the Federal Republic of Adygeya). It covers an area the size of California.

The region has a long association with oil. As early as 1000 B.C., Zoroaster (Zarathustra), the great religious figure of ancient Persia, was said to have visited the region to see with his own eyes the "eternal fires of Baku." Around 450 B.C., Herodotus wrote in his *History of the Persian Wars* about the collection of oil, salt, and bitumen from shallow wells in the region.

Shortly after the start of the modern age of oil in the United States in 1859, Russia became the world's second oil power, supplied by the fields in the Caucasus and driven initially by a refining and distribution center in Baku created in the 1870s by the Nobel family of Sweden. The Rothschilds of France, who operated an oil refinery on the Adriatic Sea, also quickly entered the market for Russian crude, along with Standard Oil and Shell.

In the 1880s, Russian drillers struck the "fountain fields" near Baku, which gushed enormous quantities of oil. Russian production rose tenfold to 23 million barrels a year, almost equal to that of the United States. But while oil production in the United States rose steadily through the first decades of the twentieth century, production in Russia peaked in 1901, and its share of world oil exports fell from nearly one-third in 1904 to less than one-tenth in 1913.

A revolutionary from the Republic of Georgia in the southern Caucasus, Yossip Djougashvili (who became Stalin), helped trigger the decline. Stationed and at times imprisoned in the region from 1901 to 1905, he incited the oil workers to a series of strikes, which eventually led to the terrifying attacks on Baku, described by Daniel Yergin in his history of the oil industry, *The Prize* (Free Press, 1993):

"Strikes and open rebellion spread throughout the empire in September and October of 1905. In the Caucasus, it was race and ethnic conflict, and not socialism, that drove events. Tartars rose up once more in an attack on the oil industry throughout Baku and its environs, intent on killing every Armenian they could find, setting fire to buildings where Armenians had taken refuge, pillaging every piece of property on which they could lay their hands. 'The flames from the burning derricks and oil wells leaped up into the awful pall of smoke which hung over the inferno,' one survivor would write. I realized for the first time in my life all that can possibly be meant by the words, 'Hell let loose.' Men crawled or dashed out of the flames only to be shot down by the Tartars.... As for the Russian oil industry itself, the tally was dismaying: two-thirds of all the oil wells in the region had been destroyed and exports had collapsed."

Production from the Caucasus recovered slowly after 1910, and by the start of World War I, Russian oil was again an important part of the world market. But production fell sharply after the Russian Revolution in 1917, and it was not until 1923, with the Soviets in power, that the U.S.S.R. was once more a net exporter of oil. Leonide Krassine, Lenin's financial expert, who had overseen the sale of precious artifacts from Russian churches, handled the negotiations with foreign oil companies. Attempts by the Nobels, the Rothschilds, and Shell to recover their original concessions failed; the entire industry was nationalized. Many western firms, including American oil companies, continued to purchase Soviet oil, which often sold well below market prices. Oil revenue, mainly from exports to Europe, was the largest source of foreign cash for the new Soviet government.

When Stalin seized power after the death of Lenin in 1924, he rejected the New Economic Policy through which Lenin had introduced a small dose of the free market into Soviet agriculture and industry. On October 1, 1928, the First Five-Year Plan went into effect. It gave priority to heavy industry and major construction works, which were helped both by foreign specialists and by cheap labor from the gulags. Enormous importance was given to the electrification of the country and its industries. During the 1920s, the role of electricity in the oil industry grew dramatically. By the end of the decade, more than two-thirds of the energy for the oil installations around Baku came from electrical power. Lenin's famous phrase – "The Communists are the Soviets, plus electricity" – was often repeated.

The connection between the Soviet oil industry and Société de prospection électrique (*la Pros*) was made by Vahé Mélikian, a young engineer from a prominent Azerbaijan family in Baku. In her memoir, Annette Doll described Mélikian as "a native of the Caucasus, with silky black hair, olive skin, almond eyes…and a pensive, rather withdrawn temperament; he seemed to brood over his mysteries."

Mélikian had fled Baku after the Soviets came to power. In France, he obtained a passport for a stateless person, and settled in Paris. (He eventually married a French woman.) He was accepted as a student at École des Mines and studied mining engineering and geophysics, graduating in 1928. He joined *la Pros* shortly after graduation and worked at the offices on rue Fabert for about a year. Then, according to Annette, "One day, in March 1929, he presented himself at the office of Conrad and Marcel, accompanied by an official. When the door was closed, the stranger revealed his identity as Professor Golubiatnikov, representing Soviet geology. He had come to propose to *Messieurs* Schlumberger a contract setting up a close working relationship in return for regular payments back from the U.S.S.R. Mélikian, the young Russian engineer, would be part of the contract. Back in the Soviet Union, he would serve as liaison between the Soviet oil trust and the

Vahé Mélikian in a class photo at École des Mines, circa 1924.

Société de Prospection Électrique. Was this proposal agreeable to Mélikian? His expressionless face gave no hint of his thoughts."

D. V. Golubiatnikov worked for NGRI (*Nieftenoïe Geologo Radziedochnoïe Institut*), the Russian research institute for petroleum geology, which directed geophysical work for the Soviet oil trusts. The three key trusts were Groznieft, which controlled the fields near Grozny in Chechnya; Aznieft, which operated the fields around Baku in Azerbaijan; and Embanieft, which operated the fields around the city of Maikop in Adygeya. Created in the late 1920s, these three trusts ran the oil industry in the Caucasus, which accounted for more than 98% of Soviet production.

The First Five-Year Plan had given the trusts aggressive targets for exploration and drilling. The slogan posted everywhere in the Soviet Union was "Run the Five-Year Plan in four years." The drillers in Baku, for example, received orders from the Central Committee to increase the drilling rate to 275 meters (900 feet) per well per month – much higher than any rate achieved before in any Soviet oil district. The only hope of meeting the targets was new technology. As Mélikian and two Russian engineers wrote in *The Azerbaijan Oil Review* in January 1932, "It is evident that the combination of the two problems which the country looks to the oil industry to solve, i.e., the maximum rate of production, and the quality, necessitates a radical transformation of all the methods constituting our present technology for 'It is by technology that all problems arising during the period of reconstruction are solved' (Stalin)."

Actually, by technology and an iron fist. If targets were not met, an accusation of incompetence or sabotage could result in exile in a gulag or execution.

The agreement Golubiatnikov proposed to Conrad and Marcel in Paris was for "technical cooperation…for the purpose of introducing [the company's] processes in U.S.S.R." Payments would be guaranteed and deposited each month at a bank in Paris. The agreement required strict conditions of secrecy: *la Pros* would not be allowed to publish results from its work in the Soviet Union without the consent of the Soviet authorities, and would have "to stay independent of any financial, banking, or political groups, and not to intervene in any internal Russian matter."

In addition, each engineer would have to sign a statement agreeing "not to mention anything of what he learned or any of the impressions that he gained while in the U.S.S.R. during the course of work, or to publish afterwards any books, articles or studies describing life in the U.S.S.R. or analyzing [its] social or political organizations." Results sent back to Paris would have be analyzed in secret and kept under lock and key. The contract also required *la Pros* to train Soviet engineers in the methods of electrical prospecting, to allow them to access the company's laboratories in Paris, and to set up new labs in the Soviet Union.

It was not an easy decision for the young French company. Conrad and Marcel knew that the Soviet engineers, with training, would quickly be able to replace the French crews. But Conrad was impressed by the attitude of the Russian scientists he had met: They had followed his early research in electrical methods and were prepared to apply it systematically on a large scale. "Very favorable conditions for the application of [our] new processes were encountered in the Russian oil fields," he and Marcel later wrote, "thanks to the great drilling activity prevailing there, to the centralized management which permits a rapid generalization of the improvements achieved in any particular district, and lastly to the scientific spirit which animates the officers of the oil trusts, and which greatly facilitates new researches and technical improvements."

Annette recalled her father pacing the floor, "his thumbs hooked in his suspenders, his head bent forward. He saw a new world opening before him, a world in which comradeship and confidence would regulate the relations of each for the good of all." Marcel was less idealistic and "read the contract over and over again…. What unknowns were concealed in this commitment? Would Soviet engineers leak the company's technical secrets? Would a contract with the Soviet Union compromise possible business in the United States? Would it jeopardize the family name in Europe?"

On July 4, 1929, Conrad and Marcel signed a contract in Paris with Groznieft. A year later, it was extended to all of the trusts through Soyousnieft, the "trust of trusts," overseeing the entire Soviet oil industry. The opportunity was too large to turn down.

The first to leave for the Soviet Union was Mélikian. In late July, 1929, he went by train from Paris to Moscow and arrived two weeks later in Grozny. There he set up the first offices of *la Pros* in the Soviet Union and visited the local oil fields with Groznieft's director of exploration.

"It's an immense plain," he wrote in a letter to Paris on August 26, 1929, "covered with tall vegetation, burnt and dried out. Countless dunes form hills that are not very prominent. The landscape is on average flat; changes in elevation, though steep on the dunes, are less than 20 meters. Transportation by car is possible, but difficult. The vegetation is a barrier, and the clay soil is covered by a thick (one meter, for example) layer of very fine dust, which slips from under the wheels of a car…. The starting point for the electrical prospecting work will be about forty kilometers from Grozny. The team will have to live in tents. The heat is very intense (30° to 35° C in the shade) but bearable. Living conditions (with the gracious help of Groznieft) will, I hope, be decent. Everyone will have to avoid drinking the natural water. There is a local 'marsh' fever, but it's not very serious. No snakes."

The description of part of his native Caucasus probably brought a smile to Mélikian, who along with the other engineers in Paris had heard the stories of exploration along the Gulf Coast, where the mud was a meter thick and snakes outnumbered people.

Mélikian was soon joined by five engineers from Paris: Roger Jost, Raymond Sauvage, Jean Lannuzel, André Poirault, and Marquehosse. The group left Marseille on August 1, 1929, with 26 boxes of equipment on the steamship *Le Rhin*, and arrived on August 25 at the eastern Black Sea port of Batum in Georgia. Agents from Groznieft met the ship at the dock and took the equipment to Grozny. A few days later, the five engineers went by train to Tiflis (Tiblisi), the capital of Georgia, about 260 kilometers (160 miles) east of Batum. Mélikian was there and took them by car over the mountains to Grozny.

Work started in September 1929. For the next five years, the oil fields of the Caucasus would serve as a giant geophysical laboratory for *la Pros*, its engineers, and their colleagues in the Soviet oil trusts. And, through a quirk of geology, the region was ideally suited to electrical prospecting for oil.

The great oil reservoirs of the Caucasus occur mainly in thick layers of sandy sediments buried at depths of several kilometers. The reservoir rocks themselves are often unconsolidated: When brought back to the surface, they are not solid rock, but are more like coarse wet beach sand. These sediments were deposited in shallow seas that covered the area during the Tertiary geologic period, which lasted from about 65 million to 1.8 million years ago. The Tertiary lies between the Cretaceous period, which ended with the extinction of the dinosaurs, and our current geologic period, the Quaternary.

Roger Jost and a Soviet engineer taking measurements near Grozny, around 1929.

At the start of the Tertiary, the geography of this part of the world was very different from today. The ancient African and Indian continents, along with uplifted pieces of ocean floor that would later become the Italian and Arabian Peninsulas, lay much farther to the south. These land masses were separated from the core of Eurasia by an ancient ocean geologists named Tethys, after the Titan of Greek mythology who with her husband Oceanus ruled the seas before Poseidon.

Carried on the backs of tectonic plates that make up the earth's crust, these land masses were all moving slowly northward and would eventually collide with Eurasia at different times during the Tertiary, creating the Alps in Europe, the Caucasus in the Middle East, and the Himalayas in Asia. Most of the ancient seafloor of Tethys was consumed in these collisions, plunging below Eurasia deep into the earth's interior; parts of the plunging seafloor were also sliced off and appear today at the tops of the mountain chains created by the collisions. A line of volcanic islands developed off the southern coast of Eurasia, separated from the continent by a long shallow sea, which covered the entire region of what is now the Caucasus. About 25 million years ago, this sea accumulated the sediments that would form the great oil reservoirs of the region.

The collision of the Arabian Peninsula with Eurasia, which started about 3.5 million years ago, lifted up the Caucasus Mountains and separated the two basins that form today the Black Sea and the Caspian Sea. This recent mountain building has created steeply tilted layers, numerous faults, and frequent large earthquakes, which make the geology of the region highly complex. Mount Elbrus (5642 meters) in the western Caucasus Mountains is the highest peak in Europe.

The underground oil traps were created during the recent mountain building, when layers of sediment sandwiched between the rising Caucasus Mountains (to the south) and the Eurasian continent (to the north) arched up, forming long underground ridges called anticlines. The cores of these ridges are coarse unconsolidated Tertiary sands, which are ideal reservoir rocks – porous and highly permeable. Equally important though is a thick layer formed from a mixture of fine sand held together with even finer-grained silt or clay, which makes it impermeable to oil. This layer of hard rock, a type of shale called *Samartien* by Russian geologists, sits above the coarse sands, and forms the cap rock of the oil reservoirs.

Samartien was good for electrical prospecting in the Caucasus: Of all the subsurface rock in the area, it is the most conductive, which means that any electrical current injected into the earth tends to concentrate towards it in seeking the path of least resistance. Moreover, this layer is close enough to the surface for its effects on electrical current to be clearly visible in surface electrical prospecting.

The first successes came in a group of oil fields in Chechnya, called the New Fields, which are south and east of the city of Grozny. The original oil fields of the region, renamed the Old Fields, lay to the north and west of the city. By the end of 1929, a crew led by Roger Jost had carried out a surface electrical survey covering a huge area, about 400 square kilometers (154 square miles), surrounding the city. The survey was designed to probe the underground to a depth of about 250 meters (820 feet). The map it produced not only showed clearly the full extent of the geological structure making up the New Fields, but also answered questions that had long puzzled the geologists at NGRI. One obvious question was: Are the Old and New Fields connected underground? Years of surface geological studies, drilling and production had not provided an answer.

The new resistivity map, however, showed clearly that both Old and New Fields were part of the same geological structure, a single anticlinal ridge, which had been cut in two by a fault running north to south along a line just west of Grozny. Russian crews trained by Jost extended this subsurface map to cover nearly 8000 square kilometers (3100 square miles) of the northern foothills of the Caucasus, and discovered two larger buried ridges flanking the one that ran through Grozny. The map produced by these surveys is still one of the largest contiguous resistivity maps of the earth's subsurface.

Oil derricks at the Bibi-Eibat oil field south of Baku, Azerbaijan, around 1931. The oil field extends along the western shore of a semi-circular bay that lies south of the city. The first marine electrical survey was carried out in the bay using the waterproof cables of the electrical logging crew.

An equally dramatic result came from the oil fields of Azerbaijan near the city of Baku, in the region operated by the Aznieft oil trust. The city of Baku itself lies at the top a small semicircular bay on the southern shore of the Aperchon Peninsula, a land mass shaped like a bird's beak that juts eastward about 70 kilometers (40 miles) into the Caspian Sea. The first electrical surveys near Baku were done over the Bibi-Eibat oil field, which lies south of the city along the western shore of the bay.

In 1929, Bibi-Eibat (which at the time was renamed "Stalin Field") was the second most productive oil field in the Soviet Union, accounting for almost 17% of Soviet production. The geologic structure of the reservoir was an anticline, which appeared to extend under the bay itself. The first production wells drilled in the 1880s ran to the edge of a cliff along the western shore of the bay; in the 1920s, new production was opened up, by filling in part of the bay and drilling to the east of the original shoreline.

To determine the field's full extent, Jost and his crew performed the first marine electrical prospecting survey by borrowing the winch and waterproof cables of the electrical logging crew. The winch and one of the current-injection electrodes were left onshore, while the three cables carrying the second current electrode and the two potential electrodes were towed in a boat about 1500 meters (about one mile) from the shore and dropped onto the sea bottom. The submerged cables and electrodes were then winched back to shore, with the crew taking measurements every 15 meters (50 feet). After a profile had been recorded,

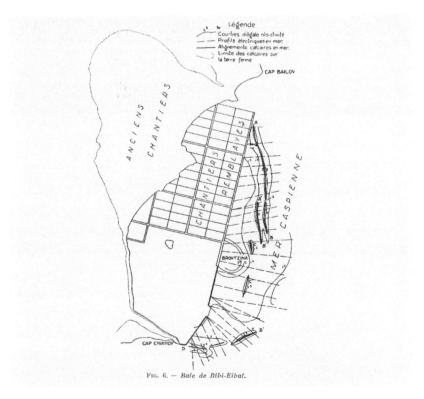

FIG. 6. — Baie de Bibi-Eibat.

Map of electrical resistivity beneath a bay of the Caspian Sea near Bibi-Eibat oil field in Azerbaijan. The map showed that the buried geological structure of the oil field (an anticline) extended another 500 meters into the bay.

the equipment was moved about 100 meters along the shore, and the process was repeated until the entire bay had been surveyed.

The resistivity map created from these sea-bottom profiles showed that the oil field renamed after Stalin extended another 500 meters into the bay.

Electrical logging for the Soviet oil trusts got off to a slower start. Raymond Sauvage, the engineer in charge of the logging team, attempted the first test in September 1929 in the New Fields at Grozny. The wells of the New Fields, however, were in poor condition. In trying to meet their quotas, the drillers had worked at a furious pace, leaving highly "deviated" wells with rough sidewalls (the faster the drilling, the rougher the walls and the more the well deviates from vertical). When Sauvage and his crew tried to lower the logging equipment into the first well, it got stuck near the surface. Several months, and many wells later, they still had not managed to get the logging equipment down to the oil-bearing layers. In December 1929, Sauvage returned to Grozny, where he learned that the local drilling director, accused of sabotage, had disappeared.

The new drilling manager was not optimistic. "You see that armchair?" he said, pointing out the director's chair to Sauvage. "It doesn't bring good luck."

Discouraged, Sauvage returned to the base camp, prepared to stop the logging tests. But on December 24, 1929, while watching the completion of a new well, he had an idea. He convinced the drillers to re-insert the hollow drill pipe into the well beyond the depth where the logging tool usually got stuck. He then inserted the logging tool into the drill pipe, where it slid down past the obstruction and sank to the bottom of the well. (Pierre Bayle, working for *la Pros* in Venezuela during this time, invented a similar method for conveying logging equipment on drill pipe to the bottom of a well.) The method worked in other wells, and within a few days, Sauvage and his crew had recorded logs showing the presence of previously unknown oil-bearing layers in the New Fields.

The best electrical logs from the Caucasus would come eighteen months later in the Soviet Union's largest oil field, which lies about 16 kilometers (10 miles) northeast of Baku, near the city of Surakhany. In June 1931, several deep new wells were being planned for Surakhany, which was producing almost 20% of Soviet oil. The goal was to tap new oil-bearing layers, which geologists believed lay several thousand feet below the existing reservoirs. The new wells would penetrate 2000 meters (6500 feet), the deepest so far in the region.

Mélikian and Sauvage suggested that the new wells could be drilled without taking any cores, by relying on the electrical logs to identify the geologic layers. The local drilling manager liked the idea, since it would be much faster and safer than coring. The geologists protested, but with the support of Golubiatnikov at NGRI, the drilling manager prevailed.

By this time, news of Doll's idea about the streaming potential and his experiments with spontaneous potential (SP) logs at Pechelbronn had reached the Soviet Union. Sauvage and Mélikian decided to try the new measurement in the deep wells of Surakhany.

Logging at Surakhany began in July 1931. The resistivity logs were excellent, but the SP logs were astonishing. The "bumps" on the curve of electrical potential opposite permeable layers were as high as 100 millivolts, more than ten times larger than anything seen at Pechelbronn. Consistent with Doll's hypothesis that the variations were caused by a streaming potential, the curve flattened opposite imperme-able zones, which helped to identify cap rock above the reservoirs.

By comparing the resistivity and SP logs, Sauvage and the local geologists were able to identify nearly all of the geological layers at Surakhany, including several deep new reservoirs. At the Geological Congress of the Transcaucasus and Central Asia in October 1931, geologists from Aznieft presented their colleagues with a startling new map of the Surakhany oil field. It showed a much more complex structure than had been previously imagined, including new production zones and fault systems, which divided the reservoir into several compartments.

The geologists at Baku wanted to push the electrical measurements even further. "It seems that geologists at several of the sites,"
Mélikian wrote in March 1931, "were trying to interpret the peaks of
the graphs in a way that was much too simplistic – transforming the
values of resistivity in ohms directly into tons [of oil]. We had to draw

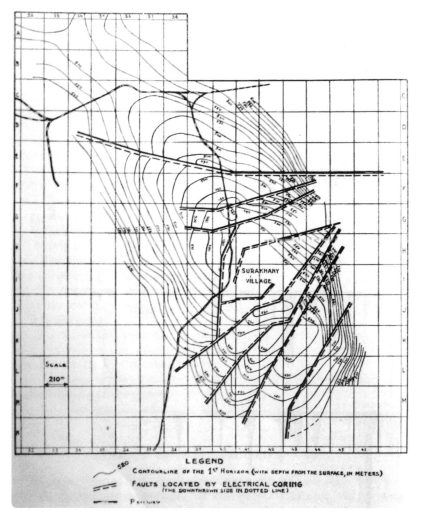

LEGEND

CONTOURLINE OF THE 1ˢᵗ HORIZON (WITH DEPTH FROM THE SURFACE, IN METERS)

FAULTS LOCATED BY ELECTRICAL CORING
(THE DOWNTHROWN SIDE IN DOTTED LINE)

Map of an oil-producing layer at Surakhany field in Azerbaijan produced by Raymond
Sauvage and Soviet engineers from resistivity and SP logs recorded in deep wells drilled
through the reservoir. The dark lines are geological faults discovered by comparing logs
from nearby wells.

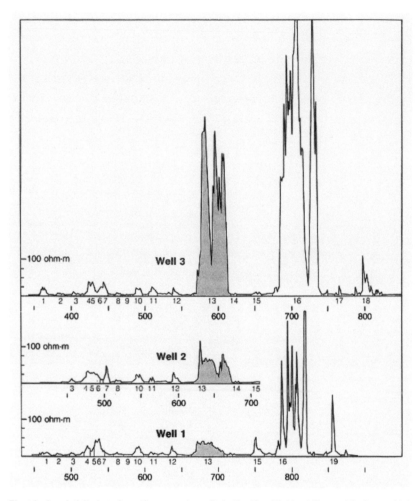

Electrical resistivity logs from three nearby wells in the New Fields at Grozny. The logs, which were assembled by Raymond Sauvage and a crew from Groznieft Oil Trust in 1932, show the correlation of electrical resistivity with oil content in the New Fields. The shaded areas highlight an oil-producing layer in wells 1, 2, and 3. The layer in well 3 has the highest resistivity (over 300 ohm-m, see scale at left) and produced only oil. The resistivity decreases to about 100 ohm-m in well 2, which produced a mixture of oil and water. Finally, the resistivity falls to 50 ohm-m in well 1, which produced mostly water.

the attention of the Geologic Office at Aznieft to the very serious risks in such an effort. Everyone now understands that Sauvage will undertake this question of the interpretation of the logs and will improve the links with the geologists."

But several months later, he also wrote, "At Surakhany, the proportionality between the resistivity of a layer and its oil content is really remarkable. The same thing is seen at Bibi-Eibat."

By the end of 1931, the Soviet oil trusts were convinced that the new logs were indispensable to meeting their quotas. "The principal advantages of electrical coring are a greater speed in bringing wells into production," Mélikian and two Soviet engineers wrote in an article published in the *Azerbaijan Oil Review* in January 1932. "A few hours at most are needed to establish a log for the whole length of the drill hole, that is to say, the same length of time needed to take a single core.... Use of electrical coring, which precludes the necessity of taking core samples, should increase the drilling speed to 275 meters (900 feet) per well per month, the figure imposed by the Central Committee."

Of the 180 wells drilled at Bibi-Eibat in 1931, more than two-thirds used electrical logs instead of mechanical coring. Early in 1932, the Aznieft Trust issued a directive forbidding the taking of cores from all but the last few meters of any well (this last section was actually impossible to log because of the length of the sonde). For the next five years, an electrical resistivity log, along with an SP log, would be recorded in nearly every oil well drilled in the Soviet Union.

Henri-Georges Doll and Annette arrived in Moscow on March 2, 1932. The visit was part of the contract, paid for by NGRI, except, as Conrad insisted, for the extra expenses of Annette. The young couple were treated as visiting dignitaries: an evening at the Bolshoi, receptions around the city, a private tour of the Tomb of Lenin in Red Square. Annette recorded her first impressions of "this new paradise of socialism" in a small black leather notebook. (Customs officials confiscated it when she left the country.)

They arrived at Grozny on March 6. Annette stayed in the city, while Doll headed for the company's base camp with several cases of equipment shipped from Paris: a new voltmeter, rubber plugs for repairing leaks in the cables, and other assorted spare parts including resistors, wires, and glass tubes.

For the first time since he had left Oklahoma at the end of 1929, Doll was back in an oil field. He wrote to Paris on March 13, describing the experiments he wanted to carry out in the Caucasus, along with a plan for setting up an experimental laboratory for the oil trusts, preferably at Grozny, where he thought the organization was better suited for research. He was excited, but "didn't expect that it would all go very fast."

Doll had brought along a new instrument, a version of the electromagnetic magnetometer which he had first tested several years earlier on the Esplanade des Invalides. Working with Conrad and Marcel, he had managed to fit the device into a thin pressurized cylindrical tube that could be lowered into a well to measure its inclination with respect to the earth's local magnetic field. They called the device a "teleinclinometer," because its main use was to determine a well's trajectory underground. Doll and Sauvage used it to show that two unproductive wells at Surakhany actually intersected about 10 meters (33 feet) below the surface.

The teleinclinometer was based on a device called an "electromagnetic compass," which had been invented in 1907 by the French physicist, Louis Dunoyer. Charles Lindbergh used a version of Dunoyer's instrument for navigation in his solo flight across the Atlantic in 1927. The instrument consists of a circular coil of wire mounted on a platform that can rotate below an electromagnet that is wound around a pendulum.

To make a measurement, the coil is spun with a motor, and the voltage induced in the coil by the earth's magnetic field and by the magnetic field of the pendulum is recorded. The measurement is then repeated with the magnetic pendulum switched off. The two different readings allow a mathematical formula to determine the two angles that determine the orientation of the device: the angle between the coil's axis and magnetic north and the angle between the coil's axis and the vertical.

The new instrument could also be used in combination with the resistivity measurement to determine the electrical anisotropy of sedimentary rocks. A substance is anisotropic when its properties change with the direction in which they are measured. A well-known example

Henri-Georges Doll calibrating the teleinclinometer in the base camp of the Surakhany oil field near Baku, Azerbaijan, in 1932. The tool, which Doll invented with Conrad and Marcel Schlumberger, contained an electromagnetic compass for determining the underground trajectory of an oil well. Raymond Sauvage is seated at the table behind Doll. Two Soviet engineers from Aznieft Oil Trust are standing next to the table.

of electrical anisotropy is the mineral selenium, whose resistivity is very high when current flows through it in one direction, and very low when it flows in a perpendicular direction. The anisotropy of selenium is caused by the mineral's crystal structure, which consists of parallel planes of atoms. Electrons can flow easily along the planes, but have to expend extra energy to jump from one plane to another. This extra energy causes the higher resistivity in the direction perpendicular to the atomic planes.

Sedimentary rocks are often anisotropic for a similar reason: Current in the fluid-filled pores of these rocks can generally flow more easily along the sedimentary layers than across them. The effect is particularly striking in rocks composed of thin oil-filled sandstone layers, separated by layers of shale, where the difference in resistivity can be 100 times or more depending on whether current flows parallel or perpendicular to the layers. A measurement of a rock's electrical anisotropy can therefore indicate the direction of its layering. The two measurements – the inclination of the well at different depths and the local direction of layering – provide geologists with important clues to a reservoir's internal geological structure, and a guide on where to drill next.

Doll tested the teleinclinometer at Grozny the week after he arrived. He and Sauvage did further tests two weeks later at Baku. The instrument was returned to Grozny, where it was used in more than 60 wells in the New Fields. A description of the device, along with some results from the Soviet oil fields, became Doll's first scientific paper, which he presented in 1933 at the World Petroleum Congress, held at Imperial College in London.

A photograph taken during the field test shows Doll and Sauvage in the base camp near Baku calibrating the instrument. Doll, wearing plus-fours, knee-high field boots, and a beret pulled down over his ears, stands next to the tool with a cigarette dangling from his mouth. Sauvage, also wearing a beret, is seated on a bench behind a wooden cross-legged table, shielding his eyes from the sun and talking with two Russian technicians who are taking measurements as Doll adjusts the angle of the tool. Wooden cabins and one-story, cinderblock buildings of the Surakhany base camp form the background.

Doll also performed experiments at Grozny and Baku to test his ideas about the streaming potential. While he and Conrad were preparing the patent applications in Paris after the tests at Pechelbronn a year earlier, they had devised a formula using the streaming potential to estimate the fluid pressure in underground reservoirs. The idea was simple: If the spontaneous potential (SP) in a well was caused by a streaming potential (as Doll had hypothesized), then the size of the effect would depend on the difference between the pressure in the column of mud filling the well and the pressure in the reservoir fluid. Changing the mud pressure would therefore change the SP signal, but the pressure in the formation would stay the same and could be estimated from the change in the SP signal. This was the basis for the formula in the patent.

Tests at Pechelbronn had shown that the SP signal did change when the mud level in the well changed (the height of the mud column determines the pressure in the mud). But the signals were so noisy that it was difficult to see if the result agreed with the formula in the patent. Doll actually doubted that the formula was accurate. "It was a bit of a pipe dream," he later wrote. "But it was worth a try."

The deep, permeable reservoirs at Grozny and Baku were perfect test beds for the formula. The first experiment was performed late at night during Doll's first week at Grozny. A technician from Groznieft lowered the sonde into the well, while Doll operated the potentiometer and dictated the first set of readings in Russian to another technician. The drillers then poured more mud into the well. Doll made a second set of readings and calculated the formation pressure from the formula. To his surprise, the result agreed with estimates the local reservoir engineers had made from the rates at which the wells produced oil. Doll telegraphed the results to Paris.

In Baku a week later, Doll attempted a second test in the Surakhany oil field, where the largest SP signals had been observed. The result this time was even more surprising. The formula predicted that the pressure in the reservoirs at Surakhany was zero!

This was impossible, and Doll knew immediately that there was something wrong with his assumption that a streaming potential was the only source of the spontaneous potential in oil wells. He later learned from Louis Bordat (an engineer from *la Pros* working with the geologists at Baku) that the largest SP signals at Baku occurred opposite permeable layers filled with highly salty water. This suggested that the SP signal might also include an electrochemical effect driven by differences between the concentrations of salt in the mud and in the reservoir fluids.

Conrad reached the same conclusion after hearing the results from Baku. From his experience with surface SP, however, he knew that salt concentrations could not generate the 100-millivolt potentials seen in the oil wells at Baku. He suspected that other elements were at work, which he guessed were clay particles. It was a natural guess from the long history of the subject, going back to original experiments by Reuss and Quincke.

Conrad immediately carried out experiments in Paris to simulate electrochemical reactions that could occur underground between drilling mud in the well, salt water in permeable underground reservoirs, and clay particles in surrounding layers. His tabletop experiments showed that the presence of clay did enhance the electrochemical signal, but not by enough to explain the logs at Baku. It would take another decade for a full understanding of the spontaneous potential in oil wells to emerge as a combination of streaming potential and electrochemical effects.

Fortunately for *la Pros*, its patents did not have to be revised. With his usual scientific foresight, Conrad had made sure that the applications were written broadly enough to cover all possible causes of SP signals in oil wells, including streaming potentials and electrochemistry. In fact, the main point of the patent was that the cause of the effect was less interesting than its uses. Whether driven by a streaming potential or electrochemistry (or some other effect), the new SP log clearly "wiggled" opposite permeable layers. This was the key observation that Doll had first made while thinking about the vibrating needle at Seminole.

The new SP log, in combination with the resistivity log, would allow oil company geologists and engineers to focus on underground layers most likely to contain and produce oil: *la Pros* now had "two measurements that worked." In 1942, ten years after Doll's experiments in the oil fields of the Caucasus, Judge Samuel Sibley wrote in an opinion for the United States Fifth Circuit Court in New Orleans, "Electrical logging…has made great practical strides in the oil well art; as is reflected by the commercial success of the logs. But neither [method] practiced by itself would have had any success. The older patent [resistivity] was a commercial failure till combined with the second [SP], and the combination made little progress until both the processes and instruments were changed to eliminate inaccuracies."

For further details on the role of "the two measurements that worked" in the success of Schlumberger, see *Science on the Run, Information Management and Industrial Geophysics at Schlumberger, 1920-1940*, Geoffrey C. Bowker (MIT Press, 1994).

May Day celebration in Grozny, May 1, 1936.

Doll was the co-inventor with Conrad Schlumberger of the SP log, but his name does not appear on the French or U.S. patent. Both were issued in Conrad's name only. "At the time it was logical," Doll recalled many years later, "because it was allowed under French law and was normal practice: All of the patents were taken in the name of Schlumberger. It was the name of the company."

Patent law is different in the United States. A U.S. patent application has to include the name of any inventor who contributed to the patent's claims; the rights can then be re-assigned to another person or company (usually to whoever paid for the work). Schlumberger's SP patent could have been challenged in the United States, perhaps even invalidated, for omitting Doll's name. In 1942, the United States Fifth Circuit Court did in fact invalidate Conrad Schlumberger's SP patent, as well as his resistivity patent – but for very different reasons.

In May 1932, after two months in the Caucasus, Henri-Georges and Annette Doll returned to Paris. In Moscow on their way back, Doll wrote a short letter to NGRI about the visit. "We have drawn…a good impression of the collaboration, both for now and for the future, and… are convinced that NGRI will rapidly become a powerful and experienced geophysical organization."

That year, *la Pros* and the Soviet oil trusts had 19 crews at work, including 14 French engineers and 50 Soviet engineers. The crews in surface electrical prospecting were mostly Soviets, trained by Jost and Lannuzel in a center they had operated at Grozny since the spring of 1930. In his notebook, Jost made a collage of photographs of the 24 graduates of "the first class of engineers in the Soviet Union trained in the methods of Professor Schlumberger."

The Soviets were pleased with the results. Conrad was welcomed as "the revolutionary professor of geophysics" when he visited the Soviet Union in November 1931 to attend conferences in Moscow, Grozny, and Baku and to see his engineers in the field. Marcel had already visited twice, the first time in 1929, to chair a special conference on electrical prospecting organized by the oil trusts, the second time in 1930, to negotiate the contract with Soyousnieft.

In November 1932, the Aznieft Trust organized a conference at Baku to celebrate two years of electrical prospecting in the Soviet Union. At the end of the conference, telegrams were exchanged between Conrad and Golubiatnikov toasting the success of the collaboration between *la Pros*, NGRI, and the oil trusts.

Two months later, Golubiatnikov disappeared from Moscow. There was no official explanation of what had happened and no easy way to find out. Conrad and Marcel sent condolences to NGRI through Mélikian. Work continued, however, and the scope of the collaboration expanded. Marcel visited again in 1933 to negotiate a new contract for work in the Emba Basin, near the Ural Mountains north of the Caspian Sea, in Kazakhstan, and in the Donetz Basin. In November 1933, Conrad visited the crews again in Baku and Grozny and attended scientific meetings organized in his honor in Moscow and Leningrad.

Conrad personally contributed 18,000 rubles by subscription to the Soviet Union's Second Five-Year Plan, and donated another 22,000 rubles through *la Pros*. He had great sympathy for socialist causes around the world, but it was also true that the Soviet oil trusts were his company's best clients. At the start of 1934, NGRI was paying *la Pros*

The first class of Soviet engineers trained in the Schlumberger method by Roger Jost.

about 250,000 francs a month for geophysical services, and were paying the expenses of the French engineers, which amounted to another 100,000 francs per month. Since the arrival of Mélikian in September 1929, *la Pros* had recorded revenues of more than 3.5 million francs from its work in the Soviet Union. It was the company's largest single contract. "Up to the beginning of the 1933," Doll wrote, "we had carried out only about 30 logging operations in the United States; in Baku alone, we had already done several hundred."

In return, the oil trusts had increased production from the oil fields of the Caucasus to levels higher than any pre-revolutionary year. (By the start of World War II, Soviet production was again second to that of the United States.) They had also trained a new generation of geologists and geophysicists in the technology of electrical surface prospecting and electrical logging. Starting in 1933, the Soviet authorities began to refuse visas to the engineers from *la Pros*, and by the end of 1934, only four French engineers (along with Mélikian) remained in the Soviet Union. Back in Paris, Doll remarked, "the Russians have decided to fly solo."

The Soviet oil trusts were also interested in the new seismic methods that were increasing the success rate of finding oil in the United States. In 1931, Conrad and Marcel decided to set up a separate company to develop seismic technology and incorporated Compagnie générale de géophysique (CGG), jointly with the French government, retaining a 50% ownership through *la Pros*. The 1934 contract negotiated by Marcel with the Soviet trusts envisaged collaboration in the development of seismic methods; that year, a separate contract was signed between CGG and a new institute created in Moscow called the Bureau of Geophysical Research (KGR).

In the spring of 1935, five seismologists from CGG, working alongside geophysicists from KGR, made the first seismic surveys for oil exploration in the Soviet Union. In November of that year, the director of KGR, M. Koslov, visited Paris to meet Conrad and discuss further collaboration on seismic technology. Koslov also wanted to reduce tensions that had developed earlier in the year, when Conrad had opened his copy of the journal *Geophysical Abstracts* and seen an advertisement for a new book entitled *Electrical prospecting by the method of steady currents*, 123 pages long and available for 3.50 rubles from a Moscow publisher. The author was a Russian geologist (Dakhnov), who had been trained by *la Pros* while he was working for NGRI.

Conrad had actually seen a copy of the book during his visit to Moscow in November 1933 and had warned the trusts that its publication outside the U.S.S.R. would be a violation of their contract. He had been reassured that the book was strictly for internal use. After seeing the advertisement, Conrad wrote immediately to Mélikian on October 7, 1935, "[It contains a] detailed description of the method of Schlumberger...[and] a considerable amount of practical material on electrical prospecting.... The disclosure of this book in *Geophysical Abstracts*, especially after my letter of December 25, 1933, seems to us to be a serious matter."

Tensions eased during Koslov's visit to Paris. He apologized for publication of the book and engaged Conrad in a long discussion about the future of oil prospecting, concluding with a personal invitation to

Conrad and Madame Schlumberger to visit Moscow in the spring of 1936, when the contract was due for renegotiation.

Marcel and Doll were less convinced of Koslov's sincerity. In February 1936, Doll wrote to Mélikian, "You know that at the present time the world is invaded by 'geophysicists for rent' who are trying by any means possible to copy the methods and equipment that more capable companies have developed, with an eye to compete with them and to do this without any of the costs involved in the research.

"On the other side, you are familiar with how little effective the protection of inventions by obtaining patents can be and you know how easy it can be to overturn them…

"It remains well understood that we will continue to furnish KGR all of the information that it may want regarding this issue [a new technology for surface electrical measurements] and to keep it informed of all of the advances that we will be able to make on this question, but this on the formal condition that no publication, even internal, will be made. Competition is becoming fiercer every day, and you will understand that we are doing everything to defend ourselves against it."

Conrad, Marcel, Doll, and Léonardon had all realized, more or less together at the start of 1936, that electrical logging was reaching a tipping point in the oil industry. In 1931, the use of resistivity and spontaneous potential logs at Baku was an innovation. Five years later (and nearly a decade after the first log had been recorded at Pechelbronn), skepticism about the new methods had dissipated. Electrical logging was now an accepted part of the oil industry, which meant that *la Pros* would have to defend itself against imitators on the one hand and anticipate the next innovation on the other.

On April 9, 1936, Conrad went to Moscow alone (his wife was unable to make the trip). Mélikian met him at the train station. The country was in the grip of the massive repression launched by Stalin after the assassination of Sergei Kirov, the Communist party chief of Leningrad. During the taxi ride to the International Hotel near Red Square, Conrad asked about the geologists and managers he had met during his last visit in November 1933:

"Zametov?"

"Arrested," Mélikian replied.

"Glutchko?"

"Arrested."

"Grigoriev?"

"Arrested."

Golubiatnikov, surprisingly, had re-appeared and would be present at the negotiations. But Mélikian warned Conrad that he would not recognize his friend and colleague, "Don't be surprised." he said. "He has aged twenty years."

The negotiations dragged on for two weeks. KGR insisted that *la Pros* remove its personnel from the Soviet Union and only furnish equipment and material for the training of Soviet engineers.

On April 17, 1936, Conrad received an urgent telegram from Paris. Humble Oil Company had obtained patents in the United States claiming "significant improvements" on the Schlumberger method of electrical logging. In negotiations with Léonardon, Humble had offered to license the patents to Schlumberger in return for a large discount on its logging services. If Léonardon did not accept, Humble would license the patents to competitors of Schlumberger.

Conrad spent the rest of the trip dealing with the two crises facing his company: On the one hand, a collapse in the negotiations in Moscow would bring an end to seven years of brilliant technical collaboration and profitable business in the Soviet Union; on the other, a refusal to accept Humble's offer would mean taking on the world's largest oil company in a competitive battle. It was clear from Léonardon's reports that Standard Oil of New Jersey, the majority owner of Humble Oil, was driving the offer for the patents.

On April 29, 1936, Conrad signed the last contract between *la Pros* and the Soviet oil trusts. He had managed to secure an acceptable deal: *la Pros* would remove its personnel from the country and provide new equipment; in exchange, the Trusts would maintain the strict confidentiality of the contract and would continue to make their monthly payments to the company's bank in Paris.

The next day, Conrad left Moscow for Leningrad, where he boarded a boat for Stockholm. He had arranged to meet with attorneys there to discuss another competitive threat in the form of two Swedish patents, which also claimed to improve on the Schlumberger method and which had been licensed to a small California company called Lane-Wells. (Lane-Wells specialized in perforating oil well casings with explosive charges to start oil production.) Conrad telegraphed to Paris that he intended to purchase the Swedish patents.

The morning he arrived in Stockholm, Conrad met with the lawyer representing *la Pros*; in the afternoon, he played golf. The next morning, he collapsed from a heart attack and was taken for medical care to a nearby nursing home. Annette was the only family member to reach him before he died, two days later, on May 15, 1936. He was 58 years old.

Conrad was buried next to his father in the graveyard of a small church near the family estate in Normandy. Condolences came to his family and to his small company in Paris from the Soviet oil trusts; from the French and Russian academies of science; from French, German, Swedish, Canadian, and American mining companies; from École des Mines and École Polytechnique; and from universities and professional societies around the world.

A few months after Conrad's death only three engineers from *la Pros* remained in the Soviet Union. Mélikian also remained in Moscow to coordinate the activities of the 40 or so crews operated by KGR. The purges continued. During his last visit, Conrad had seen that Mélikian – a Soviet citizen employed by a foreign company in a key sector of the economy – could easily become a target, and he announced at one of the meetings that Mélikian was "long overdue to return to Paris for further training."

Marcel Schlumberger and Doll immediately began writing to KGR and the oil trusts requesting Mélikian's return as "a routine matter of the company's training policy." It took nearly a year – and a series of increasingly aggressive letters from Doll, eventually threatening to stop the training of Soviet engineers – before Mélikian received an exit visa. He arrived in Paris on March 17, 1937.

Payments from the trusts stopped after Mélikian received his visa. During his stay in Paris, customs officials searched his apartment at 9 Koptielsky Street in Moscow and impounded his car, a new Chrysler which *la Pros* had imported into the country a year earlier. Soviet officials wrote to Paris informing Mélikian that he owed duties amounting to 34,000 rubles on goods he had imported from France. The sum was equivalent to many years of salary for an ordinary Soviet worker.

Mélikian's exit visa was limited to six months, and he insisted on returning. He was convinced that he could resolve the issue with customs by dealing directly with officials in Moscow. He may have also feared retaliation against his parents, who were still in Azerbaijan. "During the week preceding his departure," Annette wrote, "we no longer dared look at him. [He] was married to a French woman and was the father of an eight-year old son; he could have stayed, he should have stayed. But he was a man of his word, and left France at the appointed hour."

Mélikian arrived back in Moscow in September 1937. He resumed work for the trusts and continued to maintain a correspondence with Doll on technical subjects. He also visited Moscow Customs and discovered that it had initially asked KGR to pay the duties that he was claimed to owe. Mélikian wrote to Doll expressing confidence that he could have the duties reduced on appeal and requested Doll's help in pursuing this strategy.

On February 22, 1938, Doll wrote to the Ministry of Heavy Industry, asking for their help resolving the matter. (The Ministry had ratified the final contract with the oil trusts that Conrad signed in 1936.) A copy of the letter was sent to Mélikian.

It never reached him. At the end February, *la Pros* received news that Mélikian had been arrested at his apartment in Moscow. The charges were not specified. Marcel and Doll wrote to KGR and the oil trusts and applied for visas at the Soviet Embassy in Paris. They tried to send two of the company's directors to Paris to resolve the incident. Finally, they wrote to the Red Cross in Geneva, asking for help from their station in Moscow and enclosing a check to cover any expenses that might be incurred. A few weeks later the Red Cross wrote back that their Moscow office had been closed; the check was returned.

Doll sent a letter addressed to Mélikian at his apartment, enclosing a copy of an invoice *la Pros* had sent to the Soviet oil trusts. The amount outstanding on the invoice was nearly a million francs. The letter told Mélikian that he had the authority to handle the matter "with discretion, for whatever use was necessary."

A response came back indirectly in August 1938, in a letter from Parfenov, the new director of KGR. The letter reviewed a number of complaints against *la Pros* and concluded: "All of the above, as well as your non-performance of a series of secondary terms of the contract, have caused us material damages of about 400,000 rubles. We will not provide you with the details of this amount at this time, and will not tarry over the details of the illegal dealings of your representative Mélikian, reserving the right, if necessary, to return to this question at a later date."

By January 1939, Parfenov was also gone. In February, Doll wrote to the Federal Geophysical Trust, a new agency that had replaced KGR as the head of Soviet geophysics, and enquired again about Mélikian. The response from its first director (Prospielov) was surprisingly friendly. Although it did not specifically mention Mélikian, it encouraged *la Pros* to apply again for visas at the Soviet Embassy, with the hope that "direct discussions will end in a successful way for both parties."

Leon Migaux, the chairman of *la Pros,* and Maurice Martin received visas at the Soviet Embassy, and they visited Moscow in June 1939. The meetings went well, and on August 17, Doll wrote to Prospielov expressing his company's thanks, with the hope that "…the ground had been completely prepared for a 'renaissance' of a collaboration which had proven so fruitful in the past, and which, we have no doubt, will be equally so in the future."

One point though remained unresolved. "Unfortunately," Doll wrote, "the visit of Monsieur Migaux did not shed for us any light on the fate of our former representative in Moscow, V. Mélikian. You have noted that you know nothing in this regard, nor anything about the reasons that led to his arrest. We have to conclude – something which seemed evident a priori – that this arrest was caused by reasons purely outside his professional activities, but we cannot even conjecture what these might be. Knowing him as we do, we cannot believe that he would have let himself get involved in any reprehensible conduct, and we remain convinced that there must have been a bad misunderstanding in this affair. We will continue to try, with all our means, to straighten this out and will be most grateful to you of any clues to this, however small, that you may be able to provide."

The same day, a letter was sent from rue Fabert to Schlumberger Well Surveying Corporation in Houston. "It will probably interest you," the letter began, "to learn that the problems which have arisen in the last two years between us and the Federal Bureau of Geophysical Research of the U.S.S.R. (VKGR), regarding the execution of our contract with them, have now been resolved to the satisfaction of both parties. By means of a cash payment (representing about four months of fees of the old contract) to be made by the Federal Geophysical Trust, the legal successor to VKGR, and without any further action on our part, this contract will be deemed fully executed and all disputes on the subject resolved. In addition, the Geophysical Trust indicates its strong intention to renew a collaboration with us, the conditions of which will be defined in a new contract, which will probably be negotiated in Paris before the end of the year. We have not, however, been able to obtain any precise information on the fate of our former representative in Moscow, V. Mélikian, whose arrest, we are told by the Trust, could only have been due to causes completely independent of his professional activities."

Two weeks later, on September 1, 1939, German troops invaded Poland, in what would become the start of the Second World War. The payment by the Federal Geophysical Trust was never received.

There was no news of Vahé Mélikian. (After the fall of the Soviet Union in 1991, his family learned that he had been tried and executed shortly after his arrest in 1938.)

Only a few photographs remain from nine years of *la Pros* in the Soviet Union. One of these shows three men – Mélikian, Schiebli and Scheiderov (a Russian engineer) – riding in the back seat of a Chrysler. The picture was probably taken during the summer of 1933, near Grozny, where Schiebli was stationed. All three men are wearing field goggles. Schiebli has on a field jacket; Scheiderov, a light summer shirt; both men are sporting French berets and are turned to the camera, smiling. Mélikian, thin, bare-headed and bare-chested, is also smiling, but in the shadows and looking straight ahead.

He was 35 at the time of his arrest.

Henri-Georges Doll gardening at Marnes-la-Coquette, 1938.

Chapter 9

Back in the U.S.A.

At the time of Conrad Schlumberger's death in 1936, *la Pros* was growing rapidly. Even American oil companies had begun to notice the "Frogs" who were using their new technology with success in oil fields around the world. "This came about," Doll said in 1933, "mainly because of the 'tourists' of the oil industry – men from companies like Shell who had come to the Soviet Union where they heard about our methods.

[U]niversity professors were not at all interested. But a field engineer, from the Gulf Coast or elsewhere, saw right away its relevance. We would not have been able to return to the United States, if people had not come to have a look at the Soviet Union, or if we had not been able to hold on in places like Venezuela, the Dutch Indies, and Rumania."

Conrad was above all a first-rate scientist, but he was also a prudent businessman. In February 1921, he had written to his father, Paul Schlumberger, to explain that he and Marcel had burned through nearly all of the 500,000 francs that had been promised for their new endeavor. Their company (a predecessor of *la Pros*) needed an additional 150,000 francs to make it through the year. "If not," Conrad wrote, "the enterprise would fall back to being just a research endeavor with a modest budget and limited staff."

Salaries at *la Pros* were good, but not exceptional. One employee recalled going to Conrad's office in the early 1930s to ask for a raise. Conrad launched into a long speech about the problems the company was having with its technology and its clients, and never came back to the original question. The employee left the office disappointed. The engineers working in the Soviet Union calculated that their expenses came to about 500 rubles a month; Conrad allowed them 350.

Once the technology had proven itself in the Soviet Union, Conrad recognized that the future of *la Pros* was the oil business and relegated research in other areas to the background. Starting in 1934, the company stopped quoting a price for its logging services as an annual fee for a project or crew; instead, it worked almost exclusively on payment per unit of work, with the fee determined by the cost of getting to the site, the depth of the well, and the time in the field – to which it added a healthy margin to support research and development and for profit.

The structure of *la Pros* had also changed. During the global economic crisis of 1931 and 1932, the company had lost money, as did nearly every geophysical company. It was to survive this crisis that Conrad and Marcel had entered into the agreement to create Compagnie générale de géophysique: (CGG) in collaboration with the French government and with another French geophysical company, Société

Eugène Léonardon (second from the right) with a crew in the field in the 1920s.

géophysique de recherches minières (Geophysical Company for Mining Prospecting), which specialized in seismic and magnetic methods. CGG would combine the expertise of its two parent companies, offering commercial services in surface geophysical prospecting, including surface electrical prospecting outside the Soviet Union. CGG became one of the world's largest seismic companies (Schlumberger sold its 50% stake in CGG in 1960).

Eugène Léonardon had been the natural choice to set up the first office of *la Pros* in the United States in 1927. Born in Montaigut-le-Blanc, a small medieval town that sits on a hillside in the Massif Centrale region of France, Léonardon received degrees in law and science from Claremont College and from Saint Louis College in Paris before studying engineering at École Polytechnique. After graduating in 1912, he served a two-year commission as an artillery commander in the French army. In 1914, he was the first employee hired by Conrad Schlumberger to work in a new laboratory at École des Mines that Conrad had set up with his own funds. After serving in World War I, he rejoined Conrad and Marcel at rue Fabert.

Léonardon spent most of 1920s in the United States. Early in the decade, he worked with Sherwin Kelly, doing surface electrical surveys for mineral prospecting and civil engineering and writing some of the earliest papers published in English on these methods. He also organized the company's campaign of surface electrical prospecting for salt domes along the Gulf Coast in 1926.

In 1926, Léonardon returned to Paris and became the first employee of Conrad's and Marcel's new company. The next year he returned to the United Sates to set up an office for *la Pros* in New York City. From then on, he rarely left the United States. He applied for permanent residence in 1934 and became an American citizen in 1939.

Léonardon was convinced early on that electrical logging was the future of *la Pros*. In 1928, when Conrad and Marcel proposed to license the technology to a drilling company to obtain funds to support the company's surface business, Léonardon responded, "Are you crazy? Give away the orange and keep the rind?" A year later, when Gypsy Oil offered to continue testing the new technology in Oklahoma and Kansas – but only if Schlumberger reduced its price from $2000 to $400 a month for a full-time crew – Léonardon refused. Roger Knappen, Gypsy's consulting geologist, then offered a more substantial sum to buy the equipment. Léonardon had less than $10,000 in the bank. The American stock market had crashed a month earlier, and economic recession was spreading throughout the country. But Léonardon refused again. In January 1931, he had to close down the New York office and return to Paris.

A year later, however, Léonardon was back in the United States. In February 1932, he presented the first long scientific paper describing electrical logging to a meeting of the American Institute of Mining and Metallurgical Engineers (AIME) in New York. The paper was published two years later, under the title "Electrical Coring: A Method for Determining Downhole Data by Electrical Measurements." The authors were "Conrad and Marcel Schlumberger and Eugène

Léonardon." Several others followed. Written by Léonardon, they are classics of applied science. Nearly all of the examples were taken from the company's work outside the United States – from the original logs at Pechelbronn, from the Soviet Union (though it was not identified by name), and from Venezuela.

Schlumberger Well Surveying Company (SWSC) offices on Leeland Avenue, Houston.

In 1934, Léonardon set up a new company to represent *la Pros* in the United States: Schlumberger Well Surveying Company (SWSC) was incorporated in Delaware, but located in Houston, which had become the center of the American oil industry. Conrad was named president of SWSC; Marcel, the assistant managing director. Léonardon was the managing director and treasurer. *La Pros* gave SWSC the rights to its U.S. patents for the sum of $3 million, payable over 15 years.

Léonardon bought 2.5 acres (10,000 square meters) of land in Houston for about $9000; the site on Leeland Avenue was then on the outskirts of the downtown area. Not everyone in Paris was happy with Léonardon's choice. "Léonardon has no taste," Conrad confided to Annette. "None of us will want to live in that city." (No one, however, could fault Léonardon's eye for real estate. Over the years, as downtown Houston grew around the Leeland Avenue site, it increased in value several hundred times.)

In 1938, SWSC opened a new three-story building, which would serve as its headquarters for the next 15 years. On the first floor was an assembly line for the field trucks; on the second floor, departments for equipment and supplies; and on the third floor, company offices. Within three years, SWSC had more than 500 employees, including more than 100 engineers, most of whom were American.

After the death of Conrad Schlumberger, Henri-Georges Doll became the technical leader of *la Pros*. Louis Magne, a French engineer who joined the company in 1934 and still lives in Houston, said in a recent interview, "Fortunately Doll was there when the company was struggling. He was really needed and I don't know what the company would have done without him on the technical side, especially after Conrad died in 1936. Marcel was mainly interested in mechanical engineering.... Fortunately, Mr. Doll took up [Conrad's] baton. He was very focused. He knew what it took to succeed with technology in the oil field."

Doll also shared responsibility with Marcel for managing the company during its rapid expansion in the United States and in other parts of the world in the late 1930s. By the end of the decade, *la Pros* and its affiliates had logged more than 15 million feet of oil wells around the world – about 2840 miles (4500 kilometers) – and was operating in more than a dozen countries, including France, Germany, Indonesia, Venezuela, and the United Sates.

Conrad and Marcel had been careful to file patents on each new development of the company's technology. Nearly all of these early patents were filed in Conrad's name. By the middle of the 1930s, a dozen or so U.S. patents had given SWSC a de facto monopoly over what was becoming an indispensable technology in the exploration, evaluation, and development of oil fields.

Competition was inevitable. The first challenge, just before Conrad's death, came from a small California company called Lane-Wells, which specialized in perforating the steel casing of oil wells to start the flow of oil. (If oil-producing zones are identified underground after a well is drilled, steel casing is usually cemented into place to prevent the well from collapsing. The casing also prevents water from flowing into the well from other layers and mixing with the oil. When it is time to produce the well, the casing must be breached at the depth of the oil layers to start the flow of oil.) Lane-Wells had developed a new technology for "perforating" using bullets driven by explosive charges mounted on a device called a perforating gun, which could be lowered into a well on a cable. Supported by its own strong patents, Lane-Wells' business was growing rapidly.

Marcel had also devised a method for perforating wells by modifying a sidewall coring device he had invented in the early 1930s. Marcel's coring device used explosive charges to propel hollow cylindrical shells – about one inch in diameter and open at one end – into the side of an uncased well. The shells were then extracted from the wall by chains attached to the closed end and brought back to the surface. Under the right conditions, the cylinders would provide small samples of the rocks along the borehole wall.

> Louis Allaud, a French engineer, carried out the first tests of Marcel's sidewall coring device in the United States in the mid-1930s. After several unsuccessful shots, he finally obtained a few cores, which were saturated with oil when brought to the surface. He recalled the owner exclaiming, "The goddamn Frog took a core!"

Perforating was more profitable than coring, and Léonardon was eager to expand SWSC services. He knew that a service company that offered both techniques – logging to identify the oil zones, along with perforating to start the flow of oil – could capture a large market. In the meantime, Marcel had turned his coring device into a perforating gun, which had also been tested successfully in Venezuela. But the Lane-Wells patents blocked its use in the United States.

Walt Wells, the president of Lane-Wells, had seen the same opportunity as Léonardon and had acquired the rights to an electrical logging device called the GeoAnalyzer, which was based on Swedish patents. Doll had studied the patents and felt that the GeoAnalyzer was overly complicated and not very effective. But he was also concerned that its use could give a bad name to electrical logging in general.

Seeing his business threatened, Léonardon made a brief attempt to negotiate with Walt Wells, and then filed a lawsuit, claiming that the GeoAnalyzer service infringed a U.S. patent granted to Conrad Schlumberger in 1934. Legal proceedings began in March 1938 before the Federal District Court in Los Angeles, California.

Marcel had become the president of both *la Pros* and SWSC after Conrad's death. He thought that Léonardon had moved too quickly and asked Doll to go to Los Angeles to help with the trial, and also to try to resume negotiations with Walt Wells. Doll arrived in Los Angeles on March 8, and was met there by Roger Henquet. Léonardon had not yet arrived for the trial.

On March 11, 1938, Doll sent a letter to Marcel in Paris. "Henquet described in detail for me," he wrote, "the attitude of Walt Wells who, as you know, believes that the time is right and that he has considerable advantages over us in both skill and intelligence, and moreover, that he has in the person of Bill Lane an inventor who makes the Schlumbergers look like amateurs. According to Henquet, Wells is convinced that if he had a license from Schlumberger, that is, if he had a free hand, he could perfect electrical coring, provide a fantastic service that would allow him to raise his prices and easily make up for any royalties. Finally, Wells is not aware of our alternatives in perforating and thinks that we will make out much worse (than him) because we are not Americans. We therefore decided that it is necessary to let Wells go on talking, and increase if possible his illusions about the situation, but to make sure that we channel the terms in the best possible way, so that in the end, the deal appears to be a simple exchange, in which he receives a license for something, which he overestimates the ease of using, while we get a license that he thinks we will not be able to do much with."

With Marcel's blessing, Doll resumed negotiations with Walt Wells, while Léonardon was still on his way to Los Angeles. The trial was in the preliminary stages of technical briefs, describing for the court the scientific details and techniques of oil prospecting. To help with this, SWSC hired a consultant named Charles Aiken, who was professor of geophysics at Purdue University, in West Lafayette, Indiana. Aiken had studied chemical engineering and physics at Tulane University in New Orleans, and had obtained both a master's degree in electrical engineering and a Ph.D. degree in physics from Harvard. He had also done research in telecommunications and in geophysical prospecting at Bell Laboratories and had served as a consultant to oil companies.

Doll was impressed by the way Aiken handled himself in court, and the two scientists quickly became friends. Doll wrote back to Marcel, "Dr. Aiken started his testimony. I have to say that it's remarkably well prepared and clear. The judge understood and asked only necessary questions. Lyon [the lawyer representing Lane-Wells] was stunned, and was only able to interrupt twice to ask questions, which actually would have been better to hold back, since they gave a chance for a reply that undercut his evidence."

Before Léonardon arrived in Los Angeles, Doll and Marcel decided to offer Walt Wells a compromise. Under the deal, Lane-Wells would receive a license for electrical logging under patents, and SWSC would receive a license for perforating under the Lane-Wells patents. For this exchange, SWSC would pay a royalty of 12.5% on its perforating services to Lane-Wells; Lane-Wells, a royalty of 15% on its logging services to SWSC. SWSC would also receive a one-time payment of $250,000, recognizing that the market for electrical logging was larger than that for perforating and that its patents expired later than the patents held by Lane-Wells.

Walt Wells accepted the offer, and Léonardon dropped the lawsuit. Doll was pleased with the outcome. He already had in mind numerous ideas for improving logging methods and was convinced that a new perforating device, which Marcel had perfected in Paris, could be deployed in the United States without infringing existing patents. In a letter to Marcel on April 10, 1938, he described the reception that Walt Wells had hosted after the agreement was signed at the Ambassador Hotel in Coconut Grove: "The best orchestra in California was there. The dinner was very elaborate, and very cordial, with the menu specially prepared for us (French wines); everyone got on well (not much alcohol was consumed), and we all danced enthusiastically until one-thirty in the morning."

The episode had exhausted Doll. He fell sick with an intestinal infection and, when he returned to France, spent several weeks recovering at the Schlumberger family estate Val-Richer.

In 1938, Lane-Wells became the Dresser Atlas Company, which was later acquired by oilfield services giant, Baker Hughes. Baker Hughes itself is one of the successors to Hughes Tool Company started in 1909 by Howard Hughes, Sr., who had invented a new type of drill bit that dramatically improved the rotary drilling process.

In an interview years later, Doll described the strategy he and Marcel had devised: "The action was very positive for Schlumberger, in the sense that it freed us from the sword of Damocles suspended over our heads in the form of perforating. Schlumberger still had its doubts about starting a perforating business in the United States without a license from Lane-Wells, but the main objective of Schlumberger in launching the lawsuit was to prevent or reduce the threat that Lane-Wells might seize a large part of the logging market. Very simply, the attitude of Schlumberger was this: ...it was better to make things more difficult for ourselves with regards to perforating – by forcing ourselves to pay a royalty – so that we could make it more difficult for Lane-Wells to enter the logging market."

That same year, 1938, three young engineers of SWSC presented a remarkable paper at the third annual meeting of the Society of Exploration Geophysicists in New Orleans. The paper suggested that it might be possible to determine precisely the quantity of oil in an underground reservoir – the "Holy Grail" of oil exploration – by comparing the electrical logs with measurements made on cores and with production rates. The underlying idea was not new. Everyone had recognized that values of high resistivity on electrical logs were somehow correlated with the amount of oil in porous reservoir rocks.

In their first paper on electrical logging presented at the World Petroleum Congress in Paris in 1929, Conrad and Marcel had shown part of an electrical log through an oil layer at Pechelbronn, with the caption, "An oilsand 50 cm thick presents a resistivity about four times higher than the surrounding ground." Mélikian, Sauvage, and the engineers working for the Soviet oil trusts had tried to quantify the "remarkable proportionality" observed between the resistivity of the oil layers at Surakhany and Baku and their oil content. In 1932, Mélikian and two Soviet engineers wrote in *The Azerbaijan Oil Review*:

"The next step in the development of electrical coring will consist in studying the feasibility of determining, by means of the electrical logs, the initial production of the sands…. In a few districts…a definite relation between the resistivity and initial flow of the wells can be established. In other districts, it is not possible to locate with certainty even the position of the oil sands, so that evaluation of their initial production is well nigh impossible. The reasons for this difficulty have been explained…as well as the means of remedying it.

"In reality, the initial production…is a definite function of the thickness of the sand, of its resistivity, and of the pressure in the sand. (It is obviously indispensable to take into account the consolidation of the rocks, which increases the resistivity independently of the oil content. It is also important to make allowance for the role of the gas, the viscosity of the oil, and the amount of water present.)"

In their paper, the engineers from SWSC – William Gillingham, Maurice Martin, and G. Murray – took this analysis further and tried to quantify it in mathematical form. Their results were tentative, but their ideas would soon dominate the industry's thinking about the use of electrical logs.

During the 1930s, the business of *la Pros* and its affiliates grew rapidly. In 1933, there were 42 logging crews outside the Soviet Union; in 1934, the number grew to 72; in 1935, to 127; and in 1936, to 237. The rapid expansion was straining the company's ability to recruit and train new engineers. *La Pros* still preferred to recruit at major universities in France, but the problem of obtaining visas would soon force it to hire local engineers in every country where it was operating. The delays in obtaining American visas became so long that one of the lawyers in Paris suggested that newly-hired engineers be sent first to Mexico, where they could apply for a work visa at the U.S. consulate in Mexico City and then cross the border as tourists to start work (before the visas arrived).

Conrad Schlumberger had liked personally to oversee the recruiting of engineers. Now, Doll took over this role. He had his own way of judging candidates. Alan Morazzani, who had seen an advertisement for *la Pros*, came to rue Fabert where he was interviewed by Doll. "We talked for four hours," Morazzani later recalled in an interview. "He asked me questions about geography, history, and all kinds of things. He was trying to find out what I knew. I remember that when I came home that night my father asked me what I had done that day. I told him, 'Well, I went to interview at a company.' 'What kind of company?' he asked. I told him, 'Dad, I don't know. The guy who interviewed me didn't tell me what they did.' I didn't have even the slightest idea. I waited for about a week, and I got a letter. I was hired and I had to show up for work. Even then, I didn't know what the company did."

Between research, recruiting, and managing the business with Marcel, Doll was overwhelmed with work. Annette insisted that her husband see a doctor, who prescribed that Doll take a break from work, at least during the weekends, and get more fresh air. Henri-Georges decided to take up gardening. He and Annette had their eyes on a small house outside Paris in the town of Marnes-la-Coquette, next to an estate owned by Maurice, Marcel's youngest brother. Izaline remembers that the house her parents bought in 1938 was "nondescript, even ugly." It was made of concrete, and featureless, but was surrounded by a large property. Doll started a rose garden.

The family would go there every weekend, when Doll was not traveling. "He really was close to nature, almost like a prehistoric man," Izaline recalled. "He set up the flowerbeds, planted roses, and as always, he wanted to do it well and kept at it systematically. The result was beautiful to look at."

A year later, in September 1939, Doll would be in charge of an artillery unit; six months after that, he would drive a small tank around his rose garden.

German paratrooper burying a Tellermine during the Allied counter-offensive in the oil district of Cyrenaica in eastern Libya, 1941. These specialists were called "tank hunters." (Photo, *Établissement de communication et de protection audiovisuelle de la Défense, ministère de la Défense.*)

Chapter 10

Dangerous Ground

France declared war on Germany on Sunday, September 3, 1939. The following Saturday, September 9, the 3rd French Tank Battalion operating near the French-German border, supported by infantry and a mechanized division, came upon a field of antipersonnel mines, followed by a field of antitank mines.

The first French tank soldier killed by a mine was second-lieutenant Rousseau, whose tank – a small six-ton Renault – triggered a mine buried by the Germans to slow down a French counter-offensive.

France had about the same number of tanks as Germany (about 3000) at the start of the war, but most of the French tanks were small, about a dozen tons or less, with weakly armored undercarriages. The Germans had also experimented with new lightweight tanks during the Spanish Civil War (1936-1937), but the experience convinced them to adopt heavier tanks – notably the fearsome twenty-ton Panzer KwIV, armed with a 75-mm cannon and capable of speeds up to 40 kilometers per hour (25 miles per hour).

France's anti-vehicle mines at the start of the war were not powerful enough to disturb the tracks of the enormous Panzers, whose ten divisions formed the striking force of the German army. The anti-tank measures used by the French, including along the famed Maginot Line, consisted mainly of sections of buried railroad tracks sticking about 30 centimeters (one foot) out of the ground. The Panzer divisions simply drove around them or, if necessary, dug them up.

Within two weeks after the start of the war, French intelligence realized that the deployment of land mines was an integral part of the German strategy. Colonel Fuller, the American military attaché in France, was allowed in secret to examine a German antivehicle mine recovered intact by the French army. It consisted of a dozen kilograms of explosives, cased in steel and activated by a mechanism that was triggered by a weight of 135 kilograms (300 pounds) or more.

The Germans called it a Tellermine, after *Teller,* which means "dish" or "plate," but it actually resembled a large canister of film. It could destroy the French lightweight Renault tank, and disable larger tanks, such as the French B1, weighing 28 tons, or the American M4 Sherman and M26 Pershing tanks.

The Tellermine came in various models. The one Colonel Fuller examined was Model 35, with five kilograms (11 pounds) of explosive. The same model also came with a more resistant cover, which required

Dangerous Ground

more than 135 kilograms to trigger. Model 42 was activated by less than 135 kilograms, finally, there was Model 43, at the bottom of the scale, which could be triggered by 100 kilograms, the weight of a large soldier. The charge was normally TNT (trinitrotoluene; first synthesized in 1863 by the German chemist, Joseph Wilbrand), or ammonium nitrate. Both were powerful explosives. More than 3.5 million Model 43 Tellermines were manufactured in Germany during the war.

The variety of land mines was also astonishing. It was captured in lines spoken by the character of Captain John H. Miller early in the 1998 movie *Saving Private Ryan:* "These two minefields, or actually one big one, we tried to make our way up the middle of it, but it turned into a mixed high-density field and a little bit of everything: Sprengmine 44s, Schuhmine 42s, pot mines, A200s – the little wooden bastards that the mine detectors don't pick up. This road here they placed big mushrooms, Tellermine 43s, I guess for our tanks, from here right up to the edge of the village right here. So we marked it and called the engineers."

The Sprengmine, also known as the Schutzenmine or S-mine, was the most feared anti-personnel mine. Smaller and lighter than the Tellermines, a Sprengmine was made of two or three stacked steel cylinders, with a 500 gram (one pound) explosive charge at its base, which propelled the cylinders about a meter (3 feet) above the ground, where they exploded and sent shrapnel in all directions out to a distance of 50 meters (160 feet) or more. The Americans called the device a "Bouncing Betty;" the English called it a "Jumping Jack," or "bollocker" in reference to the castrating effect of shrapnel flying a meter off the ground.

Schuhmines, pot mines, and A200s were all varieties of small non-metallic mines developed later in the war. Schuhmines were made of plywood and cardboard in the shape of a pack of cigarettes; they were powerful enough to blow off a soldier's foot. The A200s were also called Holzmines (*Holz,* meaning "wood"). The pot mines, about 12 centimeters (five inches) in diameter, were made of glass in the shape of jelly and mustard jars. There were also mines made of concrete, like

149

the Stockmine, which was mounted on a stake and triggered by a trip-wire. By the end of the war, the Germans even perfected a chemical triggering mechanism, which dispensed with a mine's last metal piece, the firing pin.

Statistics kept by the American army illustrate the effectiveness of the new weapons: More than 20% of the tanks lost and 2.5% of the human casualties during World War II were caused by land mines. Mines continued to kill soldiers and civilians in Europe long after the end of the war. More than 15 million land mines were buried in French soil during the war, about one for every French family.

The first mine detectors were based on electromagnetic metal detectors that had been used for many years to detect underground minerals, pipes, or buried "treasure." Alexander Graham Bell invented one of the first metal detectors, which he patented in 1877. But at the start of World War II, mine detectors were not a standard piece of military equipment. A Polish engineer, Jozef Kosacki, was one of the first to build a metal detector for military use. He offered his patent to the British army.

Kosacki's detector consisted of two small radio-wave transmitters, in the form of small tightly wound coils, and a third coil which served as radio receiver. (The coils operated at a frequency of a few thousand cycles per second, which is at the low end of the radio-frequency spectrum.) Its principle of operation set the standard for nearly all other mine detectors to come. The transmitters were arranged and tuned so that their signals cancelled each other at the position of the receiver coil when the device was held above a homogenous soil. Buried metal objects, however, disturbed the delicate balance at the receiver coil, and circuits in the receiver detected this, generating a tone audible to the operator.

The "Polish metal detector" was light enough, 14 kilograms (31 pounds), to be carried by a single soldier and was generally effective at locating metallic mines. Over 100,000 units were manufactured during the war. Many of these were used by the British army in northern Africa, where the German *Afrika Korps* under General Erwin Rommel had planted hundreds of thousands of mines in the desert sands. The main problem with Kosacki's detector was that the delicate balance in its circuits required constant calibration. If not, the device generated false alarms, which slowed down mine-sweeping.

At the start of the war, the French minister of armaments, Raoul Dautry, called on several companies that he thought were capable of producing a mine detector that could be mounted in front of a tank or other moving vehicle. He did not have to look far. Dautry lived on the second floor of an apartment building on rue Casimir-Périer, in the 7th arrondissement of Paris. The apartment below was occupied by the Doll family, Henri-Georges, Annette, and their three daughters.

Doll was 37 years old when the war broke out and a lieutenant in the artillery reserve (a post he had held since his graduation from École Polytechnique). He had been mobilized and sent to the front, near the Maginot Line in northeastern France, in command of an artillery battalion of 150 men.

When he visited *la Pros*, Dautry was told that if he wanted to build a mobile mine detector quickly, he should have Doll recalled from the front. Doll received his orders to return to Paris in January 1940. In an interview many years after the war, Doll recalled his new assignment. "The idea of the minister of war and of Dautry," he said, "was that if a tank could have a detector mounted in front to 'see' the mines, it could go out on a mine field as if it had a kind of radar, like the radar mounted on a ship to alert it to presence of other ships."

Working at the Ministry of Armaments with existing metal detectors, Doll quickly realized that the requirements to see below the soil and to see far ahead of a vehicle were contradictory. Soil absorbs radio waves very effectively; moreover, a small metal mine reflects only a small fraction of the incident radio wave back to the surface. This meant that a detector using radio waves would have to get very close to a buried land mine to "see" it.

Doll began working with Maurice Lebourg and other mechanical engineers at *la Pros* on a new detector. He quickly built a simple electronic detector of essentially the same design as Kosacki's; the electronics, he later admitted, were "still very rudimentary." But his real interest at first was devising a way to mount the device in front of a tank, so that it could detect a mine in enough time to avoid disaster. The mounting would also have to be stable enough to isolate the detector from excessive vibration, which caused false alarms. Simply suspending the detector on a frame extending from the front of the vehicle, or mounting it on standard wheels, did not work, especially when the vehicle turned.

Doll solved the problem by inventing a wheel with a flexible rim: "When the tank turned, if the wheels of the device in front of it did not turn enough, it would not go in the direction steered.... We therefore made a wheel rim, and in place of a hard tire around the rim, we put a thin plate of flexible rubber in the shape of a disk. Then when the vehicle or tank turned, the rubber plates bent and slid over the ground like skis. They didn't stick. If they were made of hard rubber, it would not have worked, but the flexible disks, unlike wheels mounted on pivots, easily slid along the ground like a kind of rubber ski."

Doll tested the system himself at the front of a small gray tank that the army had delivered to his backyard at Marnes-la-Coquette. The neighbors were amazed enough to see him driving a tank around his garden, but could not imagine the purpose of the strange-looking box mounted in front on flexible rubber tires. Doll's three daughters – Izaline, Clarisse, and Henriette – liked to climb over the vehicle and watch the device light up when the tank approached metal objects which their father had buried in the garden. Izaline recalled that they were all strictly forbidden from answering any of the neighbors' questions.

By March 1940, Doll, with the help of Lebourg, had designed and built a full prototype for testing on a combat tank. (It was during this time that he was called to the American embassy in Paris to give a deposition in the legal battle between SWSC and Halliburton.) On May 10, 1940, the German army attacked Holland and Belgium. Several Panzer divisions launched an offensive through the Ardennes, whose forests were thought to be impenetrable by tank divisions. The Panzers quickly broke through the forest to the town of Sedan in northwestern France, about 20 kilometers (12 miles) from the Belgium border.

On May 30, 1940, Lieutenant Doll wrote to the Ministry of Armaments asking for a reassignment to his regiment at the front line, the 258th Heavy Artillery Division. He made clear that his prototype mine detector could be tested in the field and further improved by the team at *la Pros*. He preferred to return to the front, "persuaded that if my comrades and my men see me returning at a time when things have turned serious, they will understand that those in the rear are with them when they need it, and it will have good effect on their morale."

By June 6, 1940, Doll was back at his command. The German army had managed to split the Allied line in two, encircling the eastern half. Thousands of French and British troops were taken prisoner. But the Allies managed to evacuate 360,000 troops (about 240,000 British and 120,000 French troops) in Operation Dynamo, a flotilla of about seven hundred boats hastily assembled off the coast of Dunkerque. A massive exodus began from the north of France; more than eight million men, women, and children fled to the south.

On June 14, 1940, the German army marched down the Champs-Élysées in Paris. The next day the French government retreated to Bordeaux. On June 16, Paul Reynaud, the head of the government, refused to sue for peace and resigned. On June 17, Marshall Philippe Pétain announced that he would petition the enemy for a cessation of hostilities. On June 18, General de Gaulle broadcast from London an appeal to his countrymen to resist.

On July 6, Lieutenant Doll was awarded the *Croix de Guerre* (Cross of War) by the French army. The citation read, "Having returned voluntarily to his army during military operations, he conducted himself very courageously during the period from the 9th to the 14th June 1940."

Annette left Val-Richer in a small Simca to join her three daughters, who had been sent to the south of France to stay with Doll's parents in Lyon. The roads leading south were being strafed by the German air force. During one attack, she had to abandon the car and hide in a ditch. She found the car later, pierced with bullets but with the motor intact. Finally, with the help of her cousin, Xavier, one of Maurice Schlumberger's sons, she reached Clairac, a small town about 40 kilometers (25 miles) southwest of Bordeaux, where her mother had grown up. Xavier later took part in the resistance and died in a Nazi concentration camp. His brother Georges, attached to the second French armored division, died in combat in the Vosges just before the Allied victory.

Doll was demobilized on July 22, 1940, at the French army center of Montluçon, and he returned to his parents' home at 18 rue de Margnolles in Caluire, north of Lyon. He would not be there long. The Germans had taken control of the offices of *la Pros* in Paris. Even though Annette had managed to get rid of the mine detector and other equipment from the family's homes in Paris and Marnes-la-Coquette, she feared that the German army would come looking for her husband and warned her parents-in-law about the danger. A few days after Doll reached Caluire, German military police knocked on the front door of his parents' house, asking for Lieutenant Doll. They left when told he was not there. Doll was actually working in the backyard, dressed as a gardener.

In August 1940, the Doll family was reunited at Clairac. Engineers from *la Pros*, including Jean Mathieu, who had returned from Houston at the start of the war, had been working there for several months. The idea of evacuating the offices in Paris had been in the air since the start of the war, and Annette had offered use of several empty houses on her grandmother's property at Clairac for lodging and workspace.

Clairac was not occupied by the Germans and was designated as a "free zone" after the Armistice of June 22, 1940. (The "free zone" was later occupied by the German army when the Allies took over North Africa.) Marcel Schlumberger had sent various files and equipment there from the offices in Paris; his brother Maurice sent the files of his bank. An abandoned abbey overlooking the Lot River, which flows south of the city, served as a warehouse.

The three remaining Schlumberger brothers – Marcel, Jean, and Maurice – all came to Clairac. Annette recalled their "discussions continuing on late into the night on a terrace overlooking the river, in the

Henri-Georges Doll in uniform, 1940.

quiet of the abbey and the sweetness of the summer." Jean Mathieu also participated in these discussions. In an interview in 1974, he recalled a "sharp debate" about the future of the company. With France under occupation and the outcome, and even duration, of the war uncertain, Marcel believed that SWSC in Houston would have to sustain the company. He believed that handling SWSC's finances properly would be the main challenge for the company to survive the war, and he wanted to go to the United States to take charge of this.

"Doll believed," Mathieu recalled, "that if the war lasted four or five years, the company risked being eclipsed technically by the Americans." Doll argued that SWSC had to be built up with workshops and manufacturing, and also with an engineering department and a management team capable of developing new technology. "The force, the locomotive that drives and carries along the rest," Doll said, "is research."

Marcel quickly understood that the full center of gravity of his company would have to move from Paris to Houston. Mathieu agreed, "I jumped quickly to support Doll's idea, and in the end, we left with the Doll family."

Doll and Mathieu were joined by Maurice Lebourg, who had also been demobilized after the Armistice. In mid-September, the three engineers left Clairac for Lisbon by a circuitous route that took them through Algeria, Morocco, and Spain. Annette and Pauline Mathieu, Jean's wife, took the train for Lisbon with their children – the Dolls' three daughters and the Mathieus' two young children. They waited impatiently in Lisbon for their husbands, who arrived just in time to board the *Excalibur*, "an old cargo boat hastily outfitted for human traffic, headed for New York," Annette recalled. "After twelve days of bad seas, the Statue of Liberty…greeted us from a distance. Never had a statue seemed so enticing to me."

On November 4, 1940, one day after the election of Franklin Roosevelt to a third term as president of the United States, the Doll family boarded a train in New York for Houston.

Chapter 11

Paris in Texas

In 1940, the population of Houston was less than 400,000. Today it is a dozen times larger in a metropolitan area that extends more than 50 miles along a canal that connects the city to the Gulf of Mexico and makes Houston one of the world's largest ports. An oil field was discovered near the city in 1901, sparking a rapid industrialization of a region blessed with mineral resources (oil, gas, sulfur, and lime) and abundant agricultural production (cotton, rice, and cattle).

Schlumberger Well Surveying Corporation (SWSC) in Houston was originally under the direction of Paris. But at the start of World War II, Marcel had split management of *la Pros* and its affiliates, giving local managers complete control over their divisions. Léonardon became president of SWSC. His right-hand man was Paul Charrin, an engineer hired by Conrad in 1925, who had helped Doll to prepare the first logging experiment at Pechelbronn. When Doll arrived in Houston in November 1940, he was named chairman of the board of SWSC and its director of research. He was 38 years old.

"The first impression one has on seeing Henri-Georges is his natural elegance," Annette wrote in her memoir. "It was in his bearing and his gestures…. If you ran into him in the field, in knickerbockers, or at his work desk, in a tweed jacket, what struck you first was the ease with which he blended into the setting…. He seemed to be one of those men who could walk across the Gobi Desert without getting dust on his shoes. The passage of years only accentuated his neatness; it was like his own secret pact with the things around him. Straight, slender, his large nose looming over a trim mustache, he had the eternal youth of a young recruit."

He also inspired a natural respect among his colleagues. Jay Tittman, an American physicist hired by Doll in 1950, recalled, "When I got out of the Navy at the end of World War II, I decided that I would never again stand up when somebody walked in my office because he had a higher rank than me. Mr. Doll was the kind of man for whom, when he walked into your office, you just naturally stood up."

Doll arrived in Houston with an impressive number of achievements to his credit, including the first experiments in electrical logging at Pechelbronn in 1927, the invention of the spontaneous potential (SP) log, and the development of the teleinclinometer (the device for measuring the tilt or "dip" of rock layers below the earth's surface). He was also the company's best interpreter of well logs.

Doll was virtually unknown, however, in the American oil industry. Nearly all of the patents, including those on SP, were in Conrad's name, and the key scientific papers in English on electrical logging had appeared under the names of Conrad and Marcel Schlumberger and Eugène Léonardon. It had been a conscious and pragmatic choice. Conrad and Marcel were the founders and original technical leaders of the company that bore their name, and Léonardon was the face of Schlumberger in the American oil industry.

But Léonardon had no pretensions to technical leadership. He was focused on the well logging business. "If electrical logging had not been invented in 1927," Léonardon said in a 1971 interview after his retirement, "the adventures of Conrad Schlumberger would have had a sad ending." Through stubbornness and persuasion, Léonardon had resuscitated the company's business in the United States in the face of a slump in the oil industry during the economic depression of the early 1930s.

"I had been fighting to recreate our activity in the U.S. from before 1931," he recalled in the same interview, "and when I came back in 1932, I took it upon myself to talk to the oil companies about electrical logging. In Houston, I could find only two companies who were interested – Humble and United Gas. By 1936, everyone was convinced. The business was going well; financially it was very sound."

Doll tried to recreate in Houston the atmosphere of research and development that Conrad had set up in rue Fabert. He started recruiting talented young engineers – French and American engineers with diverse backgrounds, often from the top schools in both countries – to work alongside a small team of researchers. In less than two years, he had set up a research organization, along with a technical service group for the field, and a centralized manufacturing team. He brought several experienced engineers from the field to Houston to work with the young scientists and engineers. A large hangar-like shed at Leeland Avenue was transformed into a workshop and outfitted with offices and laboratories. "We did the best with the space available," Doll recalled later.

Doll also knew that new scientific expertise was needed within Schlumberger. Doll had already sensed potential applications spinning off the revolution in atomic physics. Shortly after arriving in the United States, he filed a patent on the use of radioactive bullets to mark key geological layers in oil wells, which could then be precisely located after the well had been cased, by logging the well with a radiation detector, such as a Geiger counter.

Many of the creators of the new physics had fled to the United States from Europe before the war. Enrico Fermi, the winner of the Nobel Prize in physics in 1938, took advantage of the voyage to Stockholm to leave fascist Italy. In October 1939, Fermi was at the University of Chicago. Along with three Hungarian physicists – Leo Szilard, Edward Teller, and Eugene Wigner, also refugees in the United States – Fermi wrote the letter that Einstein signed and sent to President Roosevelt, urging him to set up what became the Manhattan Project for development of the first atomic bomb.

Doll knew Jean Perrin, professor of physics at the Sorbonne and himself a Nobel Prize winner. Like Doll, Perrin was serving as an officer

Francis Perrin, professor of physics at the Sorbonne (Université de Paris-Sorbonne Paris IV). In 1939, Perrin and Frédéric Joliot-Curie demonstrated the possibility self-sustaining nuclear chain reactions. Perrin worked as a consultant to Henri-Georges Doll on various projects. (Photo, Institut Francis Perrin, archives CEA. ©CEA.)

in the French army at the start of the war, and had fled to the United States after the occupation of Paris. (Perrin died in New York City in 1940.) His son Francis Perrin was also a professor of physics at the Sorbonne and became a visiting professor at Columbia University in 1941. Doll invited Francis Perrin to visit Houston as a consultant.

It was most likely Francis Perrin who told Doll that Bruno Pontecorvo was in the United States. Pontecorvo, a student of Fermi, had written a research note describing the possibility of using neutrons to explore the pore space of rocks in oil wells. The idea was based on work that Fermi had done at the University of Rome. In 1934, Fermi had discovered that a beam of high-energy neutrons can pass through most materials easily, but are slowed by collisions with hydrogen atoms. Fermi's experiments demonstrated that, as the neutrons slow down after these collisions, they can be absorbed by atomic nuclei in the material in the path of the neutron beam, creating unstable isotopes that emit high-energy gamma rays.

Pontecorvo suggested that the intensity of the gamma rays emitted by a material, after irradiation by neutrons, could be calibrated into a measure of the density of hydrogen atoms in the sample. In geological formations, hydrogen atoms occur mainly in fluids (oil, water, or gas) occupying the pore space of rocks, so Pontecorvo's claim was that neutrons could be used to measure the porosity of an oil reservoir. (By a quirk of chemistry, the density of hydrogen atoms in oil and water is almost exactly the same, so the measurement cannot distinguish the two. The density is of course much less in gas, which can be detected by the "neutron-gamma" measurement.) After finishing his studies in Rome, Pontecorvo did further work on nuclear reactions with Frédéric and Irene Joliot-Curie in Paris. He then fled to the United States in 1940, after the Germans occupied Paris.

Doll suggested that SWSC hire Pontecorvo to create a research laboratory in nuclear physics for Schlumberger, but the suggestion was turned down. He later told Annette that at one point in the discussion, a manager at SWSC had complained, "You are not going to hire that Italian macaque to make some doohickey that won't do us any good."

Pontecorvo ended up working briefly at Well Surveys, Inc. (WSI), a small company in Oklahoma that was a competitor of SWSC.

Pontecorvo licensed his idea on neutron logging to WSI, and in 1942 published an article in *Oil and Gas Journal* that introduced nuclear well-logging to the oil industry ("Neutron well logging, a new geological method based on nuclear physics," *Oil and Gas Journal*, v. 40, p. 32-33, 1942). WSI made the first "neutron-porosity" logs the same year as Pontecorvo's article. It would take Schlumberger nearly a decade to catch up.

At SWSC, Doll quickly re-adapted to the rhythm of scientific work and the hectic environment of supporting field operations. Adapting to everyday life in Houston, Texas, was more difficult for Annette and their three daughters.

"It was like settling down on a new planet," Annette recalled, "far from the familiar family and cultural surroundings of Paris." Annette toured the city and found a small, red-brick house at 1824 Larchmont Road. "A pathway, also in brick, led up to a white front door," she

Henri-Georges and Annette in front of their house on Larchmont Road, Houston, Texas.

wrote in her memoir. "Oak trees surrounded the house; clumps of grey moss, like beards, hung in the branches of the trees, nourished by the humid air and swaying with the least breeze. Their swaying mixed with the chirps of insects…and helped me forget about my new residential quarter, which I really did not like very much and which quite recently was just a wild forest."

Izaline, the oldest daughter, was 15 years old when the family arrived in Houston. She remembers becoming "the young lady of the house," helping her mother with her two younger sisters and sometimes taking care of the children of the other engineers. Izaline wrote often to her maternal grandmother, Louise Schlumberger (née Delpech), who was living at Clairac in France during the war.

"The garden is not as large as the one in Marnes," she wrote in one long letter describing her new surroundings. "But Papa may make it bigger by buying the lot next door. The house is surrounded by grass; it is situated at a crossroad, which allows it to be better ventilated on hot days…. The windows are white wood. I am going to have my own bedroom, which I like a lot. It really only has three walls, because the fourth has been transformed into a bow-window, which will allow me more of a breeze than a simple window, because here the air plays a big role; one always has the impression of suffocating; it happens frequently that there are humid days, as if in a bathhouse. Papa and Mama have a large, very pleasant bedroom.

"This country is amazing for its plants; right now all of the roses are in bloom. What's more, Houston is a flower nursery, roses in particular. There is one huge inconvenience: it's the invasion of mosquitoes. Fortunately, we have a porch where we even feel very much like at home…. Today Clarisse starts her first day at the American school; a little emotional for her, since she doesn't speak English. As for Henriette, this afternoon she is going to her first lesson of ballet and tap dancing."

Annette often brought Doll his lunch at work in the pail-style metal lunchbox popular at the time with American workers. On Sundays, she sometimes went to one of the many churches in Houston (there were more than a thousand in a city of 400,000 inhabitants) – churches built of wooden planks, sometimes painted white, where the singing of "Alleluias" by the Black congregation was punctuated by the clapping of hands.

The Doll family itself was not very religious. Doll had serious reservations about the symbols of Christianity, especially the cross and blood of the crucifixion. A free thinker, he respected religious opinions, but believed strongly that they should never be imposed on others. Izaline recalled that he advised his children not to put too many coins in the alms boxes for the missionaries, whose zeal, he thought, turned people away from their own beliefs and traditions.

The Dolls were soon joined in Houston by other members of the family. Jean de Ménil, the husband of Annette's younger sister Dominique, had joined *la Pros* in 1939. De Ménil, who was working in Rumania at the start of the war, had met up with Éric Boissonnas (the husband of Annette's youngest sister Sylvie) in Syria; and the two of them succeeded in reaching Turkey. In 1943, Éric took over as head of the company's operations in the south of France. He also joined the local French resistance network and helped escaped prisoners of war to reach Spain.

De Ménil visited the company's operations in the Far East, then crossed the Pacific to the United States and stayed for a short period with the Dolls in Houston, before he and Dominique left for Venezuela. Their children – two young daughters, Marie and Adelaide, and a son Georges, the youngest – stayed in Houston with the Dolls until their parents returned to Paris in 1944.

Houston, the former cotton capital of the Deep South and the emerging oil capital of the world, had become the new home of *Société de prospection électrique (Procédés Schlumberger)*.

Chapter 12

Under Occupation

The war had emptied rue Fabert of its substance. Most of the personnel of *la Pros* had dispersed. Some who were soldiers in the French army had been taken prisoner and forced into labor camps; some had joined the resistance; others had disappeared into the countryside. Raymond Sauvage, who had worked with Doll and Mélikian in the oil fields of the Caucasus, was in the Far East as the company's director of operations when the war broke out.

He was working in a Shell oil camp in Sumatra, when Japanese paratroopers landed on the island. He hid for a year, but was later deported to Saigon, where he was ordered to work for the local French Vichy government, which was cooperating with the Axis. In Paris, Marcel walled up in the basement documents that he thought might be useful to the German army.

A few days after the occupation of Paris, officers of the Gestapo came to the offices of *la Pros*, and the following month, notices banning entry into the buildings at rue Fabert and rue Saint-Dominique were affixed to the front doors. The German geophysicist Bernt Paul came to the offices, escorted by German soldiers; his mission was to study the company's equipment and its files.

Bernt Paul knew *la Pros*. After finishing his studies in geophysics at the University of Freiburg, he had been hired by Conrad and Marcel Schlumberger in 1936 to direct the company's office in Hannover. He had also worked briefly at the offices of SWSC in Houston. After Austria was annexed by Nazi Germany, *la Pros* had to abandon its offices in Vienna, which were servicing the Zisterdorf oil field near the city. At the direction of the Germany military, Paul had taken over the offices of *la Pros* and its equipment in Vienna. After Germany invaded Poland, Paul opened an office in Galicia, where he employed several French engineers who had been taken prisoner at the start of the war. (One was Roger Jost, another veteran of the Caucasus, who was working in Germany at the start of the war.)

Paul informed Marcel that the German government considered its contract with *la Pros* to still be in force, and he arranged for the revenues from services in the oil fields of Hungary, Rumania, Austria, and Germany to be sent to Paris. Paul became an important figure in the efforts of the German government to secure oil supplies for the war. (In an interview after the war, he recalled that, despite severe gasoline rationing in Germany, he was allowed to drive his own BMW unrestricted, even on Sunday.) Oil was the fuel of modern warfare. The German army needed it above all for their Blitzkrieg style of warfare, combining quick, aggressive strikes with armored tank divisions and air force, both of which consumed gasoline at a furious pace.

In 1940, Germany imported more than half of its oil from Rumania and another third from the Soviet Union, mainly from the Caucasus. Imports from the U.S.S.R. had stopped in 1936, but resumed after Hitler and Stalin signed the German-Soviet Non-Aggression Pact in August 1939.

La Pros had documents and data from its work in the oil fields of the Soviet Union and Rumania. After Germany occupied Paris, the German command gave Paul authorization to accompany Marcel to visit his son-in-law, René Seydoux, who was being held in a prisoner-of-war camp outside the city of Nienburg-an-der-Weser.

Paul recalled that he brought Seydoux a carton of cigarettes; Marcel bought his son-in-law a pound cake. Boris Schneersohn, an employee of *la Pros* and himself a prisoner in Germany, recalled in an interview after the war that the Germans had offered to free Seydoux, but only if Marcel agreed that *la Pros* would cooperate with German industry in oil and mineral prospecting. Marcel refused, and he returned alone to Paris. Seydoux was transferred to a prisoner camp in Lübeck, where two important figures were kept under close surveillance: Vasili Djougashvili, the son of Stalin, and Robert Blum, the son of Léon Blum, the former head of the French government.

Hitler believed that a lack of oil could be fatal to his war plan and had launched a vast program for synthetic production of gasoline from coal. This process involved converting coal into hydrocarbons through the process of hydrogenation, which had been invented in 1897 by the French chemist Paul Sabatier, who shared the Nobel Prize in chemistry in 1912 for this work. In 1913, the German chemist Friedrich Berguis adapted the Sabatier process for the production of liquid hydrocarbons from lignite, a low-grade form of coal with a high moisture content, which is often called "brown coal." (Berguis himself shared the Nobel Prize in chemistry in 1931 for later work on high-pressure chemistry.)

At the start of the war in 1939, fourteen German hydrogenation factories were producing gasoline; six more were under construction. By 1940, the output had reached 72,000 barrels a day – supplying nearly all of the gasoline required by the Luftwaffe and more than half of the Wehrmacht's fuel. The large chemical company I.G. Farben, which had been appropriated by the Nazi Party and purged of its Jewish workers, constructed factories for production of synthetic fuel and rubber near the concentration camp in Auschwitz in Poland, which took advantage of the manual labor of interns deported to the camp, while they were still capable of work. These factories became key targets of Allied bombardment.

Although allied to the Third Reich at the start of the war, the Soviet Union was also viewed as a threat. In June 1940, the Soviet army occupied part of northeast Rumania, stationing its troops close to the oil fields of Ploesti. The Soviets justified these actions by terms in the Non-Aggression Pact anticipating the partition of Europe.

Oil supplies were a large factor in Hitler's decision to invade the Soviet Union in 1941. According to Daniel Yergin, in his history of the oil industry, *The Prize*, Hitler had even indulged in a bizarre calculus, estimating that the number of men lost in a war with Russia would not exceed the number of employees working in the synthetic fuel industry. On June 22, 1941, Hitler launched his surprise offensive to the East, "Operation Barbarossa," involving more than three million German soldiers and nearly another million Axis soldiers, along with thousands of tanks, trucks, and planes. (Hitler also targeted the oil fields of the Middle East, sending one of his most capable generals, Erwin Rommel, at the head of *Africa Korps*, into northern Africa, where it menaced the strategic British positions in Syria and Persia.)

By October 1941, the German army was at the outskirts of Moscow, and it appeared that Stalin would have to sue for peace. The German generals wanted to attack the city, but Hitler refused. A directive from Berlin on August 21, 1941, had set the top objective of the offensive as the occupation of Crimea, and of the industrialized coal-rich region of the Donetz River basin. Hitler wanted to cut off the Soviet Union's oil supplies from the Caucasus. The Soviet army and people offered a fierce resistance. Millions of soldiers and civilians died, including a vast number of Jews in the Ukraine and Belarus, exterminated systematically by special German troops who left mass graves that are still being discovered today.

After an exhausting winter, the armies of the Third Reich launched a new offensive into the Caucasus and the lower valley of the Volga River. They seized Rostov and cut the oil pipeline leading out of the Caucasus. On August 9, 1942, the German army reached Maikop, the western center of the region's oil industry, where a decade earlier the French engineers of *la Pros* had been working with Soviet oil trusts. The German army found that the Soviets had destroyed the oil installations at Maikop before abandoning the city. An "oil brigade" of technical experts was sent to the region to restore oil production and repair the refineries. Bernt Paul was one of the managers of the operation.

In November 1942, a final offensive of the German army, going east from Maikop toward the oil fields of Grozny and Baku, was repulsed. In the end, Hitler's calculus was wrong: More than four million Germans were lost in the war on the Eastern Front, which lasted four years. Hitler had said, "If we cannot have the oil of Baku, we have lost the war." On this point, he was right.

During the war, *la Pros* tried to stop work on its contracts in enemy territory, even though (as Marcel wrote in a letter to Doll in April 1941) the revenues from these contracts would have allowed it to continue operating profitably. A few projects continued at rue Fabert until the Gestapo occupied the buildings. These included work on a new galvanometer, a cement injector, and a circuit that allowed three logs (two resistivity logs and the SP log) to be recorded simultaneously. Marcel also invented an "electric vest," to compensate for the lack of heat in Paris. Two of the typists at rue Fabert took up knitting, and the company produced a thousand vests. Their main inconvenience was that the wearer could not stray far from an electric outlet.

Bernt Paul did not find any documents in Paris that would help the Germans exploit the oil fields of the Caucasus or Romania. Most likely, he also was the one who sent German soldiers to the home of Éric and Sylvie Boissonnas in search of seismic equipment from CGG, which he believed was hidden there. The soldiers did not recover anything from the Boissonnas' home.

"The oil had to flow," Paul recalled in an interview after the war. "It had become very important, and there was not enough [exploration] equipment. I took possession of Schlumberger's licenses and all of its equipment, the logging instruments, etc., coming from Paris."

Another German engineer of *la Pros*, Otto Hartlage, had his logging truck filled with equipment, loaded on a train, and transported to Maikop. After the failure of the assault on Baku, the truck was taken back to Germany and stored with two other Schlumberger trucks in a warehouse in Hanover.

After the war, the remains of the truck were found in the rubble of the factory, which had been destroyed by Allied bombing.

Charles Aiken in Federal District Court, Houston, Texas, 1941.

Chapter 13

Losing a Battle

On January 21, 1941, Eugène Léonardon took the stand in Federal District Court in Houston. The case was *Schlumberger Well Surveying Corporation v. Halliburton Oil Well Cementing Company*, a patent lawsuit. Schlumberger was suing Halliburton for infringement of Conrad Schlumberger's patents in electrical well logging. Judge Thomas M. Kennerly for the Southern District of Texas was presiding.

The patents at issue were U.S. patent 1,819,923, "Electrical method and apparatus for the determination of the nature of geological formations traversed by drill holes," and U.S. patent 1,913,293, "Electrical process for the geological investigation of porous strata traversed by drill holes." The first, called the "resistivity patent," described Conrad's original method for measuring the electrical resistivity of underground rock layers by injecting current into the earth through the drilling mud. The second, called the "porosity patent," described the method that Conrad and Henri-Georges Doll had invented for using the natural electrical potential in oil wells – called spontaneous potential or SP – to determine the location of permeable geological layers.

By 1941, these two methods of well logging were being used in nearly every oil field around the world. Schlumberger had created the market in the 1930s, and its technology and patents still dominated the business. Brady Cole of Baker, Botts, Andrew & Wharton, the Houston firm representing Schlumberger, asked Léonardon a series of questions to put this fact in evidence. "What percentage," he asked, "of the oil produced in the United States is produced from the fields in which you have made electrical well logging surveys by the Schlumberger process?"

"About 88 percent," Léonardon replied.

In response to another question, Léonardon compared the commercial progress of the new technology to a dam that had burst in 1934. "Suddenly," he said, "people just accepted the new idea." He had started that year with two crews in the field. The next year, 1935, he added 10 more crews, then another 10 in 1936, and 20 more in 1937. "Today," he continued, "the number of our crews in the U.S. is about 68."

After Cole finished his questioning, James Martin, the attorney from Vinson, Elkins, Weems & Francis, the Houston firm representing Halliburton, began his cross-examination. "There is another question I want to ask you," Martin said. "You have testified here about the 28,000,000 feet of surveying being done by the plaintiff. Will you state the consideration paid by the oil industry for those surveys, in round numbers?"

Cole objected to the question, and Judge Kennerly intervened.

"What is the object of the question, counsel?" Kennerly asked Martin.

Martin replied, "The only object I have is this, if the Court please. I do not wish to delve into any confidential files of the plaintiff in this action, but I do wish to bring out, through this witness, that this plaintiff has been handsomely rewarded for whatever work it has done in a commercial sense."

"Do you think his patent ought to be stricken for that reason?" Kennerly asked.

"No, I do not sir."

Kennerly allowed the question, and Léonardon responded, "Personally, I object to answering this, Mr. Martin, but if I have to, I will. ... The figure is over $3,000,000 for the year 1939, which divided by about, let us say, 600 employees, brings the revenue to $5000 per employee. Well, we have paid them. We have to do lots of things. And since this question has been brought up, I think the figure of $5000 per employee is something which may be considered reasonable. At least, it does not strike anybody as absolutely unreasonable. We have more than 100 engineers to pay, and those engineers, many of them make more than $5000."

> Trial testimony is taken from the transcript prepared for United States Circuit Court of Appeals, Fifth Circuit, No. 10063, *Halliburton Oil Well Cementing Company versus Schlumberger Well Surveying Corporation*, Appeal from the District Court of the United States for the Southern District of Texas, Transcript of Record, September 12, 1941. (On appeal, the order of the parties was reversed from the original case.)

Léonardon's objection of course was not just to testifying publicly about the finances of SWSC, which was still owned mainly by the Schlumberger family. He knew that what was at stake in the trial was his company's ability to set the price for its services under the protection of its patents. One oil company in particular had become sensitive to the Schlumberger monopoly and to its pricing.

In February 1936, five years before the trial, Léonardon had a meeting in his office with Ludwig Blau, an engineer who worked for

Judge Thomas Kennerly of the District Court of the United States for the Southern District of Houston, who presided over *Schlumberger v. Halliburton* in 1941.

Humble Oil and Refining Company in Houston. Blau described to Léonardon a method of electrical logging that he and a colleague at Humble, Ralph Gemmer, had invented and filed a patent for in 1934. The new method relied on measuring the "electrical impedance" of rocks, using alternating electrical current.

The Blau-Gemmer patent, "Method and apparatus for logging a well" (U.S. patent 2,037,306), was granted in April 1936 and was assigned to Standard Oil Development Company, a division of Standard Oil of New Jersey. "Jersey Standard" was the largest oil company created in the breakup of Standard Oil by the United States Supreme Court in 1911. In the 1920s, it had acquired part of Humble Oil, a Texas company, and eventually became Humble's majority owner.

In 1972, Standard Oil of New Jersey changed its name to Exxon, and finally to ExxonMobil in 1998, when it reacquired Mobil Oil. Mobil was originally Standard Oil of New York, another company created during the breakup of Rockefeller's monopoly. With revenues of about $350 billion in 2006, ExxonMobil is the world's largest oil company and the second largest public company, just behind Wal-Mart. The third and fourth largest companies by 2006 revenues were also oil companies: Shell, with revenues of $320 billion, and BP, with revenues of $275 billion.

Léonardon next met with Wallace Pratt, one of Humble's executives in Houston. Pratt told Léonardon that Humble Oil was satisfied with the Schlumberger logging services, but was convinced that the method in the Blau-Gemmer patent was a large improvement on existing technology. He offered Léonardon a deal in which SWSC would receive a license to the new patent and become the sole provider of well logging services to Humble and its parent company. In return, Schlumberger would provide a discount on its standard rates. Pratt indicated that Blau would work out the details of the offer.

Léonardon's report to Paris after meeting with Pratt occasioned the telegram which Conrad had received in Moscow in May 1936, during his final negotiations with the Soviet oil trusts. In part, the telegram read

```
LEONARDON CONFIRMS ENERGETICALLY HIS INTENTION
TO ACT IN RESPONSE TO THREAT BY HUMBLE AND
NECESSITY TO CHOOSE IMMEDIATELY BETWEEN EXCLUSIVE
AGREEMENT OR OPEN COMPETITION SEYDOUX NOTED
[HUMBLE'S] DETERMINED AGRESSIVENESS USING ALL
MEANS NOT CONCEALING EXTORTION CONFIRMED
TECHNICAL RESULTS ARE NOT INSIGNIFICANT CAN BE
IMPROVED QUICKLY STATES THAT LEONARDON CALM
DEUTZEN MATHIEU GUYOD ALARMED RECOGNIZING ALL
THE DRAWBACKS OF AMICABLE SOLUTION STOP
```

Conrad's telegram back to Paris recommended that Léonardon start negotiations with Humble, but also insist that the new technology be tested before a deal was completed. Negotiations between Humble and SWSC broke down shortly after Conrad's death.

By the end of 1936, Humble had sold the rights to the Blau-Gemmer patent to Halliburton Oil Well Cementing Company. Founded in 1919 in Oklahoma by Erle Palmer Halliburton and his wife Vida, HOWCO specialized in cementing steel casing into place to prevent oil wells from collapsing. In return for rights to the patent, Halliburton agreed to give Humble and Standard Oil of New Jersey a 50% discount on well-logging services; it also agreed to pay Humble a 10% royalty on revenues from its logging services for other oil companies.

The innovation claimed in the Blau-Gemmer patent was measurement of "earth strata of different electrical impedance" as a means of determining the nature of the rocks and fluids crossed by a well. Electrical impedance has essentially the same definition as electrical resistance. Both quantities are ratios of voltage to current in an electrical circuit, and both are measured in ohms.

The difference is that the term "impedance" is generally used when the current flowing in a circuit is not direct current, but instead is oscillating at a fixed frequency – like, for example, the alternating current which oscillates at 60 cycles per second ("hertz," written Hz) in electrical power lines in the United States, or at 50 Hz in Europe. The Blau-Gemmer patent envisioned measuring the impedance of rock strata at frequencies of 25 Hz to 100 kHz (kilohertz, kHz, is one thousand cycles per second).

In 1937, Halliburton started offering electrical logging services in the United States with a prototype tool built in Humble's research laboratory in Houston. A second curve was added later, an "earth potential log" measuring the natural electrical potential in a well. Even without a discount, the price of a Halliburton impedance log was much less than that of a Schlumberger resistivity log. Halliburton quickly secured a share of the market. "Halliburton was collecting bad logs," Doll later recalled, "for those who wanted to save money…. It was dangerous to let this continue, because it risked destroying the market and the technology."

The strategy of the attorneys for Schlumberger during the trial was two-fold: First, to show that the Blau-Gemmer patent contained nothing new in principle, compared to Conrad Schlumberger's original patent, and second, to show that an impedance log was exactly the same measurement as a resistivity log.

Their argument for the first point was simple: The description of the resistivity method in Conrad Schlumberger's patent did not specify that the measurement had to be made with a steady current. In fact, the words "direct current" or "steady current" appear nowhere in the patent. Moreover, shortly after the first log was acquired at Pechelbronn, Schlumberger began recording its resistivity logs with slowly alternating current, which helped to reduce the effects of random noise. Using alternating current also allowed resistivity and spontaneous potential logs to be recorded at the same time.

The attorneys for Schlumberger called on Charles Aiken as an expert witness to make their second point. Aiken had participated in the patent battle between Schlumberger and Lane-Wells three years earlier and had become a regular consultant to Doll in Houston. He did a demonstration in court to show that alternating current at the frequencies described in the Blau-Gemmer patent had no practical effect on the quantities being measured.

As Doll remarked later, "to call an electrical log an 'impedance log' was just a way of evading the patent."

Schlumberger filed its original complaint against Halliburton in August 1938. The trial itself did not start until January 1941. In May 1940, with the German army in Belgium preparing to invade France, Erle Halliburton visited Marcel Schlumberger at rue Fabert in Paris. The incident was described by Ken Auletta in his profile of Schlumberger, *The Art of Corporate Success* (Putnam, 1984):

"Everybody knew that France was going to be defeated, that Paris would be totally cut off from Houston, and that Houston could not survive by itself, without Paris.… Halliburton offered to buy Schlumberger for ten million dollars. Marcel made no reply but slowly rose from his chair and beckoned Halliburton to follow him. They walked silently to the elevator, where Marcel thanked his visitor and said goodbye."

The strategy of the attorneys for Halliburton was to apply the argument of "no invention" to Conrad Schlumberger's patents themselves. They assembled an array of experts from the oil industry and a large collection of documents detailing the history of geophysics from the

17th century to the first decades of the 20th century. Not only, they claimed, was the method described in Conrad Schlumberger's patent on electrical measurements not new (compared, for example, to work that had been done almost a century earlier by the English geologist Robert Fox in the tin mines of Cornwall), but the borehole method itself was also fully anticipated by Conrad's own papers, books, and patents in surface electrical prospecting.

Simply turning the method on its side and lowering it into a borehole, they argued, hardly constituted an invention worthy of "a vast and dominating monopoly."

Another issue was the timing of the invention and the filing of the patents in France and the United States. After the idea for an invention is disclosed, an inventor has only one year to file a patent in the United States, before the idea is considered part of the public domain. Halliburton's attorneys claimed that Schlumberger had missed this deadline. It was mainly to testify on this point that Doll was called to the United States embassy in Paris in March 1940. He also testified at length at the trial in Houston.

The trial transcripts and supporting documents run for more than 10,000 pages. Much of the testimony was intended to educate the court about the new technology and its meaning. It was not always effective. An expert witness called by Schlumberger described a logging tool as "a little reporter who visits a strange land.... He descends into a drill hole for this difficult trip and constantly reports back on each strange piece of earth that he crosses, in terms of its electrical characteristics, which we here call 'resistivity.'"

At one point, Judge Kennerly asked Léonardon why the log that measured the spontaneous potential was called a "porosity" log. Léonardon replied, "Because that's what we called it. We gave it all kinds of terrible names. We also call it permeability. The name doesn't mean anything. When you have a daughter, when she is born, you have to give her a name."

Later, James Martin, the attorney for Halliburton, asked Léonardon, "What do you mean by an electrical log?" To which Léonardon replied,

"An electrical log is the product or the result of what you get by collecting an electrical log. In other words, it's the result of electrical logging."

At times, Judge Kennerly's exasperation was evident. After listening to an expert called by Halliburton testify that no real meaning could be assigned to the apparent resistivity measured by electrical logs, he pointed to an exhibit on display of a Schlumberger log and a Halliburton log from the same well (the two logs looked very much alike): "You mean to say," Kennerly asked, "that the plaintiff measures something and the defendant measures something, but you can't say what it is?"

The trial lasted three weeks, from January 8 to 29, 1941. Judge Kennerly published his verdict on May 20 of the same year. "The evidence…produced at the trial," he wrote, "serves in most respects to illuminate (but sometimes to becloud) the questions and the issues. The witnesses (particularly the expert witnesses) disputed with each other about nearly everything. They disputed about the name, cause, movement, method of measuring, harnessing, and use of the 'earth currents.' They disputed about whether, and the extent, other natural forces and objects resist or interfere with such currents."

Kennerly ruled for Schlumberger on all counts. The main ruling was simple, "[T]he mechanism covered by [the] Patents was new and…both Patents were when issued, have been since, and are now, valid under the Law." Kennerly ruled that Halliburton's logging service infringed Conrad Schlumberger's patents; he later entered an order restraining further infringement and compensating SWSC for damages.

Halliburton appealed the ruling to the United States Fifth Circuit Court of Appeals in New Orleans. Their short ruling came in September, 1942, written by Judge Samuel Sibley. "The question," Sibley wrote, "as to each [patent] is, Does it merit the monopolization of the present art of electric logging?"

The answer of the Fifth Circuit was an emphatic "No." Kennerly's ruling of infringement was reversed, and Conrad Schlumberger's two patents were ruled invalid. The resistivity patent was overturned for lack of novelty, affirming the argument of Halliburton's attorneys: "There is hardly invention," Sibley wrote, "in the idea of using the same method and apparatus vertically that had before been used horizontally."

The porosity patent was invalidated for being too broad: "If this claim is taken at face value, it precludes anybody from measuring at any depth in an uncased mud-filled well (almost all holes are drilled full of mud), any differences in potential which spontaneously take place, where porous strata are supposed to exist.... [Schlumberger] could not thus patent generally the use of a natural phenomenon."

The opinion also ruled that the patents were deficient for failure to disclose sufficiently the invention. "The appellee [Schlumberger]," Sibley wrote, "has chosen indeed as far as possible to keep the public ignorant of its own practices and instruments. If the patents had expired the day this suit was filed, and nothing was known except what the patents disclose, neither appellant nor anyone else could have made useful electrical logs without much experimentation."

The petition by Schlumberger for a rehearing before the Fifth Circuit was dismissed, and the United States Supreme Court declined to take the case on appeal.

Between the start of the case in January 1941 and the Fifth Circuit's ruling in September 1942, the stakes for control of the technology of oil and gas exploration had risen dramatically. On December 8, 1941, the United States had declared war on Japan, after the surprise Japanese attack on Pearl Harbor the day before. On December 11, 1941, Germany and Italy declared war on the United States, which reciprocated the same day.

There is no evidence that the state of war had any effect on the ruling by the Fifth Circuit. But the public's changing attitude toward monopolies may have. It was summarized in the last sentence of Sibley's opinion: "We think that what Schlumberger in the disclosures of these patents gave to the public is not such as the statute contemplates to justify the broad monopolies claimed."

The ruling was issued on September 5, 1942. Exactly fifteen years after Doll had recorded the first electrical log at Pechelbronn, the technology fell into the public domain.

A few days after the ruling, Marcel Schlumberger and Doll were together at the train station in Austin, Texas. Marcel stretched out on a platform bench, his hat over his face. "Henri," he sighed, "it's all lost."

Doll disagreed. It was a legal, not scientific or technical, defeat – in an arena where he believed that the best science and technology could ultimately win. After Conrad's death, he had constantly argued for the priority of research, first in *la Pros* and later in SWSC, and was often frustrated by the attitudes of those he called *les financiers*. "It was a funny idea," he said later, "that what counted in a company like ours was management and finance, but as for the technical organization – well, anyone could be recruited for that!"

Many years after the trial, in an interview with Annette, he recalled the atmosphere at SWSC after the ruling. "In Houston, everyone was acting like it was the end," he said. "I was about the only one who was not all that upset. Rather than a disaster, I saw a stimulus: If I had been Standard Oil, I would have done what they did; I would have financed a competitor. The American oil industry could not and should not have been at the mercy of a single supplier. At certain times, we had made equally strong efforts ourselves not to have to rely on a single supplier of cables…not to have to dance to someone else's tune.

"In any case, it was not the superiority of our methods that was at stake, but our de facto monopoly. In fact, once it had succeeded, through Halliburton, in destroying our patents, Standard Oil became again a client of Schlumberger."

In November 1941, while the case was under appeal at the Fifth Circuit, Doll had written down a list of research topics in well logging that he thought would be important to the oil industry in the coming years. Doll's list of 21 topics anticipates nearly every development in well logging during the next 25 years – not just developments in electrical measurements, but in all types of physical measurements and sampling that can be done in oil wells: measurements of natural and stimulated nuclear radiation, measurements of sound waves, measurement of pressure, measurements of the condition of the wells themselves; samples of fluids and gases, samples of rocks, etc.

Doll was not the only person thinking along these lines. Scientists in the research laboratories of the major oil companies had begun to recognize the value of in-situ measurements in oil fields and had launched their own ambitious programs, which overlapped Doll's ideas and had started to generate results by the early 1940s.

Doll's list of projects, however, was probably the most comprehensive and wide-ranging. It would be another five years before he could start to attack it.

Chapter 14

Mine Detectors

In 1937, a new research department of the U.S. Army Corps of Engineers, called The Engineer Board, was created in Fort Belvoir, Virginia, under the direction of Captain James Young. The Board quickly became involved in a diverse set of projects including the development of new construction materials, portable bridges, and new demolition methods. In April 1940, the Board received orders to start development of new mine detectors, including a detector that could be mounted on the front of a tank or a Jeep.

By coincidence (or perhaps not), this was the same month Lieutenants Henri-Georges Doll and Marcel Lebourg performed their first tests in Paris of the vehicle-mounted mine detector that they had developed for the French Ministry of Armaments.

The Engineer Board's project on mine detectors was overseen by a new agency, the National Defense Research Committee (NDRC), which had been established in June 1940 at the initiative of Vannevar Bush to coordinate scientific research for military applications. Bush, an electrical engineer with a Ph.D. degree from MIT, was then president of the Carnegie Institution in Washington, D.C. He had worked during the First World War on the detection of submarines (during which he had invented the "differential analyzer," one of the first analog computers). In June 1941, the NDRC was itself subsumed into the Office of Scientific Research and Development (OSRD), which was established to mobilize resources and scientific personnel for the military. The OSRD would coordinate efforts of the U.S. scientific community during the war years.

Captain George A. Rote of the Army Corps of Engineers began the "vehicular-mounted mine-detector" project at Fort Belvoir by testing

'The Sad Sack,' a cartoon by George Baker in the Army weekly, *Yank* (Office of History, U.S. Army Corps of Engineers).

commercially available metal detectors. All of these operated about the same way as the mine detector that Jozef Kosacki had patented and presented to the British army: Two radio transmitters and a radio receiver were arranged so that the signals from the transmitter cancelled each other at the receiver, unless a metal object was nearby. The lightest and most sensitive commercial metal detector available in the United States was manufactured by a company from Miami, Florida, called Hedden Metal Locators. The Hedden detectors were mainly sold to treasure hunters combing beaches for buried coins.

The Hedden detector, modified and designated as the SCR-625, could detect metal mines buried as deep as 16 inches (40 centimeters). Like the Kosacki detector, its main drawback was that its circuits were fragile and overly sensitive. The balance between the transmitters could be disrupted by changes in temperature or elevation above the ground, or even by vibration as a soldier walked across a mine field. The system had to be moved slowly, and required constant calibration. ("SCR" stands for Signal Corps Radio. A large collection of SCR equipment from World War II can be purchased on eBay. An SCR-625 goes for about $10.)

Soldiers testing the SCR-625 mine detector in Belgium, 1945 (Office of History, U.S. Army Corps of Engineers).

At the beginning of 1941, Doll and Marcel Lebourg were working together again in Houston. Believing that it was only a matter of time before the United States entered the war in Europe, they had started to work again on a mobile mine detector, constructed along the lines of the prototype they had built in Paris. Doll made a scale model of the French system, which he mounted on a toy tank and showed to John Bullington, one of the lawyers with Baker, Botts, Andrew & Wharton, which had represented SWSC in the patent lawsuits against Lane-Wells and Halliburton.

Bullington had become friends with Doll and other members of the Schlumberger family in Houston and was serving on the board of directors of SWSC. Doll described him as "a very striking man, tall, handsome, very open and friendly, extremely generous and very direct; in short, someone in whom you could have complete confidence. He was a real friend, a person of high standards from all points of view, but especially ethically."

Bullington encouraged Doll and Lebourg to build an actual prototype. The work would be done in a company called Electro-Mechanical Research (EMR), which had been set up early in 1941 by André Istel, a banker and friend of the Schlumberger family, who had served as a financial counselor to the French government under Paul Reynaud before the war. Istel fled France after the armistice and was living in New York. He had helped incorporate EMR as a non-profit research company, a vehicle to allow French engineers to work for the Allied war effort. The owners of EMR were Schlumberger (through SWSC), Doll, Istel, and two American friends of Istel, who provided financing. Bullington was chairman of the board of directors; Doll was president. During the war years, EMR paid half of Doll's salary; SWSC paid the other half.

Doll picked his team leaders for the project from SWSC. Lebourg led the mechanical engineering group; O. H. Huston and G. K. Miller, two American electrical engineers, worked with Charles Aiken on the electronics. Doll bought an old Dodge sedan on which to mount the new prototype.

In November 1941, while the Halliburton lawsuit was under appeal, Doll and Annette traveled to New York City as guests of the American Institute of Mining, Metallurgical, and Petroleum Engineers and the Society of Petroleum Engineers. At the fall annual meeting of these two societies, Annette accepted the Anthony F. Lucas Gold Medal on behalf of her father and her uncle, Conrad and Marcel Schlumberger, who were honored for their "fundamental contributions to new technology for finding petroleum." The Lucas Gold Medal, established in 1936, was named after Captain Anthony F. Lucas, the prospector who had drilled the discovery well at Spindletop in Texas, on January 10, 1901. It was the oil industry's highest award for technical achievement.

> The first three winners of the Lucas Medal were all American oilmen: J. Edgar Pew (1936), the legendary executive of Sun Oil Company of Pennsylvania; Henry L. Doherty (1938), the founder of Cities Service Company; and Everette Lee DeGoyler, executive of Amerada Oil and "father of American applied geophysics," who was also a founder of the American Association of Petroleum Geologists.

The Dolls were on their way home to Houston on December 7, 1941, when news came of the Japanese attack on Pearl Harbor. Back at SWSC, Doll asked Bullington to contact the United States government and arrange for EMR to demonstrate its prototype mine detector, which was nearly finished.

Bullington was a friend of Allen Dulles, a prominent New York lawyer who in the early 1940s was in the process of setting up the Office of Strategic Services, a forerunner of the Central Intelligence Agency (CIA). (Dulles became the first civilian director of the CIA in 1953. He was the youngest brother of John Foster Dulles, who was Eisenhower's secretary of state.) Bullington also knew Robert Lovett, the assistant secretary of war, and visited Washington several times to talk with Lovett about the work at EMR.

Through Lovett, Bullington secured clearance from the U.S. army allowing EMR to work on top-secret military research projects. There was a restriction: EMR would not receive information about other projects undertaken by The Engineer Board.

According to a report written after the war, The Engineer Board made contact on February 27, 1942, with Doll and Lebourg, who "offered to sell their prototype at a price that was just a little higher than the used Dodge on which it was mounted. The offer was immediately accepted and the equipment was taken to Fort Belvoir."

See *History of the Development of Electronic Equipment I – Metallic Mine Detectors*, The Engineer Board (Fort Belvoir, 1945). Another army document about mine detectors during World War II, which is available on the internet, is *United States Army in World War II, The Technical Services, The Corps of Engineers, Troops and Equipment*, B. D. Cole, J. E. Heath, and H. H. Rosenthal (Office of the Chief of Military History, Washington, D.C., 1958).

The engineers at Fort Belvoir were interested primarily in the mounting system of the EMR device. Like the system first built in France, it had wheels made of thin flexible rubber disks, which slid smoothly along the ground when the vehicle turned. The frame on which the wheels and the detector were mounted now included a system of counter-weights, which operated a lever to reduce the weight on the wheels so that they would not trigger a typical antivehicle mine.

The army engineers also discovered that the circuits used in the EMR detector were different from the now-standard circuit in the SCR-625 (the modified Hedden detector). The EMR detector had several coils in parallel, with circuits making it much more stable than the Hedden system. In addition, one circuit was connected to a mechanical system that rapidly applied the brakes automatically to stop the vehicle when the detector sensed a metal object in the ground. The automatic braking system was also triggered when the electronics failed. (When the braking system was on, a box was lowered over the brake pedal to prevent the driver from getting his foot caught between the brake and the heavy wooden block applying the force.)

On May 11, 1942, army engineers took the EMR vehicle to Fort Knox in Maryland, where it was tested over a series of dummy mine fields. After the tests, the Board asked EMR for various modifications. The Corps of Engineers wanted the detector at the front of the vehicle to cover a swath 10 feet wide (about three meters), to operate at speeds up to 12 miles per hour (20 kilometer per hour), and to be capable of detecting mines at a depth of 14 inches (35 centimeters). They also requested that the mounting system be retractable off the ground so that the vehicle could move at high speed when the detector was not required. In the end, only the first and last requirements could be fully met. The system that EMR finally produced could operate at six miles per hour (10 kilometers per hour) and detect mines at a depth of eight inches (20 centimeters), which was usually sufficient.

Only the flexible wheels survived from the work in Paris. "What we did in Paris," Doll recalled in an interview after the war, "was not very significant compared to what we were able to do later. From the point of view of the electromagnetic detector, we didn't have the time to do much [in Paris], and I have to say, that we weren't very well equipped in electronics."

While EMR worked on the new requirements from the army, the engineers at Fort Belvoir began work on a different type of mounting system, which they called the Prairie Dog. The Prairie Dog was actually a separate lightweight vehicle on wheels, powered and steered by an electrical cable that led back to the trailing vehicle. It could advance up to 100 feet (30 meters) in front of the trailing vehicle, enough distance for the trailing vehicle to stop if the Prairie Dog detected a mine.

After several tests, The Engineer Board decided to pursue both the Prairie Dog and the EMR mounting system, and asked EMR to supply the electronics for both systems. Orders, tests, and further modifications followed at a rapid pace during 1943 as the Allies prepared for the invasion of Europe.

Not everything went smoothly. A few months into the project, one of the engineers from EMR visited the office of Allen Dulles in Washington and demanded to see Mr. Dulles. After listening to the visitor for a few minutes, Dulles excused himself and went to a nearby office to call John Bullington in Houston. He told Bullington that there was a person from EMR in his office who was claiming that Doll was a crook. "But I was reassured," Dulles added, "when he told me that you were a crook, too." When the engineer returned to Houston, he was quietly reassigned to SWSC. His motives were never determined.

Annette remembered long workdays at EMR. "Henri-Georges was always incredibly hard working," she wrote, "but I don't think I ever saw him go at it so doggedly. Several of his co-workers just about cracked from overwork." Doll was actually doing two jobs. "Schlumberger was paying half my salary to work as chairman of SWSC," he said, "even though I was spending more than half of my time at EMR working as an engineer."

Rumors were also circulating in Houston about a group of French engineers doing undercover work for the German army. Doll later recalled that if Bullington had not been the person he was – "totally above reproach and a good friend of Dulles" – the accusations could have caused him, Lebourg, and the other foreign engineers "serious trouble."

There were also lighter moments. As the orders from the army were filled, Jeeps with the mounting system installed could be seen on the grounds of SWSC in Houston (where EMR was also located). When neighbors asked about the curious-looking devices, the official explanation was that SWSC was developing and testing a new device for clearing snow from highways. It had not snowed in Houston in years.

During a test of an early prototype, an army general visiting EMR insisted on riding next to Doll, who asked the general to fasten his seat belt. The general just glared. Doll started driving, and when the vehicle approached the first dummy mine, the automatic braking system engaged, bringing the Jeep to an abrupt stop. The general ended up on the hood.

In June 1943, Captain Rote came to Houston to conduct the final tests of two mounting systems – the Prairie Dog and the EMR system – in front of army representatives. The conclusion was that the Prairie Dog was too complicated to maneuver, too fragile, and too expensive; the system was abandoned.

In July 1943, the Corps of Engineers placed an order with EMR to build twenty Jeep-mounted detectors, which had been christened the

AN/VRS-1. The first two systems were delivered in October 1943 to the Armored Board, the army division responsible for tanks and other armored vehicles. By the end of the year, another eight had been manufactured and were distributed to different branches of the military, including the Marine Corps, the Desert Warfare Board, and ETOUSA (European Theatre of Operations US Army). The Desert Warfare Board tested the systems at Camp Young in California and eventually deployed them in North Africa. Several systems also accompanied Allied troops during the invasion of Italy.

> Manuals for the AN/VRS-1 can be bought on the internet, but it appears that no actual system survives. One AN/VRS-2 system, a Prairie Dog, is listed as part of the collection of the army military museum in Fort Gordon, Georgia.

The first tests of the production systems in combat conditions showed that the EMR detectors were more stable than handheld systems, but were still giving many false alarms. They were especially difficult to use over soils rich in magnetic minerals, like the volcanic soils of Italy. In a recent memoir, Lieutenant Colonel John D. Wong of the Corps of Engineers briefly described the problems with the EMR system in Italy: "The abrupt stops were teeth rattling," he wrote. "The GIs never trusted this apparatus to work properly. No one volunteered to drive it."

> *Battle Bridges, Combat River Crossings, World War II*, John B. Wong, Lieutenant Colonel, Corps of Engineers (Trafford Publishing, 2004).

Jeep-mounted mine detector, AN/VRS-1, produced by EMR for The Engineer Board (from *History of the Development of Electronic Equipment - I - Metallic Mine Detectors*, The Engineer Board, U.S. Army Corps of Engineers, 1945).

In heavy rain, the thin mounting wheels also tended to skid and were difficult to keep on course. In the end, not much could be done about the wheels, except to put a warning in the instruction manual.

The false alarms of the detector were a different matter. "The performance was not all that great," Doll recalled in an interview after the war. "The device did not have yet the final improvements in the electronics that we put into the circuits for work over magnetic soils. Later, we were asked to make devices that could work underwater, even in salt water… I told [the Engineer Board] that I thought we could do that and that it would probably not be all that difficult. A few days later they called back from Washington, 'We're sending you a contract.' I told them…it was not a big risk for us, since in the meantime we had actually done it by modifying one of the standard army detectors. It was not so difficult. Then, in persevering along this road, I suddenly had another idea."

Doll's idea was to introduce a feedback circuit into the detector that allowed the electronics to eliminate an unwanted part of the signal. "The signal [from a mine] that one wants to detect is a sinusoid," Doll explained. "The signal from a magnetic soil is also a sinusoid of the same frequency; it gives the same tone…but the two are shifted in time with respect to each other by a fraction of a period."

As an analogy, one can imagine two choirs singing the same refrain, but with a small delay in time between the two (as in the round "Row, Row, Row Your Boat" or the French children's song *Frère Jacques*). One of the choirs sings loudly; this is the primary signal from the transmitter. The other choir sings softly and is barely audible; this is the secondary signal coming from a buried land mine. The challenge is to detect the second choir.

If the volume of the first choir is constant, one can detect when the second choir joins in by a small increase in the overall volume of the song. Unfortunately, the transmitters used in mine detectors at the time were not able to "sing" at a constant level. Their signal levels drifted with changes in temperature during the day, or even with small vibrations.

But the singing of the second choir can also be distinguished by its rhythmic offset in time from the first choir. This was the function of the feedback circuit that Doll and his colleagues at EMR designed for their final detector. The circuit stabilized the output of the transmitter by monitoring and adjusting its power; it then isolated the secondary signal by detecting its offset in time – its phase shift – compared to the primary signal.

"The key," Doll explained later, "is that the phase of the signal produced by magnetic soil is always the same as the current [in the transmitter circuit]. One only has to cancel completely the signal at this phase, which could be done by phase-selective feedback using variometer tubes.... One canceled what was called the 'inductive' component of the signal and kept the 'resistive' component. With a mine, there was always a resistive component, but not with magnetic soil. One eliminates one without spoiling the other. The system was radical."

Doll made the first prototype of the "phase-selective feedback circuit" working with Miller and Huston. The circuit also became a standard for the handheld SCR-625 metal detectors. Doll did not immediately file a patent on the circuit, but did write a top-secret report for the Army Corps of Engineers

The new electronics were added to the EMR detector in 1944. Tests by the Armored Board, which had received two of the original systems, showed that the modification significantly reduced the number of false alarms (especially over magnetic soil). The new system could also detect mines below macadam and gravel road, and even through reinforced concrete.

Before the end of the war, several hundred Jeep-mounted detectors – and many other handheld units with the new circuits – were sent into combat in Italy, France, and the Pacific. A Jeep with the new system could move across a mine field at a speed of about 6 miles per hour (10 kilometers per hour) and be stopped safely by the automatic braking system when the detector registered the presence of a mine. A soldier would then descend from the Jeep with a handheld unit, determine the precise location of the mine, and disarm it.

In June 1945, Doll received a telephone call from Lieutenant Tore N. Anderson of The Engineer Board, who asked if EMR could make a mine detector that would work underwater, at a depth of 100 feet (30 meters). Anderson had been given the assignment of finding a large number of silver coins that had been dumped in the Bay of Corregidor by General McArthur's army when the Japanese invaded the Philippines in 1942.

EMR had at its disposal the waterproof cylinders that Schlumberger used to protect the circuits in its logging tools at the high pressures and temperatures of deep oil wells. "We were able to fit a detector in one of these tubes," Doll recalled. "We did some tests and it worked."

Two days after the call from Anderson, EMR delivered a prototype underwater metal detector to the airport in Dallas, where it was put on a plane to the Philippines. Using the system, fifteen army divers led by Anderson recovered silver coins worth about 17.5 million Philippine pesos (about $8.5 million) from Corregidor.

Anderson had invited Doll to supervise the operation, but was not able to get the papers through the Department of the Army, the State Department, and the dozen other service bureaus whose approval was needed to send a foreigner on a military mission. Doll received a thank-you letter after the mission. "It would have meant more to me," he later joked, "if they had included one of the pesos."

By the end of the war, EMR had delivered 155 Jeep-mounted mine detectors to the Army Corps of Engineers at a cost of about $380,000. In 1945, the army contracted with a small Lawrence, Massachusetts, company, Plymold Corporation, to build another 2200 systems, but the order was canceled when the war ended; only 350 units were delivered. EMR also delivered ten underwater detectors at a cost of $83,000.

After the war, the American government offered France the right to copy the U.S. army's mine detectors to help with de-mining the French countryside. Doll brought the EMR detector to tests organized by the French Ministry of Defense at Fort d'Ivry, outside Paris. The ground had been prepared in advance with an assortment of soils and sands mixed with magnetic powder, "to cause the usual trouble for a metal detector...like over the reinforced concrete roads and the soils of Japan," Doll recalled. Other detectors from the Allied countries, along with detectors captured from the German army, participated in the tests. The EMR detector was picked and contributed to the de-mining of France.

During the war, EMR carried out other research for the military. One of its engineers, Pierre Mercier, who was hired at the recommendation of Andre Istel, had the idea of designing an automatic guidance system for bombs. Doll, the former artillery commander, and Charles Aiken became interested in the project; Bullington obtained clearance for EMR to work on it.

"It involved," Doll explained after the war, "a system that would allow a bomb that had been released from a plane to guide itself toward a hot spot. It would be necessary to have a servo-mechanism, but it was not a rocket as such; it was something that one could just let fall, but of course it was necessary to get it going in more or less the right direction…. It had small guide wings and instead of falling in a straight line, it fell with a little slant, it guided itself toward the target. You dropped it over a steel plant and it fell on the furnace."

The research required complex aerodynamic calculations, and it was necessary to make sure that the mathematical models were realistic. Doll invited Francis Perrin to Houston to work with him on the calculation, and had a wind tunnel built to simulate the fall of a bomb and study its aerodynamics. As with other projects, EMR was not given any information about other research the military was conducting in this area.

"The services that monitored us," Doll recalled, "gave us some indications more or less [about]…which directions to pursue. We had taken on the full problem, of course, but the services would say: 'No, it's not worth doing that, because we won't need it. They never said, 'We don't need it because someone else is doing it,' because after all, we were foreigners. They let us work, and they gave us the necessary supplies, but they did not keep us current the way you would another group that was working in the same area as you…. So, sometimes we did things that others had already done…. But all the same they let us know when something we did was interesting, or else we would have stopped work."

It was not until after the war, in 1947, that the contribution of EMR to the research in bombs and guided missiles was made public, in a book, *New Weapons for Air Warfare* (Little, Brown & Co., 1947), edited by Joseph Boyce, a professor of physics at Columbia University and special assistant director of the National Defense Research Committee. (The book confirms that the intelligence services did background checks on the motivations of the French engineers working at EMR.)

The principal contributions of EMR described in the book were a scanning system for identifying the target of guided missiles, a study of aerodynamic factors and calculations of the trajectory, the concept for an anti-roll stabilizer, and a mechanism for predicting the location and timing of impact.

"The work represented a major contribution to the fundamental theory [of scanning systems for guided missles]," Boyce wrote. Field tests under difficult conditions were carried out in a small cottage on Galveston Bay. The few neighbors who were there were of course intrigued by, and even became suspicious of, the secretive group of men who had brought in very cautiously a piece of elaborate equipment to study the boats going in and out of the port of Houston. The definitive scanner used the results of this research, and its performance was very good. A demonstration was made in a station overlooking Boston Bay, and later, at Wright Field [an Air Force base]. The result was a contract that the army made for the development of a control system for a glider bomb."

The prototype built by EMR was too big to use in the air. Charles Aiken called it the "Mack Truck." Their ideas, however, were integrated with those of the other groups and eventually led to systems used later by Werner von Braun in developing the first American guided missiles after the war.

Von Braun developed the V1 and V2 rockets used by Germany to bombard London in the final months of the war. He and his engineers were captured by the Americans and taken to the United States so that they would not fall into the hands of the Soviets.

After the war, Doll and EMR received letters and certificates of appreciation from The Engineer Board, the War Department, and the Office of Scientific Research and Development. In a letter to Doll on January 23, 1946, Vannevar Bush, director of OSRD, wrote:

"The outstanding contribution of American science and industry to the winning of the war has been recognized and commented upon throughout the country. It should always be remembered that science and industry made that contribution by teamwork – teamwork with the Armed Services and teamwork within industry itself....

"This letter gives me the pleasure of expressing to you my personal and official appreciation of the aid that the Electro-Mechanical Research, Inc., as a corporation, has given in the war effort through the work which it has performed under contract with this office.

"As we go forward into a world in which peace has been secured through this effort, our greatest assurance of a better and more fruitful life will lie in the continuance of the cooperative spirit which made possible the progress just finished."

In recognition of the work done by EMR and of the financial contribution by Schlumberger to the effort, Doll was allowed to retain patent rights to several inventions. He eventually received five patents, covering various aspects of the technology in the mine detector. The first, on the concept for the mine detector itself, was assigned to the United States through the Secretary of the Army. Two others, geared at improvements of the basic detection system, were assigned to EMR.

The final two patents covered the "radical" system for accurate phase detection of electromagnetic signals and were assigned to SWSC. They became the basis of a new resistivity measurement that would again change the oil industry.

Henri-Georges Doll around 1945.

Chapter 15

From War to Peace

Coming out of the war years, the structure, organization, and leadership of the Schlumberger companies were in flux. When Paris was cut off from the rest of the world during the war, Schlumberger Well Surveying Corporation (SWSC) in Houston became the center of operations for Schlumberger. In 1940, SWSC had 60 crews operating in the United States and was also responsible for providing equipment to Schlumberger affiliates in South America and the Far East.

Eugène Léonardon (now an American citizen) was the president of SWSC; his assistant Paul Charrin ran the day-to-day operations.

Doll had set up a research and development organization for SWSC, but from 1942 on, he was occupied mainly with the work on mine detectors and electronic guidance systems at EMR. Léonardon had also put many of the company's top engineers at the disposal of the U.S. government during the war.

Schlumberger was still a family company. Nearly all the shares of its affiliate companies – *la Pros* in Paris, SWSC in the United States, and Surenco in Venezuela – were owned by Marcel and by Conrad's three daughters, Annette, Dominique, and Sylvie. Marcel's son Pierre was the only male descendant of the two brothers. (Conrad had undoubtedly been disappointed not to have a male heir. At the time in France, and elsewhere, it was inconceivable that a woman could manage a company, especially a scientific or technical enterprise. Marie Curie, for example, in spite of her two Nobel Prizes, was poorly received when presented for nomination to the French Academy of Sciences.)

In addition to Doll, the husbands of Conrad's and Marcel's daughters all held key positions in the company: Jean de Ménil, husband of Dominique, directed the company's operations in Venezuela; Éric Boissonnas, husband of Sylvie, helped Doll manage EMR; René Seydoux Fournier de Clausonne, husband of Marcel's daughter Geneviève, helped Marcel manage what was left of the company's operations in Europe; and Henri Primat, husband of Marcel's youngest daughter Françoise, had been director of the engineering departments in Paris. (Henri Primat died in July 1945 while climbing alone in the French Alps.)

Doll's younger brother Pierre had also worked as an engineer for *la Pros*, first at Pechelbronn and later in the United States. (Pierre Doll was diagnosed with cancer while working in the United States and returned to France, where he died in the 1930s.) The youngest Doll brother Édouard declined a job with the company, choosing instead to follow in his father's steps and work at a cotton mill in Alsace.

Conrad and Marcel had shared authority equally. Conrad was the president and chairman of *la Pros*, but both brothers had full authority over the company's business and legal affairs. After the death of Conrad in 1936, Marcel shared this authority with Doll and with Eugène Léonardon.

Pierre Schlumberger had arrived in Houston in October 1941. He was 27 years old, and had worked for several years with his father at rue Saint-Dominique. Before sending his son to Houston, Marcel had written to Doll about the assignment. "With regard to Pierre," he wrote, "I want him to follow primarily the financial questions and the overall industrial management, which would put him under the orders of Jean de Ménil."

But Jean de Ménil and his wife Dominique left Houston to establish themselves in Caracas, where de Ménil took over the management of Surenco. Pierre found himself without the mentor his father had intended and in a position of ambiguous authority. Combined with his reclusive nature, the situation caused some tension in Houston.

"[Pierre] is turning out to be not very flexible, nor very talkative," Annette wrote. "His silences are disconcerting. A sandwich in hand, he surveys the offices, goes everywhere and nowhere, and leaves again in the same way." Doll complained that "Pierre does not say anything. He does not hear anything. He does not collaborate." Others were more direct in their criticism, stating bluntly that the young man was not ready yet for a position of authority in the company.

Pierre nevertheless became financial director of SWSC in 1943, then assistant general manager in 1944. Doll thought that Marcel was pushing his son too quickly towards the top. On December 3, 1945, in a handwritten letter addressed as usual "to my dear uncle Marcel," he cautioned Marcel over "the clearly premature promotion of Pierre" and the proposal to increase Pierre's salary again. "A new leap forward would currently be inappropriate and unjustified," he wrote. "[Pierre] has much experience to acquire." Doll attached to the letter a table comparing the salary progression of Pierre with that of Roger

Henquet and himself since 1926. The table shows the disproportionately fast rise of Pierre.

"During the many years when the company was not yet prosperous," Doll wrote in the letter, "I made some important contributions which were not well compensated by the very low salaries of the time – and the authorship of which, it should be said in passing, was often

Pierre Schlumberger, son of Marcel, arrived in Houston in 1941.

spirited away from me in a not very tactful way. It would thus seem to me fair that my new contract takes account of these circumstances, and provides in particular that, if I die prematurely, Annette would receive a substantial pension for a certain number of years." It is the only written evidence that Doll felt he had been treated unfairly when his name was left off the early papers and patents on well logging.

The situation with Pierre was painful for Doll, because he had helped to set up what he thought was the right leadership structure in Houston. On November 5, 1944, just after the liberation of Paris, Doll had sent a letter to Marcel at his home outside Paris. "When I leave [Houston], all will rest on Pierre," Doll wrote. "And as you know, his health has never been robust. If he had to leave Texas for any length of time, because of his health or for any other reason, the old dictatorship of Charrin would return – Léonardon is really just a puppet in Charrin's hands – and [the problems] would start all over again."

Doll had proposed a reorganization of SWSC that would take advantage of his position as chairman. His plan, to which Pierre agreed, was to appoint Roger Henquet vice-president and general manager of SWSC. Henquet, a French engineer, had been in the United States on and off for more than a decade. As a new engineer with *la Pros*, he had worked on the unsuccessful first logging campaign along the Gulf Coast, and then was transferred to Venezuela when Léonardon closed the company's American offices in 1931. He returned with Léonardon to the United States in 1932, and carried out a series of tests along the Gulf Coast that finally convinced American oil companies of the value of electrical logging. At the beginning of the war, Henquet had volunteered for commando training in Great Britain and parachuted into France before the Allied invasion of Normandy to establish connections with the French resistance.

"From all points of view," Doll wrote, "he has shown himself to be the best of our men…and has total loyalty. He conducted himself well – or rather, brilliantly – during the liberation of France…. Finally, he is very well liked by everyone and particularly by the Americans."

In Doll's plan, Charrin would remain vice president, and Léonardon would retain the title of president "to avoid spectacular changes, but will remain in the harness we have built around him. He should gradually be directed towards a golden retirement. As for myself, I will resign from the post of chairman to put it back in your hands."

Three months later, on February 1, 1945, Doll wrote again to Marcel to inform him that the plan had been carried out: "Everything went well," he wrote, "but as you thought, the conversation with Charrin was very difficult and painful…. On several occasions, [he] confirmed to me his resignation, but I maintained an attitude of very great cordiality while advising him not to let himself be influenced by the reaction of the moment…. The reaction by Léonardon on the contrary was excellent. He was never more cooperative and pleasant than on the day when the decisions were made. The difficulties [regarding the lawsuit with Lane-Wells] that we had with him at the beginning were in large part due to the fact that he was under the total domination of Charrin, and I am convinced that…he will become again exactly what he had always been."

As planned, Marcel became chairman of the board of SWSC. On April 21, 1945, he wrote to Doll: "I am very appreciative of your gesture to let me have the title of chairman and to take that of vice-chairman. I regret that this unusual title corresponds so little to the importance of your activity." In the same letter, Marcel told Doll that he would keep his salary of 2500 dollars per month, and receive a percentage (one-half percent) of the total revenues.

After more than five years in the United States, Annette was hoping to return to France, and started preparations with her daughters. Izaline was now 20 years old, Clarisse, 17, and Henriette, 11. Doll wanted to wait until the situation in Houston was fully sorted out, and rented an apartment in New York so that the children could continue their studies there.

On September 25, 1945, Annette wrote to her grandmother: "Don't worry, New York has no attraction for us, and we wait impatiently to set ourselves up on the rue de Varenne. The apartment in New York is a provisional solution until June. We will keep the house of Houston set up, even after our return to France. Henri-Georges will have his work in Houston which will require him to spend a few months there each year."

In Houston, during the war, Annette and Henri-Georges had become interested in modern painting. Dominique (Annette's sister) and her husband, Jean de Ménil, were art enthusiasts and had begun a collection of paintings, sculptures, and other objects of art. (Many of these belong to the Menil Collection, which the de Ménils donated to the city of Houston in 1987. The Menil Collection includes some 1500 works dating from 3000 B.C. to the present.)

The Dolls' interest in art also benefited from a chance encounter with someone who would change their lives. Izaline remembers that one evening, after her parents had returned from a dinner engagement, the telephone rang. A female voice on the line was asking for refuge. She identified herself as a neighbor who had had an argument with her companion and, she said, had been hit on the head with a frying pan and feared even worse. Annette and Doll told her to come over to their house. She introduced herself as Guitou Knoop. She was a painter and sculptor of Russian origin, about thirty years old; she spoke English and French with a Slavic accent.

"She knocked down our family's door," Izaline would say later. "I am not sure if it was good for us or not." Henriette on the other hand remembers Guitou as "a woman who meant a lot" in the life of her parents. "When Papa arrived in Houston, he and my mother still lacked taste," Henriette said. "It was the period of flowered chintz. Guitou Knoop, an artist rather well known at the time – she created great sculptures for the garden of the stud farm of the Rothschilds in Normandy – gave [my parents] a taste for beautiful painting, for fabrics made by hand. She became part of the family circle."

She also brought a certain carefree attitude, which contrasted with the professional preoccupations that Doll often brought home, the problems of dealing with clients and competitors, with drilling mud and ruptured cables, with antitank mines, and with the mathematical formulas that ran through his head.

"Papa was at heart a cheerful person," Henriette recalled in a recent interview. "He liked to play tennis and bridge, and he liked to dance. My mom was from a family of intellectuals who liked conversation a lot. At the Schlumbergers, we sometimes had dinners where the subject of conversation was announced in advance."

Doll also liked music. "He did not know how to read the notes," Henriette remembers, "and he invented this terribly complicated machine to read the notes by colors. The machine did not play, but it unrolled small points of color that indicated where the notes were. In reality, it was more complicated than to know how to read the music." During evenings in Houston, Doll studied the elements of harmony and composed impromptu songs on his accordion, "a large Italian accordion of very good quality."

He also liked to work around the house, a task in which he was as much a perfectionist as in interpreting logs. Once when Annette was recovering from pneumonia, he designed and built for her a small reading table. Henriette kept the object after her mother's death. "It was an astonishing piece of furniture," she remembers, "so refined, like professional cabinetmaking."

Guitou Knoop had a feeling for this other side of Henri-Georges Doll, a side that could put away professional concerns and simply have fun, a side that he rarely showed to his colleagues.

Jean-Pierre Causse, one of the young French scientists who joined Schlumberger after the war, recalls that "Doll was distinguished, elegant, and courteous – upper class, one would say. He did not say one more word than he needed. He did not fraternize, he kept a certain distance. That did not disturb us. We were all at his service."

Philippe Souhaité, an engineer who worked with Doll during Doll's last years with Schlumberger, had the same impression: "Doll was very dignified, very polite – he did not use 'tu' [the familiar form of address in French] – and did not show his feelings. It was very difficult to know what he really thought."

Jay Tittman, one of the first nuclear physicists that Doll hired, expressed similar sentiments, "Mr. Doll was not a talker, except if you put him on a platform to describe some new ideas on electric logging, then you could not stop him…. One did not imagine Mr. Doll dancing the tango."

After "knocking down the family door," it was Guitou Knoop who would introduce Doll a few years later to the woman who would be his companion for the second half of his life.

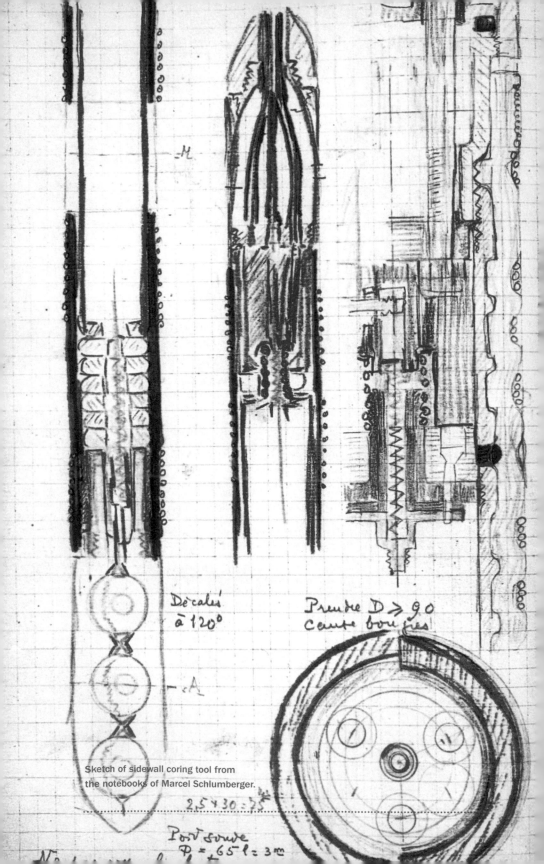

Décalés à 120°

Prendre D ≥ 90 comme bougies

Sketch of sidewall coring tool from the notebooks of Marcel Schlumberger.

2.5 × 30 = ?

Port soude
$P_l = 65$ $l = 3^{mm}$

Chapter 16

Paris, Houston, New York, or Ridgefield?

In a letter to Doll on January 15, 1946, Marcel Schlumberger listed and underlined three issues facing the future of research in his company, and expressed his own preferences for how each of these issues would be resolved:

"Location of a research center: The choice among the three cities which you talked about as the command post of research, namely, Paris, Houston or New York, seems to me personally to favor (as you indicated) Paris in preference to Houston, which itself is preferable to New York.

"Orientation of research: We will have forever to tackle this inexhaustible subject…. Personally, I think that if an inventor wants to work on something technically useful during his life, it is necessary to have the discipline not to scatter about, but rather to confine himself to a narrow domain, in our case, geophysics. The same discipline applied to business leads to something solid, as the history and evolution of our company shows.

"Surface geophysics: This leads me to talk with you about surface geophysics, which is not only a fascinating field for scientific research, but also most likely still contains some very nice financial and business opportunities."

None of Marcel's preferences had much of a chance. The choice really was Doll's to make, more so than even he may have realized. Wherever Doll ended up for the next few years would become the command post of research for Schlumberger. In the end, Doll's research center would not be located in Paris, Houston, or New York; the orientation of research would not be limited strictly to geophysics; and surface geophysics, the battleground of *la Pros* when Conrad and Marcel had launched their company, would be relegated to a back-up plan.

Doll knew that new technologies, in large part created during the war, had opened up new possibilities in applied science. The uses of electronics, which before the war had been limited mainly to radio and telecommunications, had expanded dramatically during the war, and would expand exponentially after the invention of the transistor at Bell Labs in 1947. Nuclear physics also clearly had applications in oil exploration.

"The atmosphere during the war and immediately afterwards had an extraordinarily effervescent quality," Jean-Pierre Causse recalled in an interview with Annette in the early 1970s. "America was victorious and everything seemed possible, not just because of technical progress. The U.S. had a certain superiority.... Doll understood the power of technology. He left France in 1941, that was logical; he could return immediately after the war.... For the sciences, physics, and engineering, the war years were absolutely fundamental. It generated an extraordinary effervescence. The idea, which your father Conrad shared, that anything is possible if one tackles it and works at it seriously, is hardly imaginable today. At the time [just after the war], Doll was a figure in his prime, with success behind him. He was modest, but not more so than he needed to be. He knew what he was capable of. Something needed to be done, and the right idea was to separate research and engineering in Schlumberger. If it remained in Houston, it would always be occupied with the needs of the field."

But if research was to disengage itself from Houston and expand into new areas, where should it be located?

Paris, indeed anywhere in Europe, seemed out of the question. Many European scientists had fled to the United States to escape Nazism, fascism, and (for those who could) communism. The greatest names in physics – Albert Einstein, Neils Bohr, Enrico Fermi, Edward Teller, George Gamov, Leo Szilard, Victor Weisskopf, and many others – were in the United States, doing research and teaching a new generation of American scientists, who had returned to universities after the war, helped by the GI Bill of Rights.

In his book *The Age of Extremes* (1994), the British historian Eric J. Hobsbawm relates a telling statistic. Between 1900 and 1933, there were only seven American Nobel Prize winners in science; from 1933 to 1970, there were seventy-seven, of which more than one-third were first-generation Americans. "The university environment in France had been knocked out by the war; there was no more money," Causse recalled. "France was in ruins. Doll believed that everything was going to be happening in the U.S., where he already was. Even Professor Rocard [Yves Rocard, professor of physics at École Normale

Supérieure] was sending his students to the U.S. for training. Their goal was to return to France afterwards."

A large part of the scientific establishment of the United States was still located near the major universities of the northeast: Princeton, Columbia, Cornell, Yale, Harvard, and MIT. So Doll considered several locations in New England for his research center. The choice was finally determined by Charles Aiken, his friend and colleague from the patent battles of the early 1940s, who had also become one of the founders of EMR. Aiken's wife was born in Ridgefield, Connecticut, and the couple owned a house there.

The town of Ridgefield is in Fairfield County, about 55 miles north of New York City, along the rocky ridges and valleys of southwestern Connecticut. It was settled in the early 1700s by English colonists who purchased land from Chief Catoonah of the Ramapoo Indians. In 1777, it was the site of the Battle of Ridgefield, an early skirmish of the Revolutionary War, in which Benedict Arnold participated. Originally a farming community, Ridgefield became popular in the late 1800s as a location for the summer homes of wealthy New York City residents, who built summer cottages (mansions, actually) on huge estates along the high wooded ridges overlooking the town's many small lakes.

Aiken took Doll to visit Ridgefield in 1946. Before the end of the year, Electro-Mechanical Research became the town's first industrial business. Doll purchased a small house, which he hastily outfitted as a laboratory for EMR. He immediately began working there with his colleagues from the war research: Maurice Lebourg, Charles Aiken, Joseph Bricaud, and others. He and Annette bought an old farmhouse called Ferndale, which had been turned into a country home. It was located in the woods on Spectacle Lane, a dirt lane that branched off from the main road leading south from the town, about two miles from the town center. Ferndale was a typical wooden-framed two-story New England home. White on the exterior, it had a large room with a low ceiling on the first floor, with an old fireplace surrounded by sofas and lounge chairs at one end and a large wooden dinner table at the other.

The first step out of Houston had been taken. But more was required for what Doll had in mind, which was to establish a center for long-term research, touching even on fundamental areas that he believed could lead to real breakthroughs in oil and gas exploration. In 1947, a large plot of land behind Old Dump Road in Ridgefield was purchased, and a long one-story brick laboratory was built at the site.

In August 1948, the first Schlumberger center devoted exclusively to research opened its doors. According to Earl Wallick, a lawyer from SWSC who was sent to Ridgefield to work in the patent department, the first day was spent "worrying about offices, furniture, light switches, telephone locations and whom in Ridgefield we should contact to get the street name of our new address changed." The name was changed to Old Quarry Road. The lab was named Schlumberger Ridgefield Division Research Center. Doll, who just two years earlier had been chairman of the board of Schlumberger Well Surveying Corporation, was the center's first director of research.

Schlumberger Ridgefield Division Research Center in 1948.

At age 45, Doll still had a youthful appearance. He had kept his long, thin silhouette and jet-black hair, although a few streaks of white were visible in his mustache. He always wore a jacket and tie at work, as he always had at rue Fabert in Paris, at SWSC and EMR in Houston, and almost always in the field. He was always approachable, but except for his close collaborators, he rarely socialized with the staff, generally going home to eat lunch – Ferndale was about three miles from the lab – while the scientists either went to the small restaurants along Main Street in Ridgefield, or just gathered outside the labs with lunches packed at home.

After five years of intense work during the war, the seclusion and relative tranquility of Ridgefield were ideal for Doll and for his plan to transform research in Schlumberger. He had constructed in his mind a collection of projects touching on many scientific and technical disciplines: nuclear physics, electronics, electronic computing. Some were, as he liked to say, "pipe dreams" (*châteaux en Espagne*, literally "castles in Spain"). But the company was growing at an astonishing rate, and money was no problem. "What he asked for," Annette recalled, "he got."

Annette and Henri-Georges at Ferndale in Ridgefield, around 1950.

Annette on the other hand felt isolated. "I did not realize it at the time, but the years in Ridgefield were the start of my apprenticeship in solitude. I felt more lost in New England than in the vast plains of

Texas…. I had hoped at the end of those seven fateful years [in Houston] to be on the way back to France. But against my desire to return, Henri-Georges had the needs of his work. Now that he had finally set up the research center, he couldn't shrink from the responsibility of managing it. Who else was able to put it on the right track?"

Doll rarely ordered anyone to do anything. "He was not imposing or intimidating," Jay Tittman recalled. "He was the kind of person who would ask you to do something almost in passing…. He asked me to do lots of things, but more in the way of, 'Doctor Tittman, I am very sorry to interrupt you in your work, but I was thinking that maybe you could come into my office for a few minutes to help me with something.' Always courteous, he left you with the impression that he considered you to be someone very special."

Georges Attali was a 1933 graduate of École Polytechnique whom Doll hired in 1954. "My interview with Doll lasted one hour," Attali recalled in a recent interview. "Then he told me, 'OK. You're hired.' I called up my wife and told her we were on our way to the United States." Attali started work at SWSC in Houston, and then came to Ridgefield. "Doll was a poet…of ideas," Attali continued. "His own research was more a matter of intuition than deduction. He was also a bit of a dreamer. But clearly he had the right dreams."

Doll also asked Raymond Sauvage and Jean-Claude Legrand to come to Ridgefield. Legrand, one of the first Schlumberger engineers to work in the United States in the 1920s, directed the patent department. Sauvage, Doll's old friend and colleague from the Soviet Union, set up a new department of research in the interpretation of well logs. After his ordeal in the Far East during the war, Sauvage had spent some time recovering at his grandparents' farm in Auvergne in the south of France. He arrived in Ridgefield in 1948. He was 44 years old, and had just been diagnosed with Parkinson's disease. Nevertheless, he worked at the research center for 18 years. "Sauvage was a first-rate interpreter of logs," Attali recalled. "He was really the brains behind 'Interpretation.' He was capable of making the logs talk."

Sauvage worked with two other field engineers, M. P. Tixier and Maurice Martin, who also came to Ridgefield at Doll's request. On most days, the four *anciens* (old timers) – Sauvage, Tixier, Martin, and Doll – could be heard arguing loudly the finer points of log interpretation in the hallways of the lab.

"One other characteristic of Doll," Causse recalled, "was that he never lost interest in engineering. The fact that he liked to work at his own pace, unhurried, did not mean that he was not also preoccupied… with what was going on in the rest of the company. He was also extremely attuned to field results. He put three thousand miles [between engineering and research], but he was always shuffling problems between the two…. Even though Houston often criticized Ridgefield for being 'gentlemen' scientists, it was not at all the case. We were obsessed with success in the field. For me, when I was testing my detectors in the field, I was obsessed with making them a success."

Chapter 17

Head Hunter

Under the direction of Henri-Georges Doll, Ridgefield became a multi-disciplinary research center. Electrical measurements had dominated the early years of Schlumberger. "It was Conrad's idea," Jean-Pierre Causse recalled in a recent interview. "Resistivity of course is fundamental because oil is an insulator and water is a conductor, so there is something natural and profound in using resistivity – it truly is the right measurement to identify oil."

But this idea had dominated Conrad's company for too long. In *Schlumberger, The History of a Technique* (John Wiley & Sons, 1977), Louis Allaud and Maurice Martin write: "Between 1945 and 1950, the prevailing idea was that it was possible to solve all problems of interpretation with SP and conventional resistivity measurements. This perception, which proved not just to be too optimistic, but even wrong, did not contribute much to the science of well logging."

"We discovered," Causse continued in his interview, "that it was much more complicated than just resistivity. Water is always present along with the oil and…it is really a problem of proportion. Doll had developed a new point of view, which was something we came to call the 'full suit,' in other words, that the solution required a large number of measurements that complemented each other. That pushed everyone to add in new things, because everything was welcome: a pinch of this, normal and inverse [electrical] tools, spontaneous potential; a little bit of that, natural radioactivity, neutrons, sonic, density. You sold all that to the client by telling him that if he bought everything, then there was a good chance of not just being able to measure if oil was present, but how much."

Doll reinforced the original team in Ridgefield by hiring specialists in new areas. At the recommendation of Yves Rocard, professor of physics at École Normale Supérieure in Paris, Doll hired Maurice Ferré, one of the best young *normaliens* recently graduated in physics. Shortly after he arrived in Ridgefield, Ferré was named managing director of the laboratory. It was also Rocard who suggested that his young student, Jean-Pierre Causse, go to Schlumberger to work with Doll.

Causse arrived at SWSC in 1950, at the age of 24, as a student intern. He worked on acoustics (the physics of sound waves), a subject that Rocard had discussed with Doll, including electrochemical effects that can be induced by sound waves in porous rocks. "One morning," Causse recalled, "Doll called me on the phone and told me that he had had an idea the previous night that he wanted me to work on, if it would not trouble me too much. So I went to work studying the electrical conductivity of shales, which afterwards progressed very well."

"Things went quickly back then," Causse continued. "Today, things are slower. There was an extraordinary dynamism after the war. Schlumberger was led by dynamic people, and Doll was one of them, a leader, an extraordinary man, even in his personal side. For me, Doll was the great man of the organization, someone who led the way to places where others followed."

Causse returned to France after his internship to complete his military service, but two years later he was back in the United States, working at Ridgefield.

Doll had followed the rapid development of nuclear physics and wanted to set up a research group in nuclear well logging at Ridgefield. At Houston, he had tried unsuccessfully to hire Bruno Pontecorvo, a student of Fermi's who had invented a method using neutrons to measure the porosity of rocks in oil wells.

In retrospect, the failure to hire Pontecorvo was fortunate for Schlumberger. In 1950, at the height of the Cold War, Pontecorvo left his job at the Atomic Energy Research Establishment in Harwell, England, where we was working on Britain's first nuclear bomb, and defected to the Soviet Union. Along with Fermi, Pontecorvo held basic U.S. patents on the technology of nuclear reactions, including technology used for reactors and atomic weapons. In addition to concerns about the leak of classified secrets, his defection caused complex legal problems for the United States government. See "Atomic secrets and governmental lies: nuclear science, politics and security in the Pontecorvo case," Simon Turchetti (*British Journal for the History of Science*, v. 36, pp. 389-415, 2003).

To get Schlumberger started in nuclear physics, Doll hired a consultant, Clark Goodman, a professor of nuclear physics at Massachusetts Institute of Technology (MIT). During MIT's summer break in 1949, Goodman laid out a complete program of nuclear research for Schlumberger in a manuscript several hundred pages long. He presented the manuscript, bound in a black cover with the gold lettering "Radioactivity Well-Logging," to Doll in June 1950. Nearly every nuclear measurement that Schlumberger developed for well logging can be traced to Goodman's "Black Peril." Not all of its ideas of course were original to either Goodman or to Schlumberger. Doll convinced SWSC to fund the new program at a cost of about $2 million.

A special building was constructed for nuclear research, to comply with the regulations for handling radioactive materials. One of the first scientists to work in the program was Jay Tittman. Tittman had a Ph.D. degree in physics from Columbia University, where he had studied with Isador Isaac Rabi, one of the leaders of American physics during and after the war. (In 1944, Rabi had won the Nobel Prize in physics for measuring the magnetic properties of atomic nuclei. During the war, he had helped direct the project at MIT's Radiation Lab to develop military radar systems for the Allies.)

Tittman telephoned to Ridgefield after one of his friends and fellow students at Columbia mentioned that he had been contacted by a company called Schlumberger Oil Well Surveying Company. Tittman asked what kind of job a company in the oil industry could possibly have for a nuclear physicist. "I had done quite a few interviews before," Tittman recalled, "always in the company offices, some of which were not very attractive. But I got picked up in this white Lincoln limo…and was driven to Ridgefield, to Mr. Doll's house…. The driver told me, 'You are going to have lunch there with Mr. Doll and other visitors, who are at the lab.' …So I waited in the house, walking down the living room and suddenly realized with shock that the Picasso, the Mondrian were real! I had never seen an original before…. Then they arrived: Mr. Doll, Jean-Claude Legrand, and Maurice Ferré. Harold Schwede was also there, as were Clark Goodman and Bart Fry, the first head of the nuclear section.

"Anyway, the lunch was very interesting…. Legrand did a lot of talking, so did Goodman. It was my first French lunch, and we had wine, which I was not accustomed to, being a poor graduate student. I cannot exactly remember whether dessert was *soufflé à l'orange* or *au Grand Marnier*. The cook had prepared two extra ones, and Doll, with his own ability to size up people, looked around the table and said, 'Dr. Tittman, I am sure you would like another one.' 'No, No,' I replied.

But Doll insisted, 'Please go ahead, the air will come out of it in no time so they have to be eaten.' So I had two soufflés for the first time I ever had soufflé in my life."

Staff at Schlumberger Ridgefield Division Research Center, 1948.

After lunch, Tittman visited the Ridgefield lab, and then was interviewed by Doll in his office, "…we chatted about things in general and about my background. I remember telling him that I was a little concerned because, from what I had heard and seen, geology is very important in well logging, and I had never studied geology. His response was, 'Boff! As long as you know the mathematics and physics, you will pick up the geology.' Which was true, as it turned out."

Tittman was also impressed by the long-term nature of the projects getting underway in the new lab. Doll had even talked with him about the possibility of using nuclear magnetic resonance (NMR) to distinguish oil from water. (Rabi at Columbia had been the first to measure nuclear magnetic resonance in molecular beams in 1938; Felix Bloch and Edwin Purcell developed it into a powerful way of measuring the chemical properties of liquids and solids, for which they shared the Nobel Prize in 1952.)

Two weeks after the interview at Schlumberger, Tittman received an offer from the British engineering and construction company M. W. Kellogg, which built nuclear reactors for new power plants. He called Goodman to tell him about the offer. The response was quick. Within a few days, Tittman had an offer from Ridgefield. He discovered that "Schlumberger's practice at the time was to offer twenty percent more than the going rate for industrial salaries. At the time, new Ph.D.s out of university in physics and engineering were getting about $6000 a year; Schlumberger's offer was $7200. I remember saying to my wife, 'Gosh! We can buy a new car and have a real apartment with separate bedrooms for the kids!'"

Tittman never regretted his decision. He was hired in March 1951 and worked for Schlumberger, mainly at Ridgefield, until his retirement in the late 1980s. He still lives with his wife in Danbury, Connecticut, about five miles north of Ridgefield, and consults occasionally for Schlumberger.

By the summer of 1951, Doll and Goodman had assembled the team that would lead Schlumberger into the nuclear age: Bart Fry, the first head of the nuclear section; Frank Johnson, who came with Goodman from MIT; Bill Nollingham; and Mike Morgan, who had just completed a Ph.D. degree in physics at Yale.

"Clark Goodman set up the program," Tittman recalled. "One third would be for fast results, something that would keep management happy and show that we were not a bunch of blue-sky scientists. If [a new tool] could not really make money, they were not interested. Another third was somewhat longer-term projects, one to three years, which had more meat. The last third was blue-sky, long-distance stuff. It was a very good way to lay things out like that…. Doll supported us every inch of the way and I never felt for one minute that he did not give us all the help we needed: money, consultants or whatever. On the other hand, I do want to say that he personally was never very interested in the physics of nuclear well logging. I think he was afraid of nuclear physics."

Doll also began hiring scientists to work with new electronics technologies that were developing rapidly after the war. One of these was Nick Schuster. In 1951, Schuster was finishing a Ph.D. degree in nuclear physics at Washington University in St. Louis. He had graduated from the same school in 1941 with a B.S. degree in electrical engineering, and then worked at General Electric, before serving as an officer in the U.S. Navy during the war. After the war, he participated in the nuclear tests at Bikini Atoll in the Pacific, and then returned to St. Louis to do graduate work.

"Every year, the American Physical Society had their main meeting in New York City," Schuster recalled in a recent interview. "That was also an opportunity for all young people graduating with Ph.D.s to find a job. Clark Goodman [was there] and arranged an interview with Mr. Doll and Maurice Martin, an interpretation scientist.

"Mr. Doll was going to be giving a speech in St. Louis, so they decided to interview me in Doll's room at the Radisson Hotel, one of the best hotels in St. Louis. I remember there was only one chair in his room, and Mr. Doll asked me to sit there; he sat on the bed and Mr. Martin just stood up.

"Doll was telling me about the…induction log, which had started in 1946, and I was asking a lot of questions. The interview I guess from their point of view was a little bit ticklish, because I had my Ph.D. in nuclear physics, but Mr. Doll wanted to hire me strictly for…electrical logging. But it was OK by me, because I had an undergraduate degree in electrical engineering. I was just interested in any good job that was out there. I had interviewed with a lot of companies, more than most of my friends; none of them had heard of Schlumberger and were surprised when I accepted the job. At the time, radar and other areas were much more spectacular. But I found the problems that Doll described fascinating, so I ended up going to Ridgefield, a nice place to work.

"But I guess the nicest thing was Mr. Doll. This man was chairman of the board, but that was of no consequence to him, he was primarily a scientist. I loved working with him."

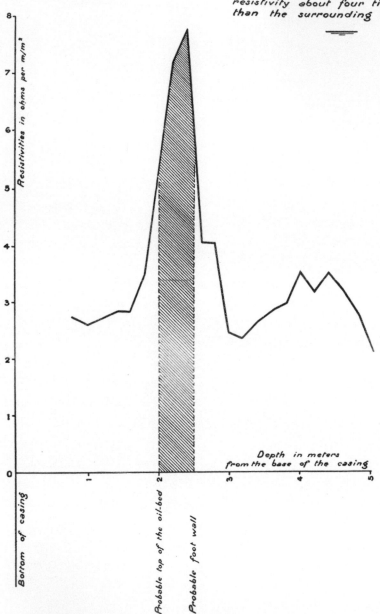

PECHELBRONN

An oilsand 50 cms. thick presents a resistivity about four times higher than the surrounding ground.

Resistivities in ohms per m/m²

8
7
6
5
4
3
2
1
0

1   2   3   4   5

Depth in meters from the base of the casing

Bottom of casing

Probable top of the oil-bed

Probable foot wall

Figure from "Electrical Coring," presented by Conrad and Marcel Schlumberger at the World Petroleum Congress in Paris, 1929.

Chapter 18

The Full Suit

One of the first breakthroughs to come from the new electronics developed during the war was the induction log. It provided a new way of measuring electrical resistivity, which was needed in wells drilled with mud having an oil base. The first drilling mud consisted of salt water mixed with clay particles. During well logging, the conductive water allowed electrical current to pass from electrodes suspended in the mud into the rock formations and fluids surrounding the well.

But certain types of shale layers, which also contained clay particles, absorbed the water in the drilling mud, causing the layers to swell and choke off the well. The problem was especially bad in deep wells drilled in California and along the Gulf Coast, which had become the premier oil and gas districts of the United States in the years following the war. To avoid this problem, drillers began mixing the drilling mud with oil, which the clay particles in geological formations would not absorb. The first oil-base drilling mud was introduced in the oil fields of Rangely, Colorado, in 1948.

Oil of course is an insulator. Electrodes suspended in oil-base mud could not make electrical contact with the rocks. New types of electrode tools were designed – with sharp points, bristles, and blades that scraped along the borehole wall to establish electrical contact – but none of these devices was very successful. The induction log solved the problem in an elegant way. If it was not possible to drive current through oil-base mud into the rocks, why not generate a current remotely in the rocks by the same physical principle used in mine detection?

In induction logging, a small antenna lowered into the borehole transmits a low-frequency radio wave into the earth, which causes currents to flow in the region surrounding the well by the phenomenon of electromagnetic induction. These "secondary" currents – the intensity of which depends on the conductivity of rocks and pore fluids near the well (conductivity is the inverse of resistivity) – generate their own radio-frequency electromagnetic field, which is measured by a second antenna (the receiver) in the logging tool.

Ralph Lohman, a California scientist, filed the first U.S. patent for an induction logging device in 1935; a year later, Charles Aiken, who was then teaching at Purdue University, filed a patent for a similar system. Schlumberger acquired the rights to both patents when they were issued in 1940. Both were based on a simple arrangement of two coils of wire, which served as the transmitting and receiving antennas.

The challenge was to develop a system that was rugged enough to survive the high temperatures and pressures in boreholes, yet capable of detecting the tiny differences in the secondary currents generated in

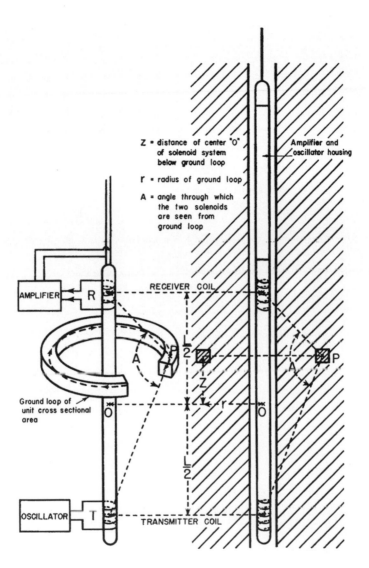

Figure from Doll's 1949 paper introducing induction logging to the oil industry. A coil transmitter fed by electrical current alternating at 20 kilohertz broadcasts an electromagnetic field (radio wave) from the borehole into the surrounding formation. The rocks and their pore fluids respond, according to Faraday's law of electromagnetic induction, by generating secondary electrical currents that circulate around the borehole. The radio-wave field of these secondary currents is detected by a receiver coil, also located in the borehole, a short distance from the transmitter. Under the right conditions, this secondary signal is proportional to the average conductivity of the region near the hole. (Reprinted with permission of the Society of Petroleum Engineers from *Journal of Petroleum Technology*, June 1949.)

water- and oil-filled rocks. The solution came from the work done at EMR during the war, in the form of the phase-selective detector that Doll, Lebourg, Aiken, and Huston had used to stabilize their Jeep-mounted mine detector.

The new phase-selective circuit was able to separate the small induction signal created by secondary currents flowing in the rocks from the large direct signal generated by the transmitter. Its precision, compared to previous circuits available before the war, was unprecedented: it could resolve a difference in phase of about one part in 10,000. The work at EMR had been declassified after the war, and Doll obtained a series of patents on the technology, which he assigned to Schlumberger Well Surveying Corporation (SWSC).

Working in Houston after the war, Doll developed the first induction tool around the design in Aiken's patent. The first log was recorded on May 3, 1946, by O. H. Huston in a well owned by Humble Oil in the Hawkins field near Tyler, Texas, about 90 miles (150 kilometers) southwest of Dallas. Several other wells were logged in subsequent months. The tests were promising, but not entirely successful. The tool detected an oil zone near the bottom of the wells, but the log was much less sensitive to the variation of resistivity along the well than a standard electrode log, which was recorded in one of the wells after replacing the oil-base mud with salt-water mud.

A new design was developed by Doll during the years of transition from Houston to Ridgefield. This time the solution was not electronics, but a tour de force of geometrical reasoning. To increase the induction tool's sensitivity, Doll arranged a series of transmitter and receiver coils at different locations along the sonde. Their combined effect was to cancel almost perfectly the unwanted signals coming from near the borehole, leaving only the signals caused by the secondary currents in the surrounding formation. To finish the design, Doll relied on a new mathematical analysis of the physics of induction that his wartime friend and colleague, Francis Perrin, had carried out at his request. (Perrin had returned to France after the war and resumed teaching at the University of Paris.)

"The tool was a bit convoluted," Doll later recalled, "like something out of Jules Verne." According to Allaud and Martin, the engineers at Houston were convinced that the tool could not, and should not, be built. "Because of [its] complexity," they wrote, "Doll had to win a psychological battle. Except for his close co-workers, no one was on his side. On the minds of management, field, and research staffs was the considerable technical and financial effort invested in the new truck…and the new recorder; they wanted a breathing spell. Many thought it foolhardy to substitute a complicated, expensive, and…unpredictable apparatus for the simplicity of three electrodes."

Doll prevailed with the help of Roger Henquet, the new assistant general manager of SWSC. Henquet had worked along the Gulf Coast and in California and knew firsthand that the industry needed an electrical logging tool for oil-base mud.

The new design was built in Houston and started making logs in 1948. In February of the following year, Doll presented the results to the oil industry at the meeting of the American Institute of Mining and Metallurgical Engineers (AIME) in San Francisco. The new induction logs were much more localized than logs from standard electrode logs, and were capable of detecting oil-bearing layers only a few feet thick. But there were still problems with the design. The delicate balance between the different coils could be carefully calibrated in the lab. But when the tool encountered the high temperatures and pressures in the borehole, Nick Schuster recalled: "It had a huge amount of drift."

The drift, Schuster explained, "was especially bad in oil zones, when the signal approaches zero. An induction tool is actually measuring the conductivity of the rocks, which has to be reciprocated to give the resistivity. In oil zones, the signal comes close to zero, and if you have any kind of error in the measurement, when you reciprocate it, it blows up. The best thing was to get rid of that drift."

Schuster had accepted the job that Doll offered him after the interview in St Louis and had started working at Ridgefield. "We actually brought five tools to Ridgefield to get started," he recalled. "There were things pretty obvious to improve on and quite a few things that were very subtle and difficult, like the capacitance between the coils. It was complicated because there was also resistance in the coils that varied with temperature and created a phase shift that was responsible for a large part of the drift. Another thing is that they were not using negative feedback, which was not too common at the time. With negative feedback, you re-inject the drift into the system with feedback resistors, so that it stabilizes. That was a success.

"By that time, Mary and I were married and I took her on a Schlumberger trip to Trinidad. They were using OBM [oil-base mud], which gave bad problems with the Schlumberger electrode log, called the ES, which could not make contact through the oil. But it did not bother the induction whatsoever.... So I gave a talk to the British oil companies who were having all these problems, and then we went

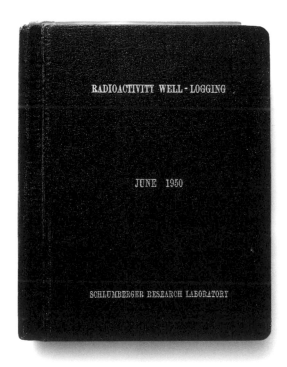

The 'Black Peril,' Clark Goodman's program for nuclear research at Ridgefield.

through Venezuela. I was introducing the induction log to the Schlumberger field organization."

Improvements in Houston increased the tool's sensitivity even further. Technicians calibrating new induction tools in the laboratory had to remove their wedding rings and belt buckles. Soon they were joking that the next thing to go would be the fillings in their teeth.

By this time (1952), the program for nuclear logging created at Ridgefield by Doll and Clark Goodman was well under way. The group had launched an ambitious program to create a new tool using neutrons to measure the porosity of underground rocks. A small company, Well Surveys, Inc. (WSI), had licensed Pontecorvo's patent on "neutron well logging" and had introduced the first porosity log in 1941. (WSI had also introduced the first nuclear log, which measured the natural radioactivity of rocks near the borehole. In the 1940s, WSI was acquired by Lane-Wells.)

Pontecorvo's patent was "Method and Apparatus for Logging a Well," U.S. Patent 2,349,753 (1941). Earlier patents on nuclear logging using neutrons included patents by Robert Fearon in 1938 and Folkert Brons in 1940.

Early on, the group at Ridgefield made a decisive choice. The source of radiation used by WSI was polonium, the first radioactive material to have been discovered in 1898 by Pierre and Marie Curie. Polonium decays into lead by emitting radioactive alpha particles; it has a half-life of 138.4 days, which means that within this period of time, half of the atoms present in any sample of polonium have transformed into lead. In another 138.4 days, half of the remaining polonium atoms also decay, leaving one-quarter of the original number, etc. For well logging, polonium is mixed with beryllium, which emits neutrons when bombarded by alpha particles. (An alpha particle is the nucleus of a helium atom, consisting of two neutrons and two protons.)

The short half-life of polonium meant that the sample had to be transported to the well and used quickly; if not, its radioactivity decayed so much that the tool had to be recalibrated. In the United

States, a tool could be loaded with the radioactive source in Houston and transported to a logging site anywhere in the country within a few days. It took longer of course to reach sites overseas, especially when dealing with customs requirements for radioactive materials.

The international presence of Schlumberger argued for use of a source with a longer half-life. The group at Ridgefield picked radium, the radioactive metal discovered by Pierre and Marie Curie in 1898. The half-life of the most stable isotope of radium is 1620 years. Radium was much more expensive than polonium and more hazardous (because it emitted higher-energy alpha particles), and was therefore subject to stricter safety regulations.

Jay Tittman, along with two engineers at SWSC, John Dewan and Denis Tanguy, designed the first Schlumberger neutron logging tool, making the key decisions about the location of the radioactive source and the distance to the gamma ray detectors. SWSC introduced the tool commercially in 1952.

At the same time, Tittman began a theoretical study of the quantitative relationship between "neutron-gamma" porosity measurement and the actual porosity of the different types of rocks. In addition, test formations were constructed at both Ridgefield and Houston to calibrate the tools. It would take nearly a decade to understand all the factors affecting the measurement, including the influence of the fluids in the borehole and variations in the gamma ray flux caused by the solid matrix of different types of rock.

In the meantime, Doll had been carrying out theoretical studies aimed at obtaining more accurate values of resistivity from the raw values on the electrical logs. Starting from Perrin's mathematical analysis, he developed a new theory that made it possible to compute from induction logs the average resistivity in different zones surrounding the borehole. Doll's "geometrical factor theory" would dominate the analysis of electrical logs for the next thirty years.

Doll also had large water-filled test pits built in a building behind the main lab, called the "Barn." The size of small swimming pools –

but called "bathtubs" in memory of Conrad's experiments in the basement of École des Mines in Paris – the pits were filled with water of different resistivities (adjusted by varying the salt content) simulating the resistivities of different underground layers. The pits allowed new induction tools to be calibrated very precisely.

After more than twenty years of electrical logging, why insist that the logs give the precise value of a reservoir's "true resistivity"?

An American electrical engineer working for Shell Oil, Gus Archie, was the first to answer this question definitively. In 1941, Archie completed a series of experiments in Shell's research labs in Houston showing how the fluid content of porous reservoir rock determined its electrical resistivity. Archie's first set of experiments demonstrated that the electrical resistivity of porous reservoir rock was simply proportional to the resistivity of the fluid filling its pores. This result was not surprising, since it was known that the solid grains of most reservoir rocks conducted almost no electricity.

The second set of experiments contained the surprise: The resistivity of most types of porous reservoir rocks varied in a simple way with the rocks' porosity (the amount of pore space) and with the fraction of the pore space that was filled with water.

Archie derived from these experiments an empirical equation for the resistivity of porous reservoir rock, which is undoubtedly the most famous equation in the history of the oil industry. It involves three terms: the porosity of the reservoir, represented by the Greek letter φ; the resistivity R_w of the water filling the pores; and the fraction of pore space filled with water, S_w – usually called the water saturation. In "Archie's law" (as it is now called), the water resistivity enters as a simple multiplicative factor, while the product of the porosity and the water saturation enters as an inverse square,

$$R = R_w \, (S_w \varphi)^{-2}.$$

Archie's law actually shows that electrical resistivity (R) is a very sensitive measure of a reservoir's oil content – if one assumes that the fraction of a rock's pore space not filled with water is filled with either oil or gas (as is the case with most rocks found deep underground). Consider an example. The resistivity of a sandstone whose pores are filled with water is normally about 10 ohm-m (S_w is 1, φ is 20% or 0.20, and R_w is 0.4 ohm-m). But if half the pore space is filled with oil (S_w is 0.5), the resistivity rises by a factor of four to 40 ohm-m. The surprising part was that this simple relationship held with minor variations for many different types of reservoir rocks, including reservoir rocks of widely different permeability.

Archie presented his work at the AIME Meeting in Dallas in 1941. His paper, "The Electrical Resistivity Log as an Aid in Determining Some Reservoir Characteristics," published in the *AIME Journal* in 1942 is a classic of modern applied science. Step by step after its publication – and its verification in oil reservoirs around the world – oil companies turned from using electrical logs only for geological correlation to using them mainly to estimate the amount of oil in their reservoirs.

In 1935, I. Kogan, an experimental geophysicist working for the Azerbaydzhan Petroleum Institut in Baku discovered essentially the same relationship pursuing the work that Mélikian and Sauvage had started with the engineers from Aznieft several years earlier. Kogan worked with a much more limited set of samples than Archie; his samples consisted essentially of rocks of two different porosities, 20% and 45%. But he was also able to correlate the decline in the reservoir resistivity over time with its production rate. Kogan's work was published in a local petroleum journal under the title "Utilization of electrical coring data for the determination of petroleum reserves," Azerb-Neft, Khozlatsvo, Baku, October 1935.

In three years, Doll's new center had grown dramatically. By 1951, the Schlumberger Ridgefield Division Research Center had 100 employees, of which more than half were scientists. The company had accepted Doll more or less unanimously as its technical leader, the intellectual successor of Conrad Schlumberger.

The engineer Jean Suau, who started in the Persian Gulf in 1950 before moving to Venezuela, met Doll in Caracas. "Doll," Suau said in a recent interview, "had a weakness for *polytechniciens* and he invited me to come to work at Ridgefield. My boss in Caracas, an American, said it was an offer that could not be refused. Doll had laid out the future of well logging, explaining that to really evaluate an oil reservoir, it was necessary to have not just one measure of its porosity or permeability (like the original SP log), but three porosity logs – neutron logs, sonic logs, and density logs – along with the resistivity log. He was pushing very hard for the development of new tools outside his own expertise. When he explained this to Houston at the company's annual planning meetings…the reaction was that Schlumberger would never be able to sell all that to the clients. No one believed it, but a few years later, it was all happening. Even things like digitizing the data for electronic transmission.

"At one of the meetings in Houston, someone joked, What are we going to measure when we get to the moon?"

Apollo 17 on the launch pad at Cape Kennedy, December 1972 (Photo courtesy of NASA).

Chapter 19

From the Earth to the Moon

The answer was photons, the elementary particles of light.

In December 1972, a rugged new sensor that EMR had developed for nuclear well logging, landed on the moon with Apollo 17, NASA's last lunar mission. The sensor was called a PMT, a photomultiplier tube. Like a solar cell, a photomultiplier tube functions by converting light into electricity.

But its purpose is not to generate electrical energy; instead, it uses energy to amplify and detect very faint sources of light.

The device is triggered by the photoelectric effect, by which certain materials create an electrical current when light shines on them. This phenomenon – the driving force in solar cells – was first observed in 1839 by the French physicist Alexandre-Edmond Becquerel (Becquerel's son Henri would later discover radioactivity). Attempts to explain photoelectricity using the classical theory of light waves failed for more than 50 years. Then in 1905, Einstein showed that the effect was understandable if light was not continuous, but instead came in discrete lumps, like particles of matter.

Photomultiplier tube, about 15 centimeters (six inches) long, for detecting gamma rays in nuclear well logging (Photo, Peter Wraight, Schlumberger Princeton Technology Center).

In Einstein's theory, particles of light (later called photons) collide like billiard balls with the electrons in matter and, if energetic enough, knock them out of their atomic orbits. Experiments by the American physicist Robert Millikan a decade later showed that Einstein's "reckless hypothesis" was correct and helped establish the reality of Max Planck's ethereal quantum of energy. Modern physics was born.

A photomultiplier tube uses the photoelectric effect to start a chain reaction. A typical device consists of a cylindrical tube of glass, a few centimeters in diameter, which is sealed at both ends and evacuated of air. Photons of light enter at one end of the tube, where they strike a thin film of material called a photocathode. Electrons ejected from the photocathode (by the photoelectric effect) are then accelerated towards a series of electrodes called dynodes, situated in the cylindrical chamber behind the photocathode. Each liberated electron that strikes a dynode produces several more electrons, which in turn are accelerated further down the tube, striking other dynodes and creating more electrons. The result after several stages is an avalanche of electrons, which are collected by a final electrode (the anode) situated at the far end of the tube. The cascade can generate more than a million electrons for every photon that enters the photomultiplier, allowing the device to detect extremely faint sources of light.

> V. K. Zworkin, a physicist working for RCA, is usually credited with the invention of the first photomultiplier tube in 1936. But a complete tube was developed by the Russian physicist, L. A. Kubetsky, in August 1930. See "On the history of photomultiplier tube invention," B. K. Lubsandorzhiev (*Nuclear Instruments and Methods in Physics Research Section A: Accelerators, Spectrometers, Detectors and Associated Equipment*, v. 567, issue 1, 2006).

The mission of the sensor developed by EMR for Apollo 17 was to detect faint sources of ultraviolet light in the heavens, against the blinding glare of visible light coming from the sun.

Why was Schlumberger developing light detectors when its main business was making measurements deep underground in oil reservoirs? The reason relates to the natural radioactivity of rocks. It had been known for many years that impermeable shale layers, which often form the cap rock of oil reservoirs, contained higher concentrations of radioactive elements than the rocks in the oil-bearing zones (usually sandstone and limestone). The naturally occurring radioactive elements are mainly potassium-40, thorium, and uranium. The radioactivity produced by these elements is emitted mostly in the form of gamma rays, which are high-energy photons of light. Thus, by recording a "gamma ray log" along the well, it was possible to identify shale layers that marked the boundaries of oil zones. The first gamma ray logs were recorded in the late 1930s by Well Surveys, Inc. (WSI), using a small Geiger counter.

W. G. Green and R. E. Fearon, 1940, Well Logging by Radioactivity, *Geophysics*, v. 40, p. 172 (presented at SEG Annual Meeting, Chicago, April 11, 1940).

In 1953, Doll learned that Jean-Pierre Causse, who had spent a year as an intern at Ridgefield, was finishing his military service at *l'Observatoire de Paris* (The Paris Observatory) in the laboratory of Professor André Lallemand, a French astrophysicist who was known for his contributions to the development of the first photomultiplier tubes and for his invention in 1937 of a sensitive electronic camera for astronomy. Doll offered Causse a job, but asked him to remain in Paris to learn about photomultipliers from Lallemand, before coming to Ridgefield to create a new photoelectric laboratory. The goal was development of a new photomultiplier for detecting gamma rays. Causse accepted.

Although gamma rays are photons, they are too energetic to be fed directly into a standard photomultiplier tube. So Causse's first task in Paris was to develop a front end to the photomultiplier in the form of a rugged "scintillator" – a material for converting a high-energy photon into several lower energy photons, which can then be channeled into the photomultiplier. Causse used a crystal of sodium iodide doped with thallium, a toxic metal used in rat poison. Crystals of sodium iodide are very stable, even at temperatures as high as 150°C (302°F), which can be encountered in deep boreholes.

The difficult part was to develop a high-temperature photocathode. The best photocathodes of the time were made from cesium and antimony (CsSb), but the cesium evaporated at temperatures as low as 50°C (122°F), which reduced the sensitivity of the photomultiplier. After many attempts, Lallemand and Causse discovered that a material made from layers of sodium-potassium-antimony (Na-K-Sb) was nearly as sensitive as cesium-antimony, but was much more resistant to heat.

This work in Lallemand's laboratory took about a year. Causse arrived in Ridgefield in 1955 and immediately set up a laboratory for producing the new detector for well logging. The first goal was a photo-multiplier tube two inches (five centimeters) in diameter, which would fit into most boreholes; the next goal was a smaller sensor, about one inch (2.54 centimeters) in diameter, which would fit into a tool that descended through the narrow inner "tubing" that is inserted into cased boreholes to isolate production from layers at different depths. Causse's new sensors were the most sensitive and rugged gamma ray detectors ever built. Manufactured by EMR, these thin sensors and their succes-sors descended through many thousands of feet of boreholes around the world, recording gamma ray logs for the oil industry.

A few of them traveled much farther in the opposite direction. The exploration of space began with the "surprise" launch of Sputnik by the Soviet Union in 1957; a few months later, President Eisenhower created the National Aeronautics and Space Administration (NASA) to respond to the Soviet challenge. One of NASA's earliest scientific mis-sions was mapping solar and stellar ultraviolet radiation in space, before it is absorbed by the earth's atmosphere. Specialists in photom-etry at NASA's Goddard Space Flight Center in Greenbelt, Maryland, heard of Causse's rugged photomultiplier and asked him to design a detector of ultraviolet radiation that would survive the rigors of a launch into outer space.

Schlumberger gave approval to Causse to work on the problem, and his research group was transferred to a small company in Princeton, New Jersey, called ASCOP, which EMR had purchased. In six months, Causse and his team delivered to NASA the first dozen rugged photomultipliers that were capable of detecting ultraviolet radiation without being blinded by visible light. These sensors were deployed on several NASA missions, and helped to advance the field of ultraviolet astronomy in the 1960s. They reached the moon with Apollo 17 in an experiment to detect weak light emitted from inter-stellar hydrogen gas, and traveled to the outer reaches of the solar system on the Pioneer probes.

Electro-Mechanical Research did other work in remote sensing for the United States military and also helped NASA develop one of the earliest digital telecommunication systems for the Apollo missions. The small company created by Doll, André Istel, and John Bullington to help the Army Corps of Engineers develop better mine detectors had traveled much farther than its founders ever imagined.

Causse left Schlumberger in the early 1960s and returned to France where he became one of the founders of France's National Center of Space Studies (CNES, for *Centre National d'Études Spatiales*). He directed the development of the first French satellites and those of the European Space Agency (ESA). In his acceptance speech for the Marcel Dassault Prize of the French Academy of Sciences in 2002, he praised "Henri-Georges Doll, who directed research at Schlumberger when I arrived there. I admire the energy and the faith in the future that he showed in launching this daring program to introduce new nuclear measurements [to the oil industry] which one day could replace his own inventions. It's a rare thing for an inventor not to favor his own inventions over those of others."

Research at Schlumberger had contributed to the space program, Causse emphasized, but Schlumberger had also benefited enormously from this work: "It was work on the space program that kept EMR-Photoelectric alive during the many years it took for Schlumberger engineering to digest the revolutionary possibilities of the photomultiplier and start to order them in large quantities."

Newer generations of the sensors developed by Causse and his team are still being improved and manufactured in a small plant in New Jersey that Causse established in 1960, which is now called Schlumberger Princeton Technology Center.

"When Doll had an idea," Causse recalled, "he wanted to follow it. He would call you at ten o'clock at night to get you started down the track. He wasn't always right, of course, and it wasn't always easy to convince him of that. But his creativity always fascinated me. It took a

Jean-Pierre Causse, around 1961 (Photo by Inge Morath, Magnum Agency).

lot of nerve to start with a modest lab and no real experience with high technology. Competing…with the world's best laboratory in photoelectricity, RCA Laboratories in Princeton, was a huge gamble.

"I went with Professor Lallemand and Doll," Causse continued, "to the home of Maurice Ponte, who was then president and managing director of CSF, the largest French company building photoelectric devices. Doll and Ponte were happy to cooperate, but the technicians of CSF were frightened by the difficulty of the project and proposed that Schlumberger take all the risk. After thinking about this, Doll decided to go it alone. I tip my hat to that. The spirit he breathed into Ridgefield was simple: No technology could be ignored that might help in finding oil."

Doll himself put it this way, "To polish what you already know today and not get on with the things of tomorrow – that's not interesting for me." It was close to something his uncle-in-law Marcel Schlumberger had said. "The moment that it's necessary to prepare for the future," Marcel had told Annette, "you have to start working with the tools of tomorrow. You can't wait a year for them."

Chapter 20

Schlumberger without the Schlumbergers

By 1956, the Schlumberger group of companies had nearly 4000 employees worldwide and revenues of more than $100 million a year. Marcel Schlumberger had turned 69 in 1953, and his health was failing. "My motor is stalling," he had told his wife early in the year. His close friends and direct employees had noticed that he had become more severe, more direct in his criticisms, and more demanding.

He was worried about the future of the company that he and his brother Conrad had created and that he had directed for more than 20 years.

"Schlumberger" was actually divided into four large entities, each under the direction of a family member, but all under the uncontested authority of Marcel.

Schlumberger operations in Europe were directed from Paris by René Seydoux, son-in-law of Marcel. Also in Paris since May 1951 was Jean Riboud, son of Camille Riboud, a prominent banker from Lyon who had been a childhood friend of Maurice Schlumberger (in their youth, Camille and Maurice had taken a trip around the world together). Jean Riboud had been hired by Marcel on the advice of André Istel. He was not a scientist, but had studied law and politics at *Sciences Po*, the Institute for the Study of Political Science in Paris.

During the summer of 1943, Riboud was taken prisoner by the Germans when he tried to join the forces of Free France in North Africa. He survived internment in Buchenwald. Released in April 1945, he had gone to New York to work with André Istel, who had founded his own company (André Istel & Company). With Istel, Riboud took part in the financial management of Schlumberger and became a friend of the family (Henri-Georges, Annette, and other Schlumberger family members attended Riboud's wedding in Connecticut in October 1949). Riboud started to work at *la Pros* in Paris in May 1951.

Schlumberger operations in South America and the Middle East were directed by Jean de Ménil, son-in-law of Conrad. De Ménil had reorganized Schlumberger networks broken by the war. He created Surenco, based in Caracas, to organize work in South America, and Schlumberger Overseas, to organize work in the Far East. He had also started the conversion of Schlumberger into a modern international company – rationalizing salaries for engineers working in different countries (by re-aligning them to the highest salaries), creating a retirement fund, and enforcing the use of English, the language of the oil field, for company business. De Ménil had also created the motto, "Wherever the drill goes, Schlumberger goes."

By the mid-1950s, Schlumberger operations in North America were being directed from Houston by Pierre Schlumberger, son of Marcel, and president of Schlumberger Well Surveying Corporation, the largest and most profitable branch of the company. Pierre was the only heir to the family name, but he had a reputation for being a fragile personality and not very communicative – at times even silent.

Pierre nevertheless had a strong business sense. "Pierre was a remarkable man," recalled Bruno Desforges, who worked at Istel & Co. and had met Pierre on several occasions. "Lepercq [an assistant to Istel and longtime board member of Schlumberger] often said to me that, of the men that he had met, Pierre was the one who had made an impression on him and influenced him, not only in a business sense, but in all ways." In April 1953, Pierre had opened up a large new center for SWSC in Houston, entertaining more than 8000 guests from the oil industry. (His father Marcel did not attend. Though he did not hesitate to travel to see a client, Marcel was not keen on receptions.)

Finally, Schlumberger research was directed from Ridgefield by Henri-Georges Doll, the husband of Conrad's daughter Annette. Two other members of the Schlumberger family were also in Ridgefield: Éric Boissonnas, the husband of Conrad's daughter Sylvie, and Jean Lebel, an engineer and the husband of Doll's daughter, Clarisse. One more member of the family soon joined Doll at Ridgefield: Arnaud de

Phillip Johnson Building at Schlumberger Ridgefield Division Research Center (Photo by Kenneth Winkler, Schlumberger-Doll Research).

Vitry, another *polytechnician,* who in 1953 married Doll's youngest daughter, Henriette.

In 1951, a new building designed by the famous American architect Philip Johnson was built to house the administrative offices and research labs at Ridgefield. Electro-Mechanical Research (EMR) was also still in Ridgefield, but its status as a Schlumberger company was ambiguous. Schlumberger Well Surveying Coporation was a part owner of EMR, but Doll, André Istel, and two of Istel's friends were major shareholders. In Houston, EMR was sometimes derisively called *la chapelle de Doll* ("the chapel of Doll"). Doll was president of EMR, but he was also preoccupied by the larger Schlumberger center at Ridgefield.

"It was a little difficult to manage," Doll recalled, "I could not spend enough time there, could not create Ridgefield and continue to take care of EMR 100%."

"The shareholders of EMR, Mr. Istel in particular," Doll continued, "had asked if it would not be better for Schlumberger to take over EMR again. The answer of the management of Schlumberger was, 'Well, we will see what it is worth.' Well, there was nothing in it at the time. There were no capital assets, no buildings, nothing of what is called 'book value.' From the point of view of the company, it was worth less than the money that had been invested in it and, consequently, was not worth the price [of its original shares]. That was more or less the response...from Pierre, and Mr. Istel thought that it was quite simply not acceptable."

But the status of EMR remained unchanged. "We put a little more money in it," Doll recalled, "and built a building that was along the road leading to the quarry." EMR continued to generate interesting new projects. A research group in analog and digital telemetry was added in the early 1950s (this group developed the telemetry systems that were used in the Apollo program); later, EMR purchased a new nuclear magnetic resonance (NMR) spectrometer and developed applications of NMR for determining the moisture content in food for cattle, paper pulp, tobacco, and cereals.

On August 20, 1953, Marcel Schlumberger died of heart failure. In addition to his many inventions, he left the company he had led for more than 20 years a striking motto, which was one of his favorite sayings: "To think for oneself, to have an independent mind. Not to follow fashion, not to become part of the establishment."

Marcel had relied on Doll for technical and scientific leadership, but also for managing people behind the scenes, for settling internal conflicts, and for safeguarding the family's interests. "[Marcel] wanted me to take over after his death," Doll said. "But when he died, nobody else wanted that; there were many candidates."

One month later, in September 1953, Arnaud de Vitry started work at EMR, helping to manage the center with Doll, who had reassured him that EMR would not be repurchased by Schlumberger. But in March 1954, de Vitry was called to New York for a meeting with Pierre Schlumberger and Jean de Ménil. He was told, to his surprise, that Schlumberger had repurchased EMR. De Ménil offered de Vitry a choice: Prove yourself to Schlumberger by working in the field at Lake Maracaibo in Venezuela for fifteen years, or prove yourself in some other company.

Henriette was present at the discussion between her husband, cousin, and uncle, and still harbors bad memories from the meeting. "I felt it was a little like a trial," she said recently. Her husband made his choice a few days after the meeting. De Vitry left Schlumberger and went on to prove himself quite successfully, including as a financer of Digital Equipment Company, the first large manufacturer of mini-computers. (DEC was one of the world's fastest growing companies in the 1960s and 1970s and was later purchased by Compaq, which itself was acquired by HP in 2002.) He always maintained cordial relations with Schlumberger and served on its board of directors.

In fact, neither Pierre Schlumberger nor Jean de Ménil had any malice toward Arnaud de Vitry. They were abiding by a new policy that Pierre and Jean Riboud had agreed on, with Marcel's blessing.

In the autumn of 1950, Marcel had spent a few days in Ridgefield during which he had long conversations with his niece. "I know that

Marcel feared," Annette wrote in her memoir, "that his end, which he felt was near, might expose conflicts that could destroy the work to which he and his brother had given the best of themselves. This premonition of Marcel materialized even quicker than he feared. With him gone, each one [of his possible successors] felt responsible for the enterprise; each wanted what the other had; each had his own reasons to destroy an edifice from the past that the present did not want."

During his visit, Marcel asked Annette what she thought of Jean Riboud. Annette, who had met and become friends with Riboud, told him, "I believe he has heart, how to say it, a human touch. It is a rare quality for somebody dedicated to high finance. If you are thinking about hiring him, it would surprise me if he disappoints you."

Marcel replied: "Yes. I find him appealing. …I would not know how to use him. Finance is not our field, and I do not believe in it."

A few months earlier, in July 1950, Marcel had invited Riboud to lunch in Paris. He learned that Riboud wanted to leave Istel & Co., but did not know what he was going to do. Perhaps open a bookstore, he

Marcel Schlumberger in a logging truck during a 1948 visit to El Tigre, Venezuela.

told Marcel. Marcel suggested that Riboud come to work for him at Schlumberger, but told him, "I do not have the least idea what you will do." Riboud accepted.

Jean Riboud joined Schlumberger in May 1951, and worked closely with Marcel. "During the first year, I did not do anything except listen to Marcel," Riboud recalled in a long interview with Ken Auletta for *The Art of Corporate Success.* "To take Jean Riboud under his wing," Annette wrote in her memoir, "form him in his school, and bequeath to him the stamp of his authority was, to his thinking, the way to avoid the worst."

Riboud eventually became CEO of Schlumberger Limited, the holding company that he helped the family set up after Marcel's death. In the 1960s, he would complete the transformation of Schlumberger into a modern multinational corporation, in part by diversifying its ownership and reducing the influence of the family.

Doll participated in the heated, sometimes "explosive discussions" (as Attali remembers them) about the future of the company following Marcel's death. But as Causse recalled, "He did not like the conflicts. Instead of managing them, he put himself in the corner."

There was another reason for Doll's detachment. He and Annette were growing apart. Doll lived by himself in Ridgefield; Annette lived in New York with her daughters, but often brought them to see him during the weekends. "He adored the children," Annette wrote. "He sometimes watched them sleep, with a candle in hand.

"When, how," she continued, "had the desire grown in me to break the bonds? By what unlikely ways did I resolve to do it? All that I know is that one day, just like all the other days of my life, the cup suddenly overflowed, and I tore up the roots of my past."

Doll, for his part, had met the woman with whom he would spend the rest of his life. The meeting took place on March 1, 1953. Henriette remembers the precise date, because it was her birthday and the year of her marriage. Guitou Knoop introduced Doll to Eugénia Delarova. Génia, as she was called, was born in 1910 in Saint Petersburg, and had attended the ballet school of the Marinski Theatre there. She immigrated to Germany with her mother, who left Saint Petersburg after the death of her husband and the rise of the Soviets. Génia then went to Paris to continue studying ballet.

Génia married Léonide Massine in 1929 and, before their divorce in 1939, the couple toured with the Russian ballet in Europe and the United States. Genia moved to New York after World War II, where she danced at the Roxy Theatre and on Broadway, and was part of the Ziegfeld Follies.

"In the beginning," remembers Henriette, "it was just to pass a few evenings, but my father was not that kind of man, and so immediately it became serious. He asked for a divorce, because he wanted to marry Génia. Mama said no. Then my father, who was a perfect gentleman, said, 'My dear, I won't bring it up again, and I will remain always your best friend.' Then, ten years later, Mama met the neurologist Jean Gruner, and it was she who asked for a divorce. But while waiting, Mama wanted her freedom and she wanted Papa to have his. So my mother bought a bachelor pad for Papa in New York. She had it set up and furnished."

Génia did not visit Doll in Ridgefield, and nobody in the center was aware that anything had changed. Doll never spoke about his private life. Nick Schuster remembers his wife, Mary, often brought the children to Ferndale, the Dolls' home in Ridgefield, so that they could play in the yard. Doll would invite them in to have lunch. "We finally got to know Mr. Doll very well," Schuster said. "To this day, Mary and I have trouble saying 'Doll' without 'Mr.' in front of it. Finally, he told us, 'Call me Henry.' But neither Mary nor I could do it. He called me by my first name, but it always sounded strange to me."

Annette no longer came to Ridgefield. Doll himself was often absent from the lab. For years, he had driven to work in the same car, an old Cadillac he had bought during the war years. Then, one day he arrived at the lab in a brand new white Jaguar convertible.

Something had changed.

Research program

①   5 galvanometer recorder.

①   3 conductor cable multifrequency equipment

2 ①   simplified recorder and circuit for core drills

①   Insulated weight adaptor

①   Insulated weight

②   Vibrator for alternating S. P.

②   Acoustic logging.

②   Gamma rays logging

④   Induction logging for oil drilled wells

④   Apparatus to measure flow of individual holes in producing wee

④   Apparatus to take average sample of liquid at different beds in producing well.

⑤   Apparatus to measure resistivity of first few inches near hole

④   New gun perforator

③   Apparatus to test pressure and permeability of porous beds.

    Photocell controled torpedo

④   Tele metering of small potential differences
(D.C. amplifier → potential to frequency converter — short wave transm
electronic frequency meter → recorder).

④   Non vibrating galvanometer.

④   Larger size sample taker —

3 ④   Formation tester

②   Caliper

④   Lateral investigation, curves

②   Lateral investigation logging. S. L. curve by multielectrode and cathode ray oscillograph.

Henri-Georges Doll's list of research projects, 1941.

Chapter 21

Epilogs

Doll made his first major presentation to the American Institute of Mining and Metallurgical Engineers (AIME) in February 1948 at the society's winter meeting in New York City. The topic was not the new induction log, for which he had just filed patents, but a subject which had fascinated him for nearly twenty years, since he had seen the needle of the potentiometer vibrating back and forth at Greater Seminole Oil Field in Oklahoma. The title of the paper was "The S.P. Log: Theoretical Analysis and Principles of Interpretation."

Five years earlier, at the May 1943 meeting of the AIME in Dallas, Texas, two scientists from Humble Oil, Whitman Mounce and William Rust, Jr., had proposed that the chief source of the spontaneous potential (SP) observed in oil wells was not a streaming potential, as Doll had hypothesized to Conrad Schlumberger in 1931, but instead was electrochemistry. The source, they claimed, was a chain of reactions driven by chemical differences between drilling mud, fluids in permeable underground reservoirs, and clay particles in impermeable beds (usually shale) surrounding the reservoirs. It was essentially the same conclusion that Conrad Schlumberger had drawn after hearing of Doll's experiments with SP logs in the oil fields at Grozny and Baku in 1932.

The first line of Mounce and Rust's paper showed how far the oil industry had come since Seminole. "The extraordinary value of electrical well logging," they wrote, "is now so universally recognized that it is not necessary to point out the ways in which it can be useful. It is sufficient to mention only the saving that has resulted from the elimination of much coring data that would have been necessary under former practices and the considerable additions to reserves resulting from the discovery of sands missed in coring."

"Paradoxically," the paper continued, "the very remarkable success that has resulted from the application of electrical logging to correlation and completion problems has cost some of its most consistent users dearly. The fact that some operators have placed unwarranted faith in erroneous interpretations of electrical logs does not reduce the value of the logs. It should, however, make one pause long enough to ask why experienced users should be misled. The answer to this question is not hard to find. In nearly every case, the fault has been oversimplification. This is illustrated very aptly by the familiar interpretation and theory of the natural potential log."

Mounce and Rust presented results from two sets of experiments performed on core samples in the research labs of Humble Oil. The first experiments showed that a streaming potential, caused by drilling mud flowing under pressure into permeable layers, could generate only about 10% of the spontaneous potential signal normally recorded by well logs. The second experiments showed that electrochemistry could generate the rest. The key ingredient was clay. The presence of clay particles in impermeable shale layers sitting atop permeable reservoirs appeared to amplify the electrochemical potential caused by differences in salt concentration between the drilling mud and the reservoir fluids.

Mounce and Rust could not explain how clay amplified the SP signal. "The mechanism is not clearly understood," they wrote (it would remain obscure for many years). But their conclusion – that electrochemistry involving clay drives "90 per cent or so" of the SP signal in oil wells – held up against later work, and is generally accepted today as the correct explanation of SP logs.

A similar proposal had been made by Parke Dickey of Forest Oil Corporation in a presentation made to the New York meeting of the AIME in April 1943. Dickey had measured natural electrical potentials between sandstone and shale in a mine shaft that passed through an oil-bearing layer. The mine was near the city of Franklin, Pennsylvania, which is close to Titusville, where Edwin Drake drilled the first oil well in 1859.

Conrad Schlumberger's tabletop experiment in Paris in 1932 was similar to the one described by Mounce and Rust in their 1943 paper, but it showed a much smaller effect of the clay. One important difference between the experiments is that Mounce and Rust used actual cores of shale, whereas Conrad used clay slurry packed in flexible porous sleeves (which the staff at rue Fabert jokingly called "Conrad's sausages").

A curious feature of Mounce and Rust's paper, which is a classic of modern geophysics, is that it contains no mention of Schlumberger. Gus Archie of Shell Oil and Carl Heiland, a professor at the Colorado School of Mines, pointed this out in the discussion following Rust's presentation (Rust was the junior author; Mounce was on war leave from Humble Oil, working at the Naval Ordnance Laboratory in Washington, D.C.) Rust explained, "The work of the Schlumberger organization was not referred to in this article because the listeners to whom it was presented were already fully aware of the very important contributions of the Schlumberger organization to the art of electrical well logging. Both Dr. Heiland

and Mr. Archie correctly point out the similarity between the experiments described in our paper and the Schlumberger experiments described in volume 110 of the *Transactions*. The difference lies in the quantitative results and, consequently, in the practical importance ascribed to the phenomena."

When Doll took the podium at the AIME meeting on February 16, 1948, his own scientific work on electrical logging was still relatively unknown. Few people outside Schlumberger knew about his contributions to development of the first electrical log and or about his invention of the SP log with Conrad Schlumberger. It may have been tempting to set the historical record straight at the meeting in New York, but Doll was more interested in the future.

His paper on SP assimilated the work of Mounce and Rust with his own work and that of Conrad and laid out the first complete theory for the practical interpretation of SP logs. The major innovation in Doll's paper was aimed directly at the "oversimplification" that Mounce and Rust had identified as a chief problem of log interpretation. Doll showed that it was possible with modern mathematical and computing methods to calculate model SP logs for much more realistic geologic formations than had ever been attempted before. The models included formations with geological layers of varying thickness and composition stacked together and penetrated by boreholes of different diameter, filled with mud of different chemical compositions.

The computations were at the limit of what was possible at the time with "paper and pencil." Doll had started the project in the 1930s at rue Saint-Dominique in Paris, much of it was done in collaboration with Géza Kunetz, a talented young Hungarian mathematician who was working as an intern at *la Pros.* (Kunetz had tutored Marcel Schlumberger's son Pierre, when he was studying for the French *baccalauréat*. Kunetz later became the chief scientist of CGG.)

For the most complex model, Doll assembled a small analog computer to carry out the computations. It consisted of a network of electrical circuits (resistors) arranged in space to simulate the path followed by electrical current as it flowed from the borehole mud into permeable underground layers and flanking shale beds. Within a few years, an entire room at the new lab in Ridgefield was devoted to assembling networks consisting of thousands of resistors and capacitors to simulate current flow in three-dimensional underground formations. These "resistor networks" were used to compute log interpretation charts for Schlumberger until the 1980s, when they were fully replaced by digital computers.

Doll's presentation on SP in New York was the first of five papers given at successive AIME meetings from 1948 to 1952, in which he helped to recast electrical logging into a modern quantitative science. In the second paper, presented in February 1949 at the AIME meeting in San Francisco, Doll introduced induction logging to the oil industry. This paper also contained Doll's new "geometrical factor theory," based on Francis Perrin's mathematical analysis of electromagnetic induction. Geometrical factor theory showed how to isolate the contributions of different regions near the borehole to the signals recorded during induction logging and how to identify the "true resistivity" of the reservoir, undisturbed by the borehole.

At the February 1950 meeting of the AIME in New York, Doll unveiled the "microlog," a device that he had invented to identify thin permeable zones intersected by the borehole. The microlog used a flexible rubber pad to push three small electrodes directly against the borehole wall. The pad was developed in Houston by André Blanchard, who had worked at Michelin before joining Schlumberger. The three electrodes on the pad were arranged in the same configuration that Conrad and Doll had used for the first electrical log at Pechelbronn: A current electrode A was situated beneath two potential electrodes M_1 and M_2, while the return electrode B was placed in the well a long distance from the pad. The distance between the electrodes on the pad, however, was only a few inches, so that the device could measure the resistivity of a small volume of rock just behind the "mudcake" that coated the borehole wall after drilling.

The first tests of the microlog along the Gulf Coast showed that it could identify, much more precisely than the SP log, the boundaries between permeable and impermeable layers that marked the top of reservoirs, and that it could also find thin permeable zones missed entirely by other logs or cores. The microlog would also prove useful in logging permeable zones in thick, highly resistive limestone formations where the SP log was ineffective, such as the huge reservoirs of the Middle East.

At the AIME meeting in St. Louis in February 1951, Doll presented a new electrode device for resistivity logging called the "laterolog." (It was at this meeting in St. Louis that Doll and Maurice Martin interviewed Nick Schuster, who was finishing his graduate studies at Washington University.) The laterolog used principles of automatic feedback – similar to ones EMR had developed in its research on guided missiles during the war – to focus "beams" of electrical current into the formation directly opposite the tool. It was the first major innovation in electrode measurements since the original conceptions of Conrad Schlumberger, and would remain an oil industry standard for almost fifty years.

Finally, at the October 1952 meeting of the AIME in Houston, Texas, Doll introduced the "microlaterolog." This tool used the same dynamic focusing principles of the laterolog, but like the microlog was deployed on a pad pressed against the borehole wall. The microlaterolog forced current through the mudcake to measure the resistivity of the region very close to the well (less than 40 inches away), which was often disturbed by drilling mud leaking out of the borehole. Knowing the resistivity of this "invaded zone," it was then possible to estimate the true resistivity of the reservoir undisturbed by drilling fluids. With the true resistivity and Archie's law – along with the porosity determined from cores or, eventually, from nuclear logs – it was possible to determine the oil saturation of the reservoir. This calculation has been performed in nearly every oil well drilled around the world for the last sixty years.

A new physical measurement was added to electrical and nuclear well logging in the years following World War II. In 1947, while preparing the move to Ridgefield, Doll wrote a memo proposing that Schlumberger resume research that he and Conrad had done in the 1930s on measuring acoustic (sound) waves in boreholes. Their idea had been to characterize different geological layers by the speed at which sound waves traveled through the rocks. The speed of sound in air is 332 meters per second (about 1090 feet per second), a figure that had been determined accurately for the first time by the French Academy of Sciences in 1738. The speed is much higher in fluids and solids and varies considerably depending on their composition, temperature, and pressure. The speed of sound in water is 1439 meters per second at 8°C (46°F) and atmospheric pressure; in sandstone, it is about 2000 meters per second; in hard limestone, it can be as high as 5000 meters per second.

In 1934, Conrad built an experimental "sonic" logging tool at rue Fabert, which was tested at Pechelbronn and patented in 1935. The source of sound was a powerful electrical horn, which was lowered to the bottom of the well. Two microphones, placed at different depths in the well, transmitted the sound recorded downhole to an operator at the surface wearing headphones. The idea was for the operator to listen for differences as the microphones were moved along the well. The tests yielded no coherent results, only an amusing anecdote: As the horn was blasting away during one of the experiments, the engineer suddenly heard a voice coming over the headphones: "It's the trilobites down here. Leave us alone!"

In the 1940s, several major oil companies, including Humble Oil, Shell, and Magnolia Oil (an affiliate of Mobil), had also done research on a sonic logging system that could be used to calibrate the seismic reflection method. By this time, the reflection method had progressed rapidly with developments in electronics during the war and dominated surface exploration for oil and gas. The chief difficulty with the method was converting the travel times of seismic reflections recorded at the surface into the depth of geological structures that generated the

Jean-Claude Legrand, Henri-Georges Doll, and Raymond Sauvage in the library at Ridgefield in the 1950s.

echoes. To do this accurately, it was necessary to know the speed of sound in all of the geological layers from the surface down to the structure of interest. This information was nearly impossible to obtain with surface measurements, but in principle could easily be obtained by measurements in a well.

Following Doll's research note, Frank Kokesh, an engineer from SWSC in Houston, developed an experimental sonic logging tool and carried out a series of tests in 1952. The new tool used a modified perforating gun as its source of sound waves. The gun could fire up to twenty-four blank charges into the borehole wall at different depths in the well, while a geophone recorded the sound waves at the surface. The charge in the gun, however, was not strong enough for use in deep oil wells. Waves generated at depths below 1000 meters (3280 feet) were too weak to be detected at the surface, and the tool was used only in shallow reconnaissance wells.

The first viable sonic logging tool came from the research laboratory of Magnolia Oil. The key development was a new electronic circuit
that was fast enough to record tiny differences in the time it took a
sound wave to travel from a source at one end of a logging tool to two
microphones placed a short distance apart at the other end. The experimental tool built by Magnolia Oil was tested successfully in 1954.
Schlumberger obtained a license from Mobil Oil for the device, which
was the basis of the sonic logging tool commercialized in the 1950s.

The sonic log found an unexpected application in Archie's law.
After its first tests, Tom Hingle, a geologist working for Magnolia,
noticed that the sound speed measured in different geological layers
was correlated inversely with the porosity measured on core samples
(the higher the porosity, the slower the sound speed). The correlation
was quantified mathematically in a "time-average formula," according
to which the time taken by a sound wave to travel a certain distance in
a porous rock was expressed as the average of the time spent in the
solid matrix and the (longer) time spent in the fluid-filled pore space
(M.R.J. Wyllie, A.R. Gregory, and L.W. Gardner, Elastic Wave Velocity
in Heterogeneous and Porous Media, *Geophysics*, 1956, v. 21, pp. 41-70).
During the 1950s and early 1960s, while the neutron porosity log was
still being perfected, porosities derived from sonic logs were used rou-
tinely in Archie's law.

In the late 1950s, a rugged new gamma ray detector built by EMR allowed
development of a new logging tool that determined the density of rocks along the
borehole by measuring the absorption of gamma rays. The source of gamma rays
was a tiny sample of cesium or americium, two highly radioactive elements. The
research on the new measurement was done by Jay Tittman, at the request of the
Schlumberger field manager in Maracaibo, Venezuela, who was familiar with
similar techniques used in laboratories. It took several years to solve problems of
deploying the new measurement in a borehole, but the "gamma-gamma" log
eventually became the standard for measuring density – and, indirectly, porosity –
in underground reservoirs.

The Schlumberger field organization in Maracaibo also discovered a new application of the sonic log. In the late 1950s, Pierre Majani, the head of the division, and Alan Rushton, a field engineer, noticed that sonic logs showed unusual features ("anomalies") at certain depths when the tool was run inside cased wells. The depths of the anomalies turned out to be correlated with levels where there was a poor bond between the steel casing and the cement used to set it in place. With a few modifications, the sonic tool generated a "cement bond log," which is still one of its chief uses.

In 1956, Schlumberger recorded its one millionth well log. Doll's scientific activity at the time was focused primarily on devising better methods of interpreting well logs. Interpretation is compared sometimes to the problem faced by Zadig, a character in Voltaire who manages to describe a horse he has never seen by observing the size of its hoof prints and their separations in the grass, the height of the tree branches broken off along a path, and the color of tuffs of hair left here and there; or to the method used by Sherlock Homes to identify a suspect by analyzing the ashes of a cigarette, the wear on a pair of shoes, and the drops of rain falling off an umbrella – a collection of things which taken individually mean nothing, but can be assembled like the pieces of a puzzle to infer a complete picture.

In log interpretation, the data collected in downhole measurements – the resistivities of different regions surrounding the wells, the diameter of the well and composition of the mud, the porosity of the rocks along the borehole wall, and the speed of sound in the rock layers – must be assimilated by the interpreter in the context of the geological history of the region.

"Doll could wear both caps," Georges Attali said in a recent interview. "He understood the physics – especially electromagnetics – but he also knew how to interpret the logs, to understand what the different curves could mean geologically." Attali remembered discussions *ad infinitum* among Doll, Tixier, Martin, and Sauvage about which logs were needed in certain oil fields to discern the full picture. In the late

1950s, the four *anciens* wrote a series of papers on the physics and geology of log interpretation. The papers are still read today.

"It was also not surprising," Attali continued, "that Doll wanted to buy powerful computers as soon as they were available. I bought the first computer at Ridgefield; it was enormous and needed its own room for special air-conditioning. I was asked, 'What are you going to do with that?' But as soon as it was installed, it was saturated."

In the mid-1950s, the induction log became a victim of its own success. This new tool for measuring the resistivity of oil reservoirs was not only providing more accurate readings than electrode tools, but it was also smaller and easier to deploy. Soon after its introduction, the induction log was being used in wells drilled with water-base mud, which created problems because the high conductivity of the mud itself generated a large signal that masked the information coming from the geological layers surrounding the borehole.

Attali had been hired by Doll in 1954 to do research in Ridgefield on induction logging, but while waiting for an American visa, he received a phone call. "We changed our minds," Doll told him. "You are going to start work in Houston." When he arrived in Houston, Attali attended a public oil-industry workshop, at which a competitor claimed that the Schlumberger induction tool was faulty. A few months later, the same competitor brought out its own induction tool, which was claimed to have a much deeper depth of investigation, and therefore less sensitivity to "borehole effects," than the Schlumberger tool.

At the time, Denis Tanguy, a French engineer who had joined Schlumberger in the early 1950s, was the head of the electrical engineering department at SWSC. Tanguy recalled arriving at work one Monday morning and being summoned immediately to the office of Bill Gillingham, the general manager of SWSC. Gillingham told him, "Denis, the competition has a better induction tool than Schlumberger. I phoned Mr. Doll who is in Paris and told him that I need a new induction with deeper radial investigation. I also phoned Nick Schuster [Schuster had been temporarily reassigned from SWSC to EMR in Sarasota]. And you, you will have to put everything together."

Within a few months, Tanguy and his team had designed a new tool by modifying Doll's original geometrical arrangement of coils. Doll had also made his own design for a radical new tool that would record only raw signals downhole and store the results for processing later by a computer at the surface.

"It's important to realize something," Tanguy recalled recently. "Doll was always ahead of his time. He always wanted to do things at full speed, sometimes much too fast. And sometimes that was a source of problems for us in engineering. He didn't always recognize that other factors were at play and that, in the end, we could not always take our time and wait for research to finish its work. We needed something that worked and could be built quickly to respond to the competition. At least, that was how I felt at the time. Doll just moved too fast for the technology that was available to us then.

"On the other hand," Tanguy continued, "you can only imagine what Doll might have been able to do if he had had today's technology at his disposal. He didn't have fast telemetry systems or the chips we now put downhole to do calculations."

Doll's idea was rejected in favor of the design made by Tanguy's team. The new tool – called the "6FF40," for its six coils designed to probe the formation a distance of about 40 inches (one meter) from the borehole – became an oil industry standard for the next forty years.

(The tool that replaced the 6FF40 in the 1990s was actually built along the lines that Doll had sketched in the late 1950s. This device, called an array induction tool, uses a series of transmitter and receiver coils operating at several different frequencies to construct an image of electrical resistivity extending outward from the borehole wall into the geological formation. The complex calculations are usually performed at a computer center far from the oil well. Modeling the new tool during its development in the early 1990s required several months of intensive calculations on a CRAY supercomputer.)

In a September 1959 article in *Sonde Off*, an internal Schlumberger publication, Doll predicted, "Someday, we will record electronic impulses on tape, rather than light on film. The tape will be processed by a computing machine, which will make the necessary mathematical interpretations automatically. It is not impossible to foresee the day when we may drop one master combination tool in a well, run a survey in a matter of minutes, and hand the customer a complete analysis of his well in addition to a log."

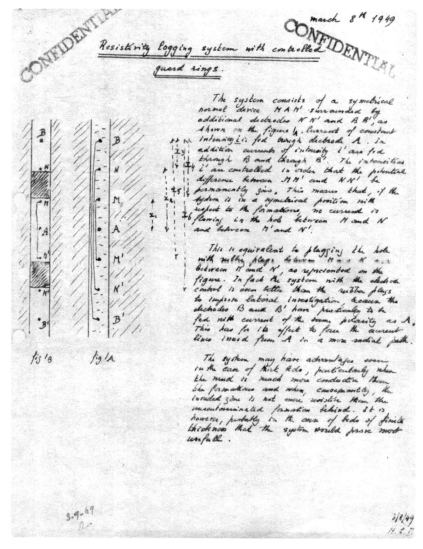

Page from Doll's notes on a new electrode device for resistivity logging, which would be called the "laterolog."

After ten years at Ridgefield, Doll had become an imposing figure in the oil industry. He held more than 70 patents in his name for inventions being used in nearly every oil field around the world. Articles in the press and in trade journals covering the oil industry spoke of "this analyst of well logs who talks like Charles Boyer, but knows physics, chemistry, and economics, and likes to solve problems." A company magazine called *Views of Schlumberger* published a cartoon by Norman James showing a man with a mustache sitting in the waiting room of the U.S. Patent Office holding in his lap a wooden log with a short electrical cord dangling from one end. There was no need to identify the person in the cartoon as Henri-Georges Doll.

Chapter 22

On Wall Street

In 1956, on the advice of Jean Riboud, the Schlumberger companies were regrouped within a single holding company, Schlumberger Limited. The new company was incorporated in Curaçao, Dutch Antilles, which was becoming a tax haven for multinational companies. Doll was elected chairman of the board, which included four other members of the Schlumberger family: Jean de Ménil, René Seydoux, Pierre Schlumberger, and Maurice Schlumberger (the younger brother of Conrad and Marcel).

Pierre Schlumberger was named president and chief executive officer of Schlumberger Limited. Jean Riboud supervised operations of the group. Éric Boissonnas remained vice president of technology and took over from Doll the responsibility for all aspects of technology development that did not touch directly on research.

Éric and his wife Sylvie built a house in New Canaan, Connecticut, about 12 miles (20 kilometers) from Ridgefield. An unusual modern design by Philip Johnson, it became one of the most architecturally famous homes of the twentieth century. Though not a creative scientist himself, Boissonnas was an accomplished organizer and kept informed of the latest research in many different areas. He was very effective at coordinating technology planning for the company.

Boissonnas shared Doll's approach to research and was not afraid to support bold projects – for example, he fully supported Doll's decision to create a photoelectric lab in Ridgefield, which put the new center into direct competition with RCA Laboratories in Princeton. But Boissonnas was often at odds with Pierre Schlumberger. "There never were two individuals," Annette wrote in her memoir, "who were less well suited to get along."

One Monday morning in the spring of 1957, the staff at Ridgefield found a notice pinned on the bulletin board just inside the entrance of the building. In the note, Boissonnas announced that he was resigning as technical director; he wished good health and a prosperous future to all of the staff at Ridgefield and their families. Shortly afterwards, the Boissonnas family returned to France.

The same year, Doll was immobilized for several weeks by a fracture of the thighbone. While walking home one evening from the lab, he had slipped on some ice and could not get back up. An operation was necessary to set the bone back in place. He was confined to a wheelchair for several months, then had to use walking sticks before recovering fully.

Doll was 55 years old, and could easily have stepped in to take over as director of Ridgefield after the sudden departure of Boissonnas. But Pierre wanted new management. It took several tries to settle on a lasting choice. Early in 1958, Clark Goodman was named director of research, but he started badly by trying to impose a rigid style of management on a lab that had been run informally for more than a decade. Within a few months, the staff was in an uproar, and Goodman was transferred to Houston (He left Schlumberger a few years later, after a controversy about his relationship to some companies Schlumberger Limited was interested in acquiring.)

André Blanchard took over as interim director for two months, until a new manager from outside Schlumberger, Paul Erlandson, an executive with Continental Can Company in New Jersey, was hired. Erlandson was a competent administrator, but was unfamiliar with the technology and business of the oil field.

In 1961, Nick Schuster, who had become the director of engineering at SWSC in Houston, was named vice president of technology, responsible for day-to-day management of both Houston and Ridgefield. "It was

In February 1962, shares of Schlumberger (SLB) were quoted for the first time on the New York Stock Exchange. Pierre Schlumberger (right) bought the first 100 shares. Henri-Georges Doll (left) was the first chairman of the board of Schlumberger Limited.

tough," Schuster recalled. "Every six weeks, I went to Ridgefield. I stayed there six weeks, and then came back to Houston for six weeks. That was my life for two years. I had two houses, two washing machines, two refrigerators, but only one wife. I could not keep it up, so they named Georges Attali director of research, and that worked very well."

Attali, whom Doll had hired after a one-hour interview in 1954, remained director of Ridgefield until his retirement in 1970.

After Boissonnas returned to France, Doll was the only member of the Schlumberger family left in Ridgefield. In October 1962, Pierre asked him to move to New York. Doll took with him a small group of engineers, including Philippe Souhaité, who had just arrived in Ridgefield from Venezuela, and Jean Dumanoir. He installed himself and the group in an office on Madison Avenue, and continued to work on problems of log interpretation that he, Raymond Sauvage, Maurice Martin, and M. P. Tixier had studied in the first years in Ridgefield. Though he spoke often with Attali and Schuster, Doll rarely returned to the research center.

"Doll could have said no, pounded on the table, and fought," Causse recalled. "But he was not like that at all. Doll's fault was that he liked too much what he was doing."

Pierre Schlumberger and the others managers of Schlumberger started tearing down *la chapelle Doll*. They sold Schlumberger Instruments Company (SICO), a small division of EMR that Doll had created to develop and manufacture systems for automation and control. Jean-Claude Legrand, who had taken over as director of EMR after Boissonnas's departure, decided to transfer the company's main division to Sarasota, Florida. Electro-Mechanical Research had developed a good business making telemetry systems for the aeronautics industry, including for NASA, and Legrand wanted to move to a region where labor was cheaper and he could build a large manufacturing center.

"It was Legrand's initiative," Schuster recalled. "Pierre approved it, but then got upset when all of the engineers quit." Legrand nevertheless managed to make the move successful and built a large telemetry business with EMR in Florida, which Schlumberger sold in the 1960s.

Doll and Génia Delarova had installed themselves in a row house on the East Side in New York, a brownstone on 78th Street, near 5th Avenue and Central Park. An original Mondrian, which had adorned Doll's office in Ridgefield, was joined by other modern paintings acquired by the couple, a mobile by Alexander Calder, and a silver box with the signatures of the 125 employees in Ridgefield, which Doll was given when he left the lab.

In 1962, Doll became an American citizen. "He was the most French of any American citizen," one of his friends remarked. That year, he also stopped smoking.

Doll and Génia rented and then purchased a house on Long Island in the town of Water Mill, near Southampton, about 90 miles (150 kilometers) east of New York City. The house, simple and functional, was close to the beach. The choice was without doubt determined by the presence nearby of a large Russian colony, where Génia had many friends.

The Dolls spent most of the summer there, and weekends during the spring. Doll bought a small sailboat and installed a workshop where his tools were carefully arranged.

At least one piece of Schlumberger business was conducted at Water Mill. In the 1960s, Riboud led negotiations for the first purchase by Schlumberger of a large public company, Daystrom, which specialized in measurement instruments and consumer electronics. At that time, Bruno Desforges was working for Istel & Co., which was financing the deal. He recalled that Riboud and Paul Lepercq (a director of Istel) were preparing the final press release for Wall Street late one Friday, when one of them suddenly said, "Hold on. Maybe before we issue this to the press, we should tell the chairman of the board!" Lepercq and Desforges chartered a small plane to Water Mill to explain the deal to Doll, and the release was issued as planned.

On another occasion, Doll wrote to Pierre to thank him for the Schlumberger annual report, which had been sent to him at the same time it was sent to the other shareholders. "A surprise to me," Doll wrote, "especially since the first page...bears my signature."

In January 1957, Pierre's wife, Claire Simone, died suddenly in her sleep, of heart failure. A mother of five children, she was only 41 years old at the time of her death. For a year and a half, Pierre Schlumberger shut himself at home, making only rare appearances at his office. He often showed up hours late for board meetings. (Pierre later met a young Portuguese woman whom he married. The couple embarked on an active social life in café society.)

Bruno Desforges recalled that Pierre had become "personally different. He slept during the day and lived at night; habits that were incompatible with the management of a big company." One day Pierre called a meeting of the treasurer, Lepercq, and Desforges. "Pierre did not speak," Desforges recalls. "We were all sitting at a table, except Pierre, who was lighting cigarettes, one after another and walking around the office like a big cat, without saying a word. We were worried about him. He was inaccessible. When you called him, he would often answer the phone and then stay silent for a long time, to the point that the operator intervened to ask if the communication was over."

Schlumberger Limited went public on the New York Stock Exchange on February 2, 1962. A total of 4,703,767 shares of "SLB" were created; an additional 629,820 shares were distributed to shareholders of Daystrom, which became a subsidiary. Most of the shares of SLB were still held by members of the family. Pierre Schlumberger paid $8450 to buy the first 100 shares sold on the market.

Annette Doll kept the shares she had inherited from her father, Conrad, which now represented a considerable fortune. Doll had acquired his own shares through stock option grants and through an employee stock-option purchase plan (which de Ménil had put in place). Doll rarely discussed his personal finances with colleagues, but Jean Suau remembers that one day, when the subject came up in conversation, Doll said, "When I have money, I give it to Lepercq. When I need some, I ask Lepercq." Doll also became a multimillionaire after the public offering.

Pierre Schlumberger's erratic behavior began to concern the other members of the family, including Doll, Jean de Ménil, and René

Jean Riboud presenting Henri-Georges Doll a commemorative medal at his retirement in 1967.

Seydoux, all of whom were on the board of directors and were approaching retirement. Paul Lepercq, also on the board, talked with the major shareholders in the family, who all agreed that Pierre should be replaced.

"There had been 'coups d'état' at Schlumberger before," Desforges recalled, "but to remove Pierre was the most dramatic, a classic Greek tragedy in that it required the vote of his mother, his sisters, his first cousins, etc. It was necessary to save the company, but of course they could not tell Pierre before the vote. He might have tried to stop it." The family persuaded Pierre to resign and asked Riboud to become president and CEO Schlumberger Limited. He accepted on May 13, 1965. Doll remained chairman of the board.

About two years later, in July 1967, Doll retired, at the mandatory age of 65, which Riboud had fixed for all officers of the company.

But his career as a scientist was not over.

Génia and Henri-Georges Doll in their apartment on 5th Avenue in New York.
(Photo by Elizabeth Heyert for the magazine *Town and Country*, May 1983.)

Chapter 23

Patrons of the Arts

At the end of the 1960s, Annette Doll decided to remarry, and granted Henri-Georges a divorce. After more than ten years together, Doll married Eugénia Delarova, his *solnoutchka* ("little sun"). The civil ceremony was followed by a party at the St. Regis Hotel in New York City. About the same time, Annette married Jean Gruner, a neurologist. She and Doll remained good friends; when he wrote, he always addressed her as *ma chérie*.

When Doll retired from Schlumberger in August 1967, Jean Riboud presented him with a commemorative medal struck in his honor, resembling two medals the company had commissioned many years earlier in honor of Conrad and Marcel.

In a memo distributed to everyone in the company, Bill Gillingham, vice-president of Schlumberger Limited, summarized the enormous contribution Doll had made to Schlumberger: "Mr. Doll viewed the invention of the electric log as only a beginning. If the first rough measurements of resistivity were so interesting to the oil industry, what potential existed for more accurate measurements, for measurements of other physical properties? It is not an exaggeration to say that he was responsible for almost every one of the resistivity services we offer today, services that account for 40% of our wireline income.... Probably more important than his own technical achievements has been his influence on our research and development."

Though Doll missed working with the scientists at Ridgefield, he had found in New York City a new world that enthralled him. He had loved dance and ballet from a young age, and Génia introduced him to the artistic world that she had lived in since her childhood in Saint Petersburg.

"He discovered a world that he had not known before, the world of music and of culture," said Marina de Brantes, one of the couple's friends in New York. "Suddenly, he was confronted with real live artists, and for him, it was exciting." Many Russian artists, who had defected during tours in the West, found refuge at the home of the Dolls in New York City, including the violinist Mstislav Rostropovitch and his wife, the soprano Galina Vichnievskaya; and the dancers Rudolf Nureyev, Mikhail Baryshnikov, Sacha Godounov, and Nathalia Makarova. Makarova and Doll became friends, and she asked him to be a witness at her marriage to Edward Karkar; the couple and their baby lived for a time with the Dolls.

In an article featuring their apartment in *Town and Country* magazine in May 1983, Génia recalled, "People asked me how they knew about us. It was the ballet grapevine. Word got around that 'the Dolls take care of artists: See Eugénia in New York.' One guest wrote to his mother in Moscow – '*Mamushka*, America is terrific. I live on Fifth Avenue for free!'" Many American artists also participated in the Dolls' informal circle of friends.

Through Guitou Knoop and Dominique de Ménil, Doll had come to appreciate modern art and sculpture and began to collect a few works, which at the time were still available at reasonable prices. To the Mondrian, which he had at Ridgefield and which he brought to New York, he added over the years paintings by Max Ernst, Braque, Miro, Matta, Zadkine, Victor Brauner, Leonor Fini; two mobiles by Calder; and some sculptures – Giacometti, Max Ernst, Guitou Knoop, Henri Laurens – along with an engraving by Jean Cocteau portraying the legendary ballerina Anna Pavlova. Doll also found and brought back to New York old photographs, taken in France in the 1840s and tinted with watercolor, of the ancestors of his father's parents.

The Dolls like to take long walks in the city. They often walked from their apartment on Fifth Avenue down to Greenwich Village in Lower Manhattan to visit friends or attend an exhibition, and also often walked around Central Park, which was right across the street. In 1963, their house at Water Mill was struck by lightning and burned to the ground. Doll and Génia decided to rebuild it along the same plan, but on a grander scale. Doll supervised the lighting. "A nightmare of electrical wiring," recalled Guy de Brantes. "There were light switches everywhere. And, self-adhesive labels to show what each switch controlled." Génia often objected that it was much too complicated, "I preferred to have just one switch that turned on all the lights."

Bruno Desforges recalled that Doll decided not to insure the house. "I will be my own insurer," Doll told him. "They tell me, 'That's idiotic.' But I'm not an idiot, Bruno. You know me well. Do you think I'm an idiot? After all, what I did for Schlumberger wasn't peanuts!"

Water Mill also became a meeting place for artists. Jerome Robbins, the choreographer of *West Side Story*, stayed there for a time while composing a ballet entitled *Watermill*, a meditation on the passage of life. Arthur Gold and Robert Fitzdale, pianists and composers, often practiced their new compositions there. The de Brantes and their children could often be found along the beach in front of the house or at the backyard pool. Doll's daughter Henriette, who still lived in New York, visited often with her children.

At the end of the 1970s, Doll and Génia purchased a large top-floor apartment on Fifth Avenue, overlooking Central Park. Doll worked with the architect to soundproof the apartment and to improve the acoustics of a room where the Dolls hosted concerts around a Steinway grand piano. Génia also had an exercise room and a room that served as a dance studio. Doll continued to take dance lessons, from the waltz to the rumba to the mambo – a dance with staggered beats, which was fashionable. He followed the classes with the diligence of a *polytechnicien*, taking notes and making sketches, but never quite acquired the spontaneity of a born dancer.

"He danced like an engineer," commented both Bruno Desforges and Nathalia Makarova. Doll also offered to pay for dance classes for his secretary, Caroline Lambert, a young French teacher who started working for him in 1970. Caroline took to dance very well and later won several amateur competitions.

The Dolls created a foundation, the Eugenia and Henri Doll Foundation for the Performing Arts, which was a patron of the New York City Ballet, the American Ballet Theatre, the Metropolitan Opera, Carnegie Hall, the Dance Theatre of Harlem, and the Brooklyn Academy of Music. Doll, former chairman of the board of Schlumberger Limited, became chairman of the board of the American Symphony Orchestra, founded by Léopold Stokowski. They also helped finance several ballets for their friends – *Bayadere* for Makarova and *Don Quixote* for Baryshnikov.

Marina de Brantes remembered that one cold winter day, the choreographer George Balanchine visited Doll to talk about his plans to create a ballet company. Balanchine was wearing an old, lightweight, camel-hair coat and was shivering from the cold. Doll gave Balanchine a brand new overcoat, which he had just bought for himself, and also a check, which Balanchine slipped into his pocket. A few days later he wrote to Doll thanking him for the coat, but forgetting to mention the check, made out for $200,000.

The engineer Jean Suau, who spent nearly ten years working at Ridgefield, and often saw the Dolls in New York, recalled that Génia spoke with a strong Russian accent, "playing with the words to make her audience laugh and showing the love of life and spontaneity that one associates with the Slavic people." One day, Nureyev was admiring a small painting in their apartment and Génia took it off the wall, "Take it, if you like it," she told him. Doll later joked, "Fortunately, he was not admiring the Mondrian."

Many of Doll's former colleagues from Schlumberger visited him and Génia in New York. The Schusters recalled many invitations to the ballet and gifts of ballet dolls for their daughters. Génia and Doll often hosted parties at their homes in Manhattan and Long Island, or at one of the city's grand hotels. When Valéry Giscard d'Estaing was president of France, they helped his wife organize a reception at their apartment. Meals with the Dolls were always carefully prepared. "It was Génia who did the cooking, and she did it very well," Marina de Brantes remembers. "She took a lot of care with the dishes he liked."

Doll dancing at a party with Karin von Aroldingen, a ballerina with the American Ballet.

WHAT DOES THE FLOWMETER DO?

The DRI non-invasive blood flowmeter operates on principles similar to those governing the well-documented invasive electromagnetic type. However, the DRI model uses a strong, external permanent magnet and skin electrodes instead of the implanted electromagnetic probe that requires a surgical operation.

The DRI equipment provides a flow waveform tracing, which represents the instantaneous pulsatile flow from the aggregated arteries at any selected segment of the limb. The contour of the waveform, i.e.,the steepness of its slopes and the proportions of the retrograde flow, supply hemodynamic information which forms the basis for the clinical assessment of the arteries. The electronic equipment enhances the quality of the biological pulsatile signal by eliminating unwanted disturbances and noise. The quantitative information derived takes into account the geometry of the limb.

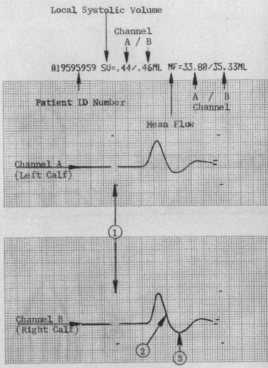

1 - Calibration Marker (R-Line Location)

2 - Slope related to run-off.

3 - Flow related to vascular elasticity.

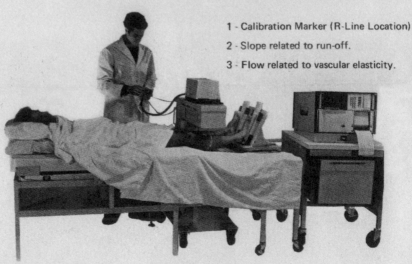

DOLL RESEARCH, INC.

Brochure from Doll Medical Research, Inc., 1977.

Chapter 24

Blood, After Oil

Doll did not abandon research after leaving the oil field. At the time of his retirement, he had become interested in diabetes, which had afflicted one of his daughters. He started by giving money to a clinic in Boston that was studying ways of administering insulin in a controlled fashion. Then, in the early 1970s, at age 67, he set up a laboratory in his home in New York City.

He launched an ambitious project to develop a new method of monitoring blood flow in the human body using the principles of electromagnetic induction that he had applied earlier to mine detection and oil well evaluation.

He had already converted a kitchen on the first floor of the apartment into an office with make-do furniture and shelves filled with scientific publications. The room opened into a small garden at the back of the row house. An adjoining guest room was converted into an office for his secretary.

The basement became a workshop and laboratory where Doll, helped at times by a young engineer, Hans J. Broner, assembled a large ring-shaped electromagnet about 32 inches (81 centimeters) in diameter. A narrow bed was placed near the magnet; it resembled a hospital bed, except that it was made entirely of wood. The setup was designed to measure blood flow of a patient lying on the bed.

Caroline Lambert (now, Caroline Corwin) was Doll's secretary and assistant for nearly 20 years after he retired from Schlumberger. She had married a scientist who was one of the pioneers of computer science. "It's important to understand how scientists like Mr. Doll feel," she said in a recent interview. "Research was something very important and fundamental to his nature. 'It is something I have to do,' he would say. 'I'm a scientist. Research is what's in me.' He let himself be absorbed in his work, because it was his mission. He didn't expect to get anything from it, except the satisfaction of doing his duty."

The project to build a new device to monitor blood flow got started after a discussion in New York City with Dr. Gabriel Nahas, a French anesthesiologist who taught and practiced medicine at Columbia Presbyterian Medical Center, the large research hospital associated with Columbia University. Nahas knew the Schlumberger family and had often talked with Doll about the difficulty of measuring blood flow in the human body

Steady blood flow is of course vital to human health, but it is very difficult to measure accurately. The rate of flow is especially diagnostic of the condition of arteries carrying oxygenated blood away from the lungs; monitoring the flow can help detect vascular disease or provide information on a course of treatment. It is particularly interesting to determine the flow during the increase in pressure at the early phase of the heart beat. This flow diminishes rapidly in the early stages of arterial disease and can therefore be diagnostic of its onset.

The two main techniques for monitoring cardiovascular health are echocardiography and radiography. Echocardiography uses reflections of sound waves at high frequencies, along with the Doppler effect, to monitor the condition of arteries and the rate of blood flow. The Doppler effect is the familiar change in pitch – that is, of frequency – of a sound wave that occurs when the source of sound moves with respect to the listener. In echocardiography, sound waves of high frequency (ultrasound) are directed into the body by a sensor called a transducer that is placed on the surface of the skin. As with sound waves penetrating the earth in the seismic method, sound waves penetrating the human body are partially reflected off internal structures, generating echoes that return to sensors on the surface where they are recorded. Echoes coming from particles moving in the blood stream are shifted in frequency by the Doppler effect; the amount of shift is roughly proportional to the speed of the particles – that is, to the speed with which blood is moving.

The important diagnostic quantity, however, is the blood flow rate, which is the volume of blood that passes a point along the artery in a given period of time. The blood flow rate is the speed of flow multiplied by the cross sectional area of the vessel (assuming of course that the speed is uniform in the cross section). It is difficult to measure both the speed and the cross-section precisely using only ultrasound.

Radiography probes the cardiovascular system by injecting a contrasting material that is opaque to X-rays into the bloodstream and observing its progress with a series of X-ray images. Radiography can determine size and shape of the arteries or veins, and identify obstructions, but like echocardiography, it can not directly measure the total blood flow rate. Before Doll's work, accurate measurements of blood flow could be made only with an instrument called a plethysmograph, which is a device usually placed directly on an artery or vein by surgery and measures the change in volume of the vessel over time as blood flows through it.

Doll's idea was to measure blood flow using an effect discovered by the British physicist Michael Faraday early in the 19th century. While studying connections between electrical currents and magnetic fields, Faraday found that a conducting fluid such as salt water creates an electrical potential when it flows in the presence of a magnetic field.

Blood is a conductor. In vertebrates, about half its volume is plasma, which is chemically similar to salt water. The rest is solid blood cells: mainly red blood cells (for carrying oxygen), white blood cells (for the immune system), and platelets (for coagulation). The resistivity of blood is also very close to that of sea water, about 0.25 ohm-m. This makes it much more conductive than most water-filled sedimentary rocks and many thousand times more conductive than dry rock.

Faraday described his discovery in 1832 in an article for the *Philosophical Transactions of the Royal Society*, "Experimental research in electricity, terrestrial magneto-electric induction" (2nd Series, v. 122, pp. 163-177). He could not explain in detail the cause of the effect, which actually was not be worked out until much later. What happens at the molecular level is that the magnetic field exerts forces on charged particles in the fluid (for example, dissolved ions) in a way that moves positive and negative charges to opposite sides of the flow. Although the fluid as a whole stays neutral, the separation of charges within the fluid creates a voltage. The phenomenon is related to a similar effect, called the Hall effect – after Edwin Hall, who discovered it in 1879 – in which a voltage develops when electrical current flows in the presence of a magnetic field. Unlike the streaming potential, in which the voltage develops in the direction of flow, the voltage in the Faraday or Hall effect develops in a direction that is perpendicular both to the flow and to the direction of the magnetic field. The effect is related to the law of electromagnetic induction, which Faraday published in the same 1832 article and which revolutionized physics. Richard Feynman gives a delightful description of the two effects in his *Lectures on Physics* (Addison-Wesley, 1964, vol. II, Lecture 17).

The principle of Doll's electromagnetic flowmeter is as follows: Imagine the patient is lying on a bed, in the presence of a magnetic field that is pointing vertically (from the floor to the ceiling). When blood flows through an artery in the patient's leg, for example, a voltage develops around the circumference of the artery. This voltage is communicated to the surrounding tissue, and can be measured by electrodes placed on the skin around the leg. The voltage induced by the flow pulsates with the heart beat, but the difference in voltage between opposite walls of an artery is tiny. The voltage present at the surface of the skin is several times smaller still (the voltage decreases with the distance from the artery to the skin surface).

The challenge for Doll was to measure these tiny voltages accurately. "The only real problem is the difficulty of creating a strong enough [magnetic] field without using too much power," he wrote in 1970 in a letter to his old colleague Pierre Charrin. "Even with a kilowatt, one only achieves voltages of a few tens of microvolts, and that is in the presence of the [electrical] signals produced by the heart and other sources of noise which are several orders of magnitude larger. In any case, it's very interesting work, which had helped me forget about well logging."

Doll followed the same rule that he imposed on the scientists at Ridgefield: If a path of research is theoretically possible, then it should be pursued aggressively to obtain results. "I have built an electromagnet 32 inches in diameter," he said one year later in an interview. "We now have an 80% chance of success (versus 5% at the start). There is no doubt that this is going to work. And, if a device can be placed in every hospital, it will mean that it will be possible to save several lives every day."

Doll created a new company called Doll Research, Inc. Not everyone understood its purpose, as was clear from a letter that arrived at the house one day and that Génia framed and placed in her husband's office. The letter, written by a Mrs. F. Lewis, was addressed to Doll Research, Inc., and was dated April 7, 1971. It read, "Dear Sir, I am interested in obtaining a doll that is no longer in production, namely, Kuddly Kewpie No 67K4, from Cameo Doll Products. I would be very grateful if you could let me know where I could obtain one." The company was renamed Doll Medical Research.

In September 1972, Doll met a young doctor with whom he would work for several years. Henri Boccalon had served an internship in a cardiovascular unit at a hospital in Toulouse, France. At the end of his stay, his supervisor in Toulouse asked him to do further training in New York, working with Nahas at the Presbyterian Medical Center. "A stay of one year was planned at the start, in the narrow field of surgical cardiac resuscitation," Boccalon recalled recently. "At the end of two months, I had identified fairly well the areas that I wanted to concentrate on, and just by chance had made contact with Mr. Doll. It all began with an interview."

During the interview, Doll told Boccalon, "Oil can be compared to the blood that circulates in a blood vessel. Oil is buried underground; the blood vessel is buried in a mass of tissue. In my specialty, I managed to detect a layer of oil thanks to a magnetic field measured at the earth's surface. Why shouldn't I be able to apply this electromagnetic method to the detection of blood flow?"

"It started like that," Boccalon said. "Trying to measure externally – that is, with a noninvasive method – something which had already been done internally by placing a magnetic ring around a blood vessel in experiments with animals, sometimes even in humans during surgical intervention. The method [Doll] was developing would measure the signal caused by blood flow by fixing two electrodes to the skin, like in an electrocardiogram. The magnet creating the magnetic field would also stay outside the body.

"My job was to be the guinea pig and intermediary for Mr. Doll – the interface between the engineer and inventor that he was and the medical application. I was also the guinea pig on the bed, where I spent hours. We presented the work at a medical congress in Atlantic City."

At the time, there was concern that exposure to strong magnetic fields was increasing the risk of cancer in workers at power plants. "In the discussion that followed our presentation at Atlantic City," Boccalon continued, "an objection was raised: 'Be careful. Verify that the action

Georges Attali and Henri-Georges Doll in front of one of the first computers used in a Schlumberger logging truck.

of the magnetic field does not cause problems with the capillaries.'" A series of studies with animals exposed to magnetic fields of much higher intensity than used in the blood flowmeter, and for much longer intervals, showed no adverse effects.

Boccalon's wife and one-year old child were with him in New York. The salary that he received as an intern at Presbyterian Hospital was not enough to pay the bills, so he took a job as a waiter and dish washer at a local restaurant. Doll dined there one night, and saw his young assistant working the tables. He took him aside after the meal. "He told me," Boccalon recalled, "'Mr. Boccalon, this is not what you are supposed to be doing.' The next day, he offered me a subsidy that allowed us to live much better." Doll also arranged for Boccalon to stay in New York longer than originally planned.

The main problem in the new measurement was to isolate the blood flow signal from the background noise, which required sophisticated signal processing. Doll hired a young engineer named Hans Broner to work on the problem. He also asked for help from his colleague, Georges Attali, who had retired from Ridgefield.

During the second half of 1974, the system developed by Doll Medical Research, named an "electromagnetic arterial flowgraph," was put into service by Nahas in a study evaluating arterial blockage in more than 60 patients. Comparison with other methods for monitoring circulation and clinical evaluation of individual patients confirmed that the noninvasive measurement was effective. It even allowed evaluation of "collateral circulation," which develops around an artery that is partially obstructed, of "retrograde circulation" (back flow), and of vascular elasticity – none of which was possible with other techniques. The main drawbacks were the size of the equipment and its cost.

The study looked at blood flow in nearly every part of the body. "We deployed magnets around the limbs," Nahas wrote, "using a large circular magnet capable of measuring flow in the entire arterial system, and in very specific locations, like the femoral artery and carotid artery. To do that, we put two square magnets on the neck above the artery, with electrodes on each side of the neck."

The experiments also helped to answer a fundamental question about the digestive system. It was known that digesting a meal required the expenditure of energy by the body. "But it was generally believed," Boccalon pointed out, "that circulation increased in the digestive system after a meal at the expense of the peripheral circulation. This is what had been measured in animals by invasive methods, with catheters placed on the arteries. We found exactly the opposite: The heart is involved in the task (of digestion), and all of the peripheral arteries just follow its lead."

Although the first clinical results were promising, no American company was interested in following up the research, which Doll had financed with his own funds. At the end of his second year in New York, Boccalon returned to Toulouse. Doll sent the equipment with him. "He had a lot of confidence in me," Boccalon recalled. "He financed the transportation of the equipment with his own money, made three trips to

Toulouse, and arranged to have the equipment delivered and installed at the cardiovascular unit at the university hospital center at Rangueil."

In the meantime, Doll continued the work on signal processing with Broner and Attali. Attali had purchased the first computers installed at Ridgefield, and had followed closely the explosive development of information technology during the 1960s and 1970s. He came to New York in November 1977 to work for a few days with Doll. He recalled going with the Dolls to a recital by Rostropovitch. During the performance, Rostropovitch announced that Anwar Sadat had traveled to Jerusalem and shaken hands with Golda Meir. "Doll was delighted," Attali recalls.

Attali worked with Doll on using a computer to calculate the background noise and subtract it from the measurements. The different components of this noise were the electrical signals coming mainly from the heart, lungs, and muscles. If these signals could be isolated and subtracted from the measurements in real time, the instrument would record only the small voltages induced by the flowing blood.

"The computers," Attali said in a recent interview, "could barely keep up with the calculations that were needed to determine the 'base line' of the signal – that is, subtract the parasitic noise – not just from the heart beat, but also from the breathing, which was not at the same rhythm, and noise from the muscles." Doll bought two more computers, each the size of a bookcase. One was installed at Presbyterian Hospital, where the clinical research was being done; the other in an office that he rented at New Hyde Park, an industrial tract on Long Island, about an hour by car from Manhattan.

"Doll's idea was right," Attali recalled. "But the computers at the time were not powerful enough to do the calculations."

In 1976, Doll turned 74. He began to suffer lapses of memory. The first person he talked to about this, in confidence, was Caroline Lambert. "Caroline, you know that I have total trust in you," he said. "From now on, you will have to be my memory." At the time, Alzheimer's disease was not as well known as it is today; one talked instead of "precocious dementia" or "gatism." In Doll's case, the progress of the disease was very slow, and he was able to continue to work for several years after its onset. Attali worked with Doll until 1979 and remembered that he "had lapses of memory; he barely was able to recognize us from morning to evening. If you gave him a problem and put all of the data in front of him at the same time, he understood and was able to think it through perfectly. But if you didn't do that, he started to forget some of the pieces, and just got lost."

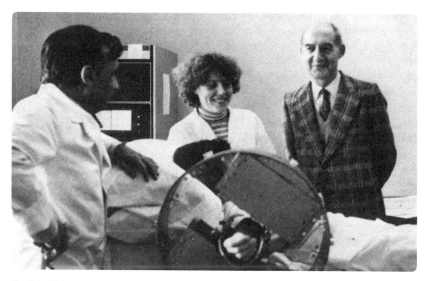

Dr. Gabriel Nahas (left) and Henri-Georges Doll testing the electromagnetic blood flowmeter at Presbyterian Medical Center of Columbia University (Photo, Archives & Special Collections, Columbia University Health Sciences Library).

After 1975, most of the tests and clinical studies of Doll's electromagnetic blood flowmeter were conducted in the cardiovascular unit of Professor André P. Enjalbert at the Hospital Rangueil in Toulouse. In March 1975, Boccalon wrote a report reviewing clinical results obtained with the system. He first described the instrument, which consisted of an electromagnet, placed under a non-magnetic bed where the patient lay. The field produced by the magnet at the location of a typical artery was about 500 gauss. (The "gauss" is a unit of magnetic field, named after the German mathematician Carl Fredrick Gauss, who made some of the earliest measurements of the earth's magnetic field, which has a value of about 0.5 gauss at the surface.)

The measurement in the blood flowmeter was made by two electrodes on the skin. Amplifiers boosted the signal level from about a microvolt to one volt. A computer digitized the output and averaged the signal over several heart beats, with some of the cycles being measured with the magnetic field turned on and some with the field off, in order to get a measure of the background noise. The voltages were directly proportional to the strength of the magnetic field and to the total blood flow, and inversely proportional to the diameter of the blood vessel being measured.

The readings were expressed in microvolts per unit of time and graphed in a continuous curve. (The area under the curve was directly proportional to the blood flow.) A mathematical formula was devised to transform the readings into physical blood flow, expressed in milliliters per second, for a typical artery running down the center of a large mass of tissue, such as the femoral artery in the thigh.

The computer recorded the results in real time. It was even possible to monitor variations in blood flow over time – for example in studying the administration of medication, or a surgical intervention – by keeping track of the percentage variation in the signal compared to a starting value.

Boccalon's study, which was directed at arterial diseases, measured the flow in the peripheral vessels of patients at different locations in all four limbs, which allowed both diagnosis of disease and its monitoring after treatment with drugs or surgery. The noninvasive measurement was especially helpful for patients with existing disease, such as diabetes for which invasive techniques were too risky.

In follow-up work, the team at Toulouse used the same technique to evaluate the elasticity of cardiac muscles after open heart surgery. In this case, a small magnet was placed in contact with two electrodes situated on the neck on either side of the carotid artery. Measurement of the pulsating flow through the carotid artery allowed a determination of the maximum rate of acceleration of the blood flow, which is directly related to the elasticity of the myocardium, the cardiac muscle. The small magnets could also be used to study specific locations along particular arteries, and were even used to study impotence in men, which is often caused by vascular disease.

In the 1970s, a special unit was created for functional vascular evaluation at Hospital Rangueil. In 1981, Boccalon and his collaborators reviewed the results of the ten years of research and clinical trials of the noninvasive blood flowmeter. The research had been supported by Doll Medical Research and also by a grant from the central regional hospital of Toulouse. A paper describing the work was published in the journal *Medical & Biological Engineering & Computing*. It was the last scientific paper on which Henri-Georges Doll appeared as an author.

The paper touched on the factors that could influence the readings: the diameter and shape of the blood vessels; the composition of the blood, whose conductivity increases as ratio of plasma to blood cells increases and is influenced by the concentration of electrolytes, mainly sodium and chloride ions, in the plasma; the influence of surrounding tissue, muscle, fat, and bone (the conductivity of bone is negligible compared to that of blood, fat, or muscle); the effects of interfering electrical signals coming from the heart-lung system and from muscular contractions; and voltage drifts caused by sweating and drying of the skin at the point of contact with measuring electrodes.

The paper also included a mathematical model of the measurement, which was checked by experiments using conducting paper cut in the shape of cross sections through different parts of the body (an example was shown of a cross section through the calf muscle of the leg). Finally, it presented results of invasive blood flow measurements carried out on anaesthetized animals, which confirmed the readings of the electromagnetic blood flowmeter.

Boccalon, H., Lozea, A., Newman, W., and Doll, H. G., 1982, Noninvasive electromagnetic blood flowmeter: Theoretical aspects and technical evaluation, *Medical and Biological Engineering & Computing*, v. 20, pp. 671-680.

In 1984, Boccalon contacted a small company in the Toulouse area to discuss commercialization of the new instrument. The company Diatecnic was part of the regional technology center for the Toulouse-Labège area of southern France, and specialized in development of medical electronics for functional and diagnostic evaluation of vascular disease. Diatecnic already sold other types of blood flowmeters: a programmable Doppler ultrasound unit, a venous plethysmograph, and a photo-plethysmograph that used infrared light.

Diatecnic requested a formal evaluation of the electromagnetic flowmeter under a protocol for testing new medical equipment in France called TEP (for "transfer and evaluation of prototypes"). The TEP was directed by the National Association for the Evaluation of Research and supported by the French government agency, CNEH (National Center for Hospital Equipment).

Diatecnic received a grant to build an improved version of Doll's instrument, and produced the DIADEM 700. The magnet used in this second-generation instrument had a magnetic field of 700 gauss. In July 1988, Diatecnic built six instruments for clinical evaluation at six regional hospitals in France: in Dijon, Montpellier, Paris, Saint Étienne, Marseille, and Nîmes. The trials were directed at using quantitative measurements of pulsating blood flow in the lower limbs for the screening and monitoring of arterial disease.

In 1989, Dr. Michel Dauzat of the unit for exploratory vascular medicine of the regional hospital at Nîmes coordinated the trials and presented the results of studies involving 588 patients at a public meeting of the French Ministry of Research and Technology in Paris. The study concluded that the new instrument was an effective method for obtaining accurate blood flow readings that allowed the screening of patients with arterial disease, but with no external symptoms, and the evaluation of therapeutic treatments. "It would be a major benefit for public health," Dauzat concluded in his report, "if an instrument such as the DIADEM 700 were developed and commercialized as a tool for medical scientists and clinicians to better fight against arterial disease."

But the DIADEM 700 was never commercialized on a large scale. The field of medical ultrasound progressed rapidly in the 1970s and 1980s, and today dominates the clinical diagnosis of arterial disease related to blood flow. More recently, magnetic resonance imaging has also produced ways of studying functional blood flow in the body, especially in the brain. In 2007, the instrument catalog of Diatecnic included only Doppler echocardiographs using ultrasound.

"But Doll's method is still valuable," Boccalon said. "It gives the doctor more information than he can obtain with an echocardiograph."

In 1989, Doll turned 87. He had kept his tall, lean, straight silhouette; but a Basque beret, not jet black hair, now covered his head. His loss of memory had progressed significantly. "At the end, Madame Doll really dedicated her life to her husband," Caroline Corwin recalled. "And she knew how to take care of this marvelous man whom she loved, as did everyone who knew him. Madame Doll had to go through all the stages: first, the denial that it was happening, then the realization that the person was no longer the companion that you once had, and then the last stage, the impossibility of communicating at all, the end."

"She was occupied with him day and night," remembers Marina de Brantes. "She took care of him better than if he had been in a specialized treatment center. She kept him occupied. It was progressive. He was able to remember things from a very long time ago, but forgot what he had been doing two minutes earlier."

During the summer of 1989 at Water Mill, Génia suffered from dizzy spells. A little while later, she underwent a brain scan that discovered a brain tumor. At the end of November 1990, she underwent surgery, insisting that her husband not be informed. Sensing that her own end was near, Génia wrote to Annette trusting that she would take care of Doll until his death.

Marina de Brantes remembered that Doll "had moments of lucidity, and was asking 'Where is Génia?' We told him that she would be coming back. She died fifteen days after the operation." She died on December 13, 1990.

Annette asked a relative, a doctor, to bring Henri-Georges back to Paris. After a short stay with the Gruners, he was placed in a home for specialized treatment at Montfort-l'Amaury, a small town outside Paris where two of his daughters lived. They furnished his room with familiar objects. There were times when he was completely lucid. When his brother Édouard visited him, he smiled and said, "Hello, old friend."

Doll died at Montfort-l'Amaury on July 25, 1991. He is buried as he wished next to his mentor Conrad Schlumberger in the small cemetery near Val-Richer in Normandy.

Henri-Georges and Génia on the beach at Watermill, at sunset.

Epilogue

IN THE SPRING OF 2004, Philippe Lacour-Gayet, chief scientist of Schlumberger, invited Henriette de Vitry, the youngest daughter of Annette and Henri-Georges Doll, to visit the research center in Ridgefield, which her father had created in 1948 and which the company had renamed Schlumberger-Doll Research upon his retirement in 1967. Early in 2004, Schlumberger had announced that it was planning to close the facility.

Henriette visited in June of that year. It was her first time back in Ridgefield since the early 1950s, when she had often come down from Boston during weekends and summer vacations to see her parents at Ferndale, their home a few miles from the town center. Philippe asked her to say a few words to the staff, and at the end of the day, everyone gathered in the auditorium to listen to Henriette reminisce about the early years at Ridgefield, when her father was director of research, and to ask questions about this person who had become a near-mythical figure in the thirty-seven years after his departure from Schlumberger and the oil industry.

Henriette also spoke about the early days of *la Pros,* recalling stories about her parents' adventures on the road and in the field, from the deserts of Bakersfield and Baku to the plains of Oklahoma and Alsace. She remembered that, after World War II, her father   who at the start of the war had headed a French artillery battalion and at the end had headed a U.S. army project on mine detectors – had picked Ridgefield as the site for the new research center almost by chance, relying on the advice of his friend and colleague Charles Aiken, who showed him this quiet town in the Connecticut woods, a setting about as far from an oil field as any place can be.

Henri-Georges Doll left nothing to chance, however, in his choice of projects for research. The list he had written down in 1941 touched not only on new areas, like nuclear physics and electronics, advancing rapidly as the world prepared for war, but also on old standards, like SP, needing a fresh approach. His genius was a sense for applied science – what was required to do it well and how best to go about it. "In all these efforts," Jay Tittman wrote in a tribute to Doll published after his death, "he was guided by faith that practical technical success rests on scientific research and engineering of the highest quality."

Jean Mathieu, who had accompanied Doll on the long trip out of France in 1940, remembers being invited to Ridgefield in the summer of 1948 to see the new center and spend a few days with Doll at Ferndale. "Doll was there alone," Mathieu recalls, "the rest of the family was on vacation. Every morning, as we were on the way to the office – it took about 15 or 20 minutes – he told me about his ideas during the night. André Blanchard told me that Doll would spend his time going from one office to the next during the day, explaining his ideas to the scientists. At any one time, there are often many different avenues that research can take. Doll had the extraordinary knack, 90% of the time, of finding one that would lead to the final result. He could have spent his entire career just doing that – providing direction to the people around him. He was born to do research." It was his sixth sense.

"Ridgefield became the center of my father's life," Henriette said to the staff at the lab in June 2004. "It was as if he had been cloistered in a monastery. He worked seven days a week, every week of the year."

What had convinced Doll to stay in the United States after the war was the optimism of American science – an optimism fueled by scientists from around the world who had come to America in the years surrounding the war, an optimism driven by the belief that anything was possible. It fit well with Doll's own conviction that "anything was worth exploring" if it might lead to a practical result.

Nicolaï Andréich Sebastianov, president of the Russian society of applied geophysicists and a leading figure in the Russian oil industry, called him "the Edison of geophysics."

Most experts agree that the world is nearing the halfway point of its oil age, which is usually said to have started in 1859 when Edwin Drake drilled the first oil well in Titusville, Pennsylvania. In the century and a half since then, we have consumed about 1200 billion barrels of oil, mostly in transportation, power plants, and plastics. Estimates are that roughly the same amount of oil, another 1200 billion barrels, can be produced from known reservoirs using current methods of drilling and pumping (which, it should be said, still leave as much as two-thirds of the oil trapped underground in the pores of rocks).

These "known reserves" of oil will not last another 150 years at the rate of consumption in 2006, which was about 85 million barrels a day, or roughly thirty billion barrels for the year. They represent only a forty-year supply at that rate – or much less if demand continues to grow at its current pace of about 5% a year, as developing countries like China and India begin consuming oil in amounts comparable to those of Europe and the United States.

No one knows how much more oil remains to be found. Estimates vary wildly, from less than 100 billion barrels on the low side to over 1000 billion barrels on the high side. These estimates, moreover, do not include "unconventional reserves" – for example, heavy oil in the tar sands of Canada and Venezuela or shale oil in the mountains of the western United States – which are difficult to exploit, but are truly gigantic in size.

One thing is sure. When tallies are made of the amount of oil in reservoirs around the world, the data and calculations will rely on the ideas and methods of Henri-Georges Doll. These tallies use vast quantities of data, but the calculations themselves are actually very simple: First, the volume of a reservoir is determined from underground maps, which today are made from three-dimensional images created by the seismic reflection method. Then, the amount of oil in the reservoir is estimated by multiplying the reservoir's volume by its oil saturation, which is determined from well logs.

Epilogue

All oil industry professionals know that this calculation relies on Archie's law – the connection between resistivity, porosity, and oil discovered by the American electrical engineer Gus Archie in the laboratory of giant Shell Oil in Houston in the early 1940s. But many do not know that the ingredients on which the result depends – the resistivity and porosity of the reservoir – derive their accuracy from the inventions of a French-American scientist, Henri-Georges Doll, and the scientists from around the world that he brought to a small laboratory in the woods of Connecticut in the years following World War II.

In January 2007, a new Schlumberger research facility opened its doors at Kendall Square in Cambridge, Massachusetts. Over a hundred people moved from Connecticut, and others came from Schlumberger locations all around the world, to work at the new site, which is within walking distance of MIT and a short subway ride from Harvard University. The center is named Schlumberger-Doll Research.

The idea for this book arose at a dinner with Henriette de Vitry in the Inn at Ridgefield during her visit in June of 2004. A first version was published in May 2007 in France under the title, *Le sens du courant: La vie d'Henri-Georges Doll, inventeur* (Le Cherche Midi, Paris, 2007).

The authors thank the Doll family and Schlumberger Limited for putting at their disposal a large collection of documents on the history of the company and its employees. Most of these documents can be found in two collections: the archives of Marcel Schlumberger at the Musée Schlumberger in the town of Crèvecœur in Normandy, France, and the archives of Conrad Schlumberger and Henri-Georges Doll at École des Mines in Paris. We thank Christophe de Ceunynck, director of Musée Schlumberger, and Fondation Musée Schlumberger, presided over by Didier Primat, for giving us full access to the archives at Crèvecœur.

Claude Suter, former director of communications for Schlumberger Limited, helped to assemble the documents from Crèvecœur and École des Mines and from the company's archives in Paris, Houston, and New York. Claude also directed a project to digitize a large part of the assembled collection, some of which will be made available to the public in an historical web site. Josephine Ndinyah helped the authors to find documents in the libraries of Schlumberger and other libraries around the world, including some of the early papers on electrical prospecting in the Soviet Union. Caroline Corwin, Doll's personal assistant at Doll Medical Research, and Dr. Henri Boccalon provided material on the electromagnetic blood flowmeter.

We thank especially Doll's friends, colleagues, and family members who contributed recollections, photographs, and letters or other documents to the project. Dr. Anne Postel-Vinay (Doll's granddaughter) assembled the family's documents. Henriette and Arnaud de Vitry, Izaline Davidson (Doll's oldest daughter), and Guy and Marina de Brantes, long-time friends of the family, kindly agreed to be interviewed for the book, along with many of Doll's former colleagues, including Jean-Pierre Causse, Georges Attali, Louis Magne, Nick Schuster, Philippe Souhaité, Jean Suau, Denis Tanguy, Géza Kunetz, and Jay Tittman. We also thank Bruno Desforges, financier and friend of Henri-Georges, and Serge Mélikian, the son of Vahé Mélikian. Lisa Stewart, editor at Schlumberger *Oilfield Review*, and James Kent helped prepare the English version of the book.

Finally, we thank Anne Mikoulinsky-Devanneaux, of the communications department of Schlumberger Limited in Paris, who helped with all aspects of the project, and Philippe Lacour-Gayet, chief scientist of Schlumberger, who made it happen.

Note on Sources

The best original sources for the history of Schlumberger are the archives of Marcel Schlumberger at the Musée Schlumberger in Crèvecœur, Normandy, and those of Conrad Schlumberger and Henri-Georges Doll at École Nationale Supérieure des Mines in Paris. The archives were cataloged by Bowker (1994); his bibliography contains a short description of their organization.

Material quoted from letters between Société de prospection électrique *(la Pros)* in Paris and the different branches of the company are taken from these archives, especially AC-101 through AC-108 (AC = Archives Conrad; AM = Archives Marcel), which cover the period in the Soviet Union from 1929 to 1935; and AC-109 to AC-120, which cover the period in the United States from 1926 to 1938. The volumes of the Halliburton trial are in AM-556 to AM-606.

The Doll family provided access to Henri-Georges Doll's technical notebooks, along with his personal and business correspondence, including letters not contained in the archives.

The memoir by Anne (Annette) Gruner Schlumberger (1977) is a wonderful source of personal stories and other original material from the early years of *la Pros*. Quotes from Annette in the text were translated from the French edition. In writing her memoir, Annette conducted numerous interviews that are available in the archives. Schlumberger Limited started a history project around the same time (early 1970s) and conducted interviews with nearly all of its surviving engineers, which are also available in the archives. The profile of Schlumberger by Auletta (1984) is an excellent source of material for the years of transition from *la Pros* and its affiliates to Schlumberger Limited.

For this book, interviews were conducted with Henriette and Arnaud de Vitry, Izaline Davidson, Guy and Marina de Brantes, Bruno Desforges, Jean-Pierre Causse, Georges Attali, Louis Magne, Nick

Schuster, Philippe Souhaité, Jean Suau, Denis Tanguy, Géza Kunetz, Jay Tittman, and Serge Mélikian.

Technical material from the years in the Soviet Union can be found in a reprint of several articles from the *Azerbaidjan Oil Industry Review,* which was published by *la Pros* in English in 1932 as "Applications of Electrical Coring in Russian Oil Fields." The reprint includes the three articles:

"I – A new technique in geological exploration," by Pefenov, Mélikian, and Nikitine.

"II – Results of the application of electrical coring in the Stalin district (Bibi-Eybat)," by M. Babaian, V. Listengarten, V. Gorine, and G. Tsatourov

"III – Results of the applications of electrical coring in the Ordjonikidze District (Surakhany)," by D. Jabrev and K. Emilianov.

Aside from the original papers, Allaud and Martin (1976) is the best source of material on the history of technology in Schlumberger, starting with the early researches of Conrad. Two useful sources for the early history of the seismic method are Sweet (1978) and the monograph by Lee, Bates, and Rice (2001) in the SEG Geophysical references series. Other valuable sources are the biography of DeGolyer by Tinkle (1970) and the early textbooks by Ambronn (1928), Jakosky (1940), Heiland (1940).

The monumental AAPG memoir by Owen (1975) is the most comprehensive source for the history of oil and gas exploration, mainly from a geological perspective, but with asides on the technology and business. Yergin (1991) is now the classic history of the oil industry.

Francis Segesman, one of Doll's colleagues in the early years of the Ridgefield, maintained a remarkably complete collection of reprints from the early years of Schlumberger, including nearly all of Doll's work. This collection is now part of the archives of Schlumberger-Doll Research. The bibliography below of Doll's technical publications was assembled from this collection.

References

Allaud, Louis A., and Martin, Maurice H., 1976, *Schlumberger histoire d'une technique,* Berger-Levrault. (Published in the United States as *Schlumberger, The History of a Technique,* John Wiley & Sons, New York, 1977.)

Ambronn, R., 1928, *Elements of Geophysics,* translated by Margaret Cobb, Mc-Graw Hill, New York.

Archie, G.E., 1942, The Electrical Resistivity Log as an Aid in Determining Some Reservoir Characteristics, *Trans. AIME, Petroleum Technology,* Tech. Pub. No. 1422 (presented at Dallas Meeting, October 1941).

Auletta, Ken, 1984, *The Art of Corporate Success,* The Story of Schlumberger, Putnam, New York.

Blanche D. Cole, B. D.; Keith, J.E.; Rosenthal, H. H., 1958, *United States Army in World War II, The Technical Services, The Corps of Engineers, Troops and Equipment,* Office of the Chief of Military History, Washington, D.C.

Blau, L., and Gemmer, R., 1936, Method and Apparatus for Logging a Well, U.S. Patent 2,037,306.

Bernstein, Jeremy, 1978, *Experiencing Science,* Basic Books.

Blau, L., 1936, Black magic in geophysical prospecting, *Geophysics,* **1**, 1-8.

Bowker, Geoffrey, 1994, Science on the Run, Information Management and Industrial Geophysics at Schlumberger, 1920-1940, MIT Press.

Cathcart, Brian, 2004, The Fly in the Cathedral, How a Group of Cambridge Scientists Won the International Race to Split the Atom, Viking.

Cooper, John M., Jr., 1990, *Pivotal Decades: The United States, 1900-1920,* W.W. Norton & Co.

The Engineer Board, 1945, History of the Development of Electronic Equipment: I – Metallic Mine Detectors, Fort Belvoir.

Faraday, M., Experimental research in electricity, terrestrial magneto-electric induction, *Philosophical Transactions of the Royal Society,* 2nd Series, **122**, 163-177.

Feynman, R., Leighton, R., and Sands, M., 1964, *The Feynman Lectures on Physics,* Addison-Wesley, 1964.

Gilbert, William, 1958, *De Magnete,* Dover, New York (republication of the translated edition published in 1893).

Hamilton, James, 2002, *A Life of Discovery, Michael Faraday, Giant of the Scientific Revolution,* Random House, New York.

Halliburton Oil Well Cementing Co. versus Schlumberger Well Surveying Corporation, No. 10063, Circuit Court of Appeals, Fifth Circuit, Sept. 5, 1942

Heiland, C. A., 1940, *Geophysical Exploration,* Prentice-Hall, New York.

Helmholtz, H., 1879, Studien uber electrische Grenzschichten, *Annalen der Physik und Chemie,* Neue Folge **VII**, no. 7, 22-382.

Jakosky, J. J., 1940, *Exploration Geophysics,* Times-Mirror Press, Los Angeles.

Johnson, H. M., 1962, A history of well logging, *Geophysics,* **28**, 507-527.

Lawyer, L. C.; Bates, Charles C.; and Rice, Robert B., 2001, *Geophysics in the Affairs of Mankind,* 2nd ed., Society of Exploration Geophysicists, Tulsa.

Lubsandorzhiev, B.K., 2006, On the history of photomultiplier tube invention, *Nuclear Instruments and Methods in Physics Research* Section A: Accelerators, Spectrometers, Detectors and Associated Equipment, **567**, 236-238.

References

Mounce, W. D., and Rust, W. M., Jr., 1943, Natural Potentials in Well Logging, *Trans. AIME*, **155**, 49-57 (presented at Dallas Meeting, May 1943).

Quincke, G., 1859, Ueber eine neue Art elektrischer Strome, *Annalen der Physik und Chemie*, **107**, no. 5, 1-47.

Reuss, F.F., 1809, Sur un nouvel effet de l'électricité galvanique, *Mémoire de la Société Impériale de Naturalistes de Moscou*, **2**, 327-337 (lue le 14 Avril 1808).

Rust, W. M., Jr., 1938, A historical review of electrical prospecting methods, *Geophysics*, **3**, 1-6.

Owen, Edgar Wesley, 1975, *Trek of the Oil Finders: A History of Exploration for Petroleum*, American Association of Petroleum Geologists, Tulsa, OK.

Pontecorvo, Bruno, 1942, Neutron well logging, a new geological method based on nuclear physics, *Oil and Gas Journal*, **40**, 32-33.

Pontecorvo, Bruno, 1941, Method and Apparatus for Logging a Well, U.S. Patent 2,349,753.

Roberts, Roy T., 1999, The History of Metal Detectors, *Western & Eastern Treasures*, September.

Rosaire, E. E., and Stiles, M. E., 1936, Exploration on the Gulf Coast, to 1936, *Geophysics*, **3**, 142-148.

Raymond Sauvage: Recollections of Schlumberger Wireline's First Four Years, *Technical Review*, Schlumberger, 1987.

Schlumberger, Anne Gruner, 1977, La boite magique, Fayard, Paris. (Published in the United States as *The Schlumberger Adventure*, Arco Publishing, Inc., New York, 1982.)

Schlumberger, Clarisse, 1997, *Schlumberger, racines et paysages*, Éditions Oberlin.

Schlumberger, Conrad, 1920, *Etude sur la Prospection Electrique du Sous-sol*, Gauthiers-Villars et Cie., Paris.

Schlumberger, Conrad, 1931, Electrical method and apparatus for the determination of the nature of geological formations traversed by drill holes, U.S. patent 1,819,923

Schlumberger, Conrad, 1933, Electrical process for the geological investigation of porous strata traversed by drill holes, U.S. patent 1,913,293.

Schlumberger, C. and M., and Charrin, P., 1932, Application de la prospection électrique aux recherches de pétrole en U.R.S.S., *Science et Industrie, La technique des industries du pétrole*.

Schlumberger, C. and M., and Charrin, P., 1935, Etudes géophysiques par les méthodes électriques en U.R.S.S., *La Revue Pétrolifère*, no. 614 et 615.

Schlumberger, C. and M., and Léonardon, E.G., 1934. Electric coring: a method of determining bottom-hole data by electrical measurement, *Trans. AIME*, **110**, 237-272.

Schlumberger, C. and M., and Léonardon, E.G., 1934. Some Observations concerning Electrical Measurements in Anisotropic Media and their Interpretation, *Trans. AIME*, **110**, 159.

Schlumberger, C. and M., and Léonardon, E.G., 1934, A New Contribution to Subsurface Studies by Means of Electrical Measurements in Drill Holes, *Trans. AIME*, **110**, 273.

Société de Prospection Électrique, 1932, Application of Electrical Coring in the Russian Oil Fields, extracts from *The Azerbaidjan Oil Industry*, No. 1, January.

Sweet, George Elliott, 1978, *The History of Geophysical Prospecting*, Neville Spearman, Suffolk.

Tinkle, Lon, 1970, Mr. De, *A Biography of Everette Lee DeGolyer*, Little Brown, Boston, 1970.

Turchetti, Simon, 1003, Atomic secrets and governmental lies: nuclear science, politics and security in the Pontecorvo case, *British Journal for the History of Science*, **36**, 389-415.

References

Westby, G.W., and Scherbatskoy, S.A., 1940, Well logging by radioactivity, *Oil and Gas Journal*, Feb. 22.

Whittaker, Edmund, 1951, *A History of the Theories of Aether & Electricity*, reprinted 1989, Dover, New York.

Wong, John B., 2004, *Battle Bridges, Combat River Crossings, World War II*, Trafford Publishing, UK.

Yergin, Daniel, 1991, *The Prize, The Epic Quest for Oil, Money & Power*, Free Press, New York.

Publications of Henri-Georges Doll

Schlumberger, C. et M., Doll, H.G., 1930, Le pendagemètre électromagnétique et la détermination de l'orientation du pendage des couches sédimentaires recoupes par les sondages, *Congres International des Mines de la Métallurgie et de la Géologie Appliquée*.

Maillet, R., et Doll, H.G., 1932, Sur un théorème relatif aux milieux électrique ment anisotropes et ses applications à la prospection électrique en courant continu, *Ergänzungs-Hefte für angewandte Geophysik*, 3, 109-124.

Schlumberger, C. and M., and Doll, H.G., 1933, The electromagnetic teleclinometer and dipmeter, *World Petroleum Congress*, Imperial College, London.

Schlumberger, C. et M., et Doll, H.G., 1934, L'Exploration électrique des sondages, *La Revue Pétrolifère*.

Schlumberger, M., Doll, H.G., and Perebinosoff, A.A., 1936, Temperature measurements in oil wells, One Hundred and Seventy-second Meeting of the Institution of Petroleum Technologists.

Doll, H.G., 1942, The S.P. dipmeter, *Trans. AIME*.

Doll, H.G., Lebourg, M., and Miller, G.K., 1946, Vehicular-mounted mine detector, *Electronics*, Jan., 105-109.

Doll, H.G., and Schwede, H.F., 1947, Radioactive markers in oil-field practice, *Transactions AIME*.

Doll, H.G., Legrand, J.C., and Stratton, E.F, 1947, True resistivity determination from the electric log – Its application to log analysis, *Oil and Gas Journal*.

Doll, H.G., 1948, The S. log: Theoretical analysis and principles of interpretation, *Transactions AIME, Petroleum Technology*, 11, 146-185.

Doll, H.G., 1949, Introduction to induction logging and applications to logging of wells drilled with oil base mud, *J. Petroleum Technology*, 1, 148-162.

Doll, H.G., 1949, The SP log in shaly sands, *J. Petroleum Technology*.

Doll, H.G., 1950, Selective S. logging, *Petroleum Transactions, AIME*, 189, 129-142.

Doll, H.G., 1950, The Microlog – A new electrical logging method for detailed determination of permeable beds, *J. Petroleum Technology*, 2, 155 164.

Doll, H.G., and Martin, M., 1950, Recent developments in electrical logging and auxiliary methods, *Quarterly J Colorado School of Mines*, 45, 49-78.

Doll, H.G., and Martin, M., 1951, Electrical logging in limestone fields, *Proceedings of the Third World Petroleum Congress*, 394-417.

Doll, H.G., 1951, The Laterolog: A new resistivity logging method with electrodes using an automatic focusing system, *J. Petroleum Technology*, 3.

Doll, H.G., Sauvage, R., and Martin, M., 1952, Application of micrologging to determination of porosity, *Oil and Gas Journal*, 51.

Doll, H.G., 1953, The Microlaterolog, *J. Petroleum Technology*, 3.

Doll, H.G., 1953, Two decades of electrical logging, *J. Petroleum Technology*, 5, 33-41.

References

Doll, H.G., and Martin, M., 1954, How to use electrical log data to determine maximum producible oil index, *Oil and Gas Journal.*

Doll, H.G., 1955, Filtrate invasion in highly permeable sands, *The Petroleum Engineer,* B53-B66.

Doll, H.G., and Stout, T.M., 1957, Design and analog-computer analysis of an optimum third-order nonlinear servomechanism, *Transactions ASME,* 513-525.

Doll, H.G., 1958, Considérations sur la diagraphie des sondages et sur l'évolution des techniques électriques, *Bulletin de l'Association Française des Techniques et du Petrole,* **127**, 17.

Doll, H.G., Martin, M., and Tixier, M. P., 1959, Review of the progress of well logging since the 4th World Petroleum Congress, Fifth World Petroleum Congress, 645-666.

Doll, H.G., Dumanoir, J. L., and Martin, M., 1959, Trends in electrical logging, Presented at 29th Annual Meeting, Society of Exploration Geophysicists.

Doll, H.G., Dumanoir, J. L., and Martin, M., 1960, Suggestions for better electric log combinations and improved interpretations, *Geophysics,* 25, 854-882.

Doll, H.G., Martin, M., and Tixier, M. P., 1960, Application of wire-line logging to subsurface geology, *Report of the International Geological Congress, XXI Session,* 121-136.

Doll, H.G., 1960, On the Earth, *Electronics,* Jul., 74.

Doll, H.G., 1960, Possibilities of wire-line logging methods in the mohole, Abstracts, AAPG-SEPM Meeting.

Doll, H.G., Tixier, M. P., Martin, M., and Segesman, F, 1961, Electrical Logging, in *Petroleum Production Handbook,* T. Frick (ed.), McGraw-Hill, New York.

Doll, H.G., Tixier, M. P., and Segesman, F, 1963, Recent developments in well logging in the U.S.A., *Proceedings Sixth World Petroleum Congress.*

Boccalon, H., Candelon, B., Leblanc, A., Doll, H.G., Puel, P., et Enjalbert, A., 1978, Contractilité myocardique: Evaluation non sanglante âpres chirurgie cardiaque, *Revu Med. Toulouse,* XIV, 225-228.

Boccalon, H.J.L., Candelon, B.J.L., Doll, H. G., Puel, P.F., and Enjalbert, A.P., 1978, Non-invasive electromagnetic measurement of the peripheral pulsatile blood flow: Experimental study and clinical application, *Cardiovascular Research,* **XII,** 66-68.

Boccalon, H.J.L., Candelon, B.J.L., Leblanc, A.J., Puel, P.F., Enjalbert, A.P., and Doll, H.G., 1979, Computer monitoring of cardiac performance from patients recovering from cardiac surgery, *Anesthésiologie und Intensivmedizin,* **116,** Acute Care, 282-286.

Boccalon, H., Lozes, A., Newman, W., and Doll, H.G., 1982, Non-invasive electromagnetic blood flowmeter: Theoretical aspects and technical evaluation, *Med. & Biol. Eng. & Comput.,* **20,** 671-680.

U.S. Patents of Henri-Georges Doll

Method and apparatus for developing intermittent venous blood flow and measuring total blood flow, U.S. Patent 4134396A, Doll, H. G., Jan. 16, 1979.

Apparatus and method for eliminating perturbations of a kinetic origin in the blood flow waveform, U.S. Patent 4036215A, Doll, H. G., Jul. 19, 1977.

Non-invasive electromagnetic blood flow measuring system with rejection of noises, U.S. Patent 3809070A, Doll, H. G., and Broner, H. J., May 7, 1974.

Electromagnetic flowmeter, U.S. Patent 3759247A, Doll, H. G., and Broner, H. J., Sep. 18, 1973.

References

Electromagnetic flowmeter, U.S. Patent 3659591A, Doll, H. G., and Broner, H. J., May 2, 1972.

Method and apparatus for logging spontaneous potentials in wells, U.S. Patent RE27079E, Doll, H. G., Mar. 2, 1971.

Methods and apparatus for investigating earth formations wherein the vertical resolution of a first exploring means is altered to approximate vertical resolution of a second exploring means, U.S. Patent 3493849A, Doll, H. G., Feb. 3, 1970.

Induction logging apparatus with reduced diameter auxiliary coil means, U.S. Patent 3466533A, Doll, H. G., Sep. 9, 1969.

Method and apparatus for providing improved vertical resolution in induction well logging including electrical storage and delay means, U.S. Patent 3166709A, Doll, H. G., Jan. 19, 1965.

Methods and apparatus for investigating earth boreholes by means of electrodes constructed to contact the borehole walls, U.S. Patent 3132298A, Doll, H. G., and Dumanoir, J.L, May 5, 1964.

Apparatus for investigating earth formations, U.S. Patent 3060373A, Doll, H. G., Oct. 23, 1962.

Electrical measuring systems, U.S. Patent 3072844A, Doll, H. G., Jan. 8, 1963.

Electrostatic shields, U.S. Patent 3013102A, Doll, H.G., Dec. 12, 1961.

Multiple frequency alternating current network, U.S. Patent 3012190A, Doll, H. G., Dec. 5, 1961.

Capacitive detector, U.S. Patent 3012189A, Doll, H.G., Dec. 5, 1961.

Automatic computing apparatus, U.S. Patent 2915242A, Doll, H. G., Dec. 1, 1959.

Phase responsive alternating current networks, U.S. Patent 2983874A, Doll, H. G., May 9, 1961.

Electro-optical function generator, U.S. Patent 2884195A, Doll, H. G., Apr. 28, 1959.

Tabular function generator, U.S. Patent 2879942A, Doll, H. G., Mar. 31, 1959.

Automatic computing apparatus, U.S. Patent 2859916A, Doll, H. G., Nov. 11, 1958.

Function generator of two independent variables, U.S. Patent 2859915A, Doll, H. G., Nov. 11, 1958.

Flow measurement in wells, U.S. Patent 2842961A, Doll, H. G., Jul. 15, 1958.

Automatic computing apparatus, U.S. Patent 2829825A, Doll, H. G., Apr. 8, 1958.

Methods and apparatus for exploring boreholes, U.S. Patent 2826736A, Doll, H. G., Mar. 11, 1958.

Methods for logging the formations traversed by a borehole, U.S. Patent 2814017A, Doll, H. G., Nov. 19, 1957.

Well logging apparatus, U.S. Patent 2813249A, Doll, H. G., Nov. 12, 1957.

Coil assembly for geophysical prospecting, U.S. Patent 2807777A, Doll, H.G., Sep. 24, 1957.

Phase rejection networks, U.S. Patent 2788483A, Doll, H. G., Apr. 9, 1957.

Apparatus for electrical well logging, U.S. Patent 2786178A, Doll, H. G., Mar. 19, 1957.

Induction well logging apparatus, U.S. Patent 2761103A, Doll, H. G., Aug. 28, 1956.

Methods and systems for maintaining alternating current networks in a reference condition, U.S. Patent 2753520A, Doll, H. G., Jul. 3, 1956.

Electrical logging in non-conductive drilling liquids, U.S. Patent 2749503A, Doll, H. G., Jun. 5, 1956.

References

Methods and apparatus for determining hydraulic characteristics of formations traversed by a borehole, U.S. Patent 2747401A, Doll, H. G., May 29, 1956.

Differential pressure well logging, U.S. Patent 2747402A, Doll, H. G., May 29, 1956.

Induction caliper, U.S. Patent 2736967A, Doll, H. G., Mar. 6, 1956.

Methods and apparatus for logging spontaneous potentials in wells, U.S. Patent 2728047A, Doll, H. G., Dec. 20, 1955.

Multiple coil apparatus for induction well logging, U.S. Patent 2725523A, Doll, H. G., Nov. 29, 1955.

Spontaneous potential well logging method and apparatus, U.S. Patent 2713146A, Doll, H. G., Jul. 12, 1955.

Electrical well logging method and apparatus, U.S. Patent 2712632A, Doll, H. G., Jul. 5, 1955.

Methods and apparatus for electrical logging of wells, U.S. Patent 2712630A, Doll, H. G., Jul. 5, 1955.

Electrical logging of earth formations traversed by a bore hole, U.S. Patent 2712629A, Doll, H. G., Jul. 5, 1955.

Electrical logging apparatus, U.S. Patent 2712628A, Doll, H. G., July 5, 1955.

Electrical resistivity well logging method and apparatus, U.S. Patent 2712627A, Doll, H. G., Jul. 5, 1955.

Selective spontaneous potential well logging method and apparatus, U.S. Patent 2712626A, Doll, H. G., Jul. 5, 1955.

Systems for investigating spontaneous potentials in wells, U.S. Patent 2707266A, Doll, H. G., Apr. 26, 1955.

Electrodes for electrical well logging, U.S. Patent 2704347A, Doll, H. G., Mar. 15, 1955.

Resistivity apparatus for obtaining indications of permeable formations traversed by boreholes, U.S. Patent 2669688A, Doll, H. G., Feb. 16, 1954.

Resistivity method for obtaining indications of permeable formations traversed by boreholes, U.S. Patent 2669690A, Doll, H. G., Feb. 16, 1954.

Method and apparatus for determining earth formation factors, U.S. Patent 2669689A, Doll, H.G., Feb. 16, 1954.

Method and apparatus for logging static spontaneous potentials in wells, U.S. Patent 2592125A, Doll, H. G., Apr. 8, 1952.

Differential coil system for induction logging, U.S. Patent 2582315A, Doll, H. G., Jan. 15, 1952.

Electromagnetic well logging system, U.S. Patent 2582314A, Doll, H. G., Jan. 15, 1952.

Well logging method and apparatus, U.S. Patent 2554174A, Doll, H.G., May 22, 1951.

Well logging method and apparatus utilizing periodically variable spontaneous potentials, U.S. Patent 2550005A, Doll, H. G., Apr. 24, 1951.

Well logging equipment, U.S. Patent 2475354A, Doll, H. G., Jul. 5, 1949.

Well surveying apparatus, U.S. Patent 2475353A, Doll, H. G., Jul. 5, 1949.

Automatic control system for vehicles, U.S. Patent 2463362A(A), Doll, H. G., Mar. 1, 1949.

Method of establishing markers in boreholes, U.S. Patent 2550004A, Doll, H.G., Apr. 24, 1951.

Electrooptical function synthesizer, U.S. Patent 2497042A, Doll, H.G., Feb. 7, 1950.

Method of positioning apparatus in boreholes, U.S. Patent 2476137A, Doll, H. G., Jul. 12, 1949.

References

Method and apparatus for locating predetermined levels in boreholes, U.S. Patent 2476136A, Doll, H. G., Jul. 12, 1949.

Frequency stabilization of alternating current networks, U.S. Patent 2463252A, Doll, H.G., Mar. 1, 1949.

Recording device, U.S. Patent 2457214A, Doll, H. G., Miller, G. K., Dec. 28, 1948.

Method and apparatus for investigating earth formations traversed by boreholes, U.S. Patent 2433746A, Doll, H. G., Dec. 30, 1947.

Method and apparatus for determining the dip of strata traversed by a borehole, U. S. Patent 2427950A, Doll, H. G., Sep. 23, 1947.

Method for determining the oil content of subterranean formations, U.S. Patent 2395617A, Doll, H. G., Feb. 26, 1946.

Delayed action fuse, U.S. Patent 2363234A, Doll, H.G., Nov. 21, 1944.

Method and apparatus for investigating boreholes, U.S. Patent 2357178A, Doll, H. G., Aug. 29, 1944.

Method and apparatus for conducting different investigations simultaneously in boreholes, U.S. Patent 2357177A, Doll, H. G., Aug. 29, 1944.

Well surveying apparatus, U.S. Patent 2338029A, Doll, H. G., Dec. 28, 1943.

Well-surveying instrument, U.S. Patent 2338028A, H. G. Doll, Dec. 28, 1943.

Device for determining the strata traversed by drill holes, U.S. Patent 2317259A, Doll, H. G., Apr. 20, 1943.

Apparatus for measuring temperatures in boreholes, U.S. Patent 2316942A, Doll, H. G., Apr. 20, 1943.

Recording apparatus, U.S. Patent 2258700A, Doll, H. G., Oct. 14, 1941.

Arrangement for measuring temperatures at a distance, particularly in boreholes, U.S. Patent 2249751A, Doll, H. G., Jul. 22, 1941.

Resistance thermometer and method of manufacturing the same, U.S. Patent 2238015A, Doll, H. G., Apr. 8, 1941.

Method of indicating spontaneous potentials in shallow wells, U.S. Patent 2230999A, Doll, H. G., Feb. 11, 1941.

Method and arrangement for determining the direction and the value of the dip of beds cut by a bore hole, U.S. Patent 2176169A, Doll, H. G., Oct. 17, 1939.

Index

A

Adygeya 99, 103
Aiken, Charles 141, 172, 179, 188, 197, 198, 214, 228, 230, 301
AIME
 See American Institute of Mining and Metallurgical Engineers (AIME)
Alsace 27, 44, 55, 202, 301
American Institute of Mining and Metallurgical Engineers (AIME) 54, 136, 231, 236, 257, 258, 259, 260, 261, 262
ampere 31, 34
Ampère, Marie 31
André Allégret 63
Anglo-Persion Oil Company
 See British Petroleum
anisotropic 116, 117
anisotropy 116, 117
Anthony F. Lucas Gold Medal 189
anticline 44, 109, 110
Aperchon Peninsula 109
Apollo 17 238, 239, 241, 243
Archie, Gus 235, 259, 304
Archie's law 235, 262, 265, 303
Armored Board 193, 195
array induction tool 268
ASCOP 243
Attali, Georges 217, 253, 266, 267, 274, 291, 292, 293, 294, 305
Azerbaijan 99, 102, 103, 109, 110, 113, 115, 117, 128, 143
Azerbaijan Oil Review 103, 115, 143
Aznieft oil trust 103, 109, 112, 113, 115, 117, 122, 236

B

baccalauréat 18, 260
Bakelite 44, 58
Baker, Botts, Andrew & Wharton (attorneys for Schlumberger) 174, 188
Baku 99, 100, 101, 102, 103, 109, 112, 113, 117, 118, 119, 120, 122, 123, 125, 143, 169, 170, 236, 258, 301
fountain fields 100
Balanchine, George 84, 282
Barn 234
Baron, Pierre 63
Barton, Donald 71

Baryshnikov, Mikhail 280, 282
Batum, Georgia 105, 106
Becquerel, Alexandre-Edmond 240
Belgium 13, 49, 152, 153, 179, 187
Bell Laboratories 141
Bergius, Friedrick 167
Bibi-Eibat 109, 110, 115
black box 34, 40
Black Magic 41
Black Peril 222, 232
Black Sea 99, 105, 107
Blau, Ludwig 41, 175
Blau-Gemmer patent 176, 177, 178, 179
Blum, Léon 167
Boccalon, Henri 290, 305
Bohr, Neils 85, 213
Boissonnas, Éric 164, 170, 202, 249, 272, 274
Boissonnas, Sylvie (née Schlumberger) 164, 170, 202, 249, 272
Borotra, Jean 20
boulevard Saint-Germain 17
Bouncing Betty
 See Schutzenmine
Boyce, Joseph 198
Bricaud, Joseph 214
British Petroleum 83
Broner, Hans J. 286, 292, 293
Brons, Folker 233
Bullington, John 188, 189, 191, 192, 197, 244
Bureau of Geophysical Research 124, 130
Bureau of Geophysical Research (KGR) 124, 130

C

Caluire 17, 64, 154
Camp Coëtquidan 22, 23
Camp Mailly 22
carottage 48, 52
carottage électrique 52
Caspian Sea 99, 107, 109, 110, 123
Caucasus 83, 97, 99-123, 165-169
Cenozoic 68
Chabas, Paul 95, 96
Chadwick, James 85
Charrin, Paul 53, 158, 202, 205, 206, 289, 310
Chatelier, Louis 64

Index